A Theory *of* Adaptation

A Theory of Adaptation explores the continuous development of creative adaptation, and argues that the practice of adapting is central to the storytelling imagination. Linda Hutcheon develops a theory of adaptation through a range of media, from film and opera, to video games, pop music and theme parks, analysing the breadth, scope and creative possibilities within each.

This new edition is supplemented by a new preface from the author, discussing both new adaptive forms/platforms and recent critical developments in the study of adaptation. It also features an illuminating new epilogue from Siobhan O'Flynn, focusing on adaptation in the context of digital media. She considers the impact of transmedia practices and properties on the form and practice of adaptation, as well as studying the extension of game narrative across media platforms, fan-based adaptation (from Twitter and Facebook to home movies), and the adaptation of books to digital formats.

A Theory of Adaptation is the ideal guide to this ever evolving field of study and is essential reading for anyone interested in adaptation in the context of literary and media studies.

Linda Hutcheon is Distinguished University Professor Emeritus of English and Comparative Literature at the University of Toronto, Canada.

Siobhan O'Flynn is Senior Lecturer in the Canadian Studies Program at the University of Toronto, Canada and Adjunct Graduate Faculty in the OCADU/CFC Media Lab Digital Futures Masters Program at the Canadian Film Centre's Media Lab.

A Theory *of* Adaptation

Second edition

Linda Hutcheon with
Siobhan O'Flynn

Routledge
Taylor & Francis Group

LONDON AND NEW YORK

First edition published 2006
by Routledge
This second edition published 2013
by Routledge
2 Park Square, Milton Park, Abingdon, Oxon OX14 4RN

Simultaneously published in the USA and Canada
by Routledge
711 Third Avenue, New York, NY 10017

Routledge is an imprint of the Taylor & Francis Group, an informa business

British Library Cataloguing in Publication Data
A catalogue record for this book is available from the British Library

Library of Congress Cataloging in Publication Data
Hutcheon, Linda, 1947-
A theory of adaptation / Linda Hutcheon with Siobhan O'Flynn. -- 2nd ed.
p. cm.
Includes bibliographical references and index.
1. Literature--Adaptations. 2. Music and literature. I. O'Flynn, Siobhan. II. Title.
PN171.A33H88 2012
809--dc23
2012011960

ISBN: 978-0-415-53937-1 (hbk)
ISBN: 978-0-415-53938-8 (pbk)
ISBN: 978-0-203-09501-0 (ebk)

Typeset in Caslon
by Saxon Graphics Ltd, Derby

Adapting is a bit like redecorating.

—**Alfred Uhry**

The content of a movie is a novel or a play or opera.

—**Marshall McLuhan**

After all, the work of other writers is one of a writer's main sources of input, so don't hesitate to use it; just because somebody else has an idea doesn't mean you can't take that idea and develop a new twist for it. Adaptations may become quite legitimate adoptions.

—**William S. Burroughs**

[T]he theatre itself is much less high-minded than those who keep a watchful eye on its purity; the stage has always cheerfully swiped whatever good stories were going.

—**Philip Pullman**

CONTENTS

ILLUSTRATIONS

Preface to the second edition

Epilogue

PREFACE TO THE FIRST EDITION

If you think adaptation can be understood by using novels and films alone, you're wrong. The Victorians had a habit of adapting just about everything—and in just about every possible direction; the stories of poems, novels, plays, operas, paintings, songs, dances, and *tableaux vivants* were constantly being adapted from one medium to another and then back again. We postmoderns have clearly inherited this same habit, but we have even more new materials at our disposal—not only film, television, radio, and the various electronic media, of course, but also theme parks, historical enactments, and virtual reality experiments. The result? Adaptation has run amok. That's why we can't understand its appeal and even its nature if we only consider novels and films.

Anyone who has ever experienced an adaptation (and who hasn't?) has a theory of adaptation, conscious or not. I am no exception. *A Theory of Adaptation* is one attempt to think through not only this continuing popularity but also the constant critical denigration of the general phenomenon of adaptation—in all its various media incarnations. Whether it be in the form of a videogame or a musical, an adaptation is likely to be greeted as minor and subsidiary and certainly never as good as the "original." This critical abuse is one of the provocations of this study; the other is the sheer number and kinds of adaptations both across genres and media and also within the same ones. Most of the work done on adaptation has been carried out on cinematic transpositions of literature, but a broader theorizing seems warranted in the face of the phenomenon's variety and ubiquity. Adaptations seem so common, so "natural," so obvious—but are they?

On a more personal note, I have learned that obsessions (intellectual and other) rarely disappear, even if they do mutate. There have been common threads in my past critical work that reappear in this book. First, I have always had a strong interest in what has come to be called "intertextuality" or the dialogic relations among texts, but I have never felt that this was only a formal issue. Works in any medium are both created and received *by people*, and it is this human, experiential context that allows for the study of the *politics* of intertextuality. This has also always been my concern, and it continues to be so in this book. A second constant has been a perhaps perverse de-hierarchizing impulse, a desire to challenge the explicitly and implicitly negative cultural evaluation of things like postmodernism, parody, and now, adaptation, which are seen as secondary and inferior.

Once again, I have tried to derive theory from practice—as wide a cultural practice as possible. I have used many different examples here in order to make it easier for readers to "hook onto" some familiar work and thus onto my theorizing from it. My method has been to identify a text-based issue that extends across a variety of media, find ways to study it comparatively, and then tease out the theoretical implications from multiple textual examples. At various times, therefore, I take on the roles of formalist semiotician, poststructuralist deconstructor, or feminist and postcolonial demythifier; but at no time do I (at least consciously) try to impose any of these theories on my examination of the texts or the general issues surrounding adaptation. All these perspectives and others, however, do inevitably inform my theoretical frame of reference. So, too, does the very fact that, as Robert Stam has noted

(2005b: 8–12), all the various manifestations of "theory" over the last decades should logically have changed this negative view of adaptation. There are many shared lessons taught by Kristevan intertextuality theory and Derridean deconstruction and by Foucauldian challenges to unified subjectivity and the often radically egalitarian approach to stories (in all media) by both narratology and cultural studies. One lesson is that to be second is not to be secondary or inferior; likewise, to be first is not to be originary or authoritative. Yet, as we shall see, disparaging opinions on adaptation as a secondary mode—belated and therefore derivative— persist. One aim of this book is to challenge that denigration.

I should also explain what this book is *not*, what it does *not* aim to do. It is not a series of extended case studies of specific adaptations. Many fine books like this exist, especially in the area of cinematic adaptations of literary works, no doubt because of the impact of George Bluestone's seminal 1957 work *Novels into Film*. Brian McFarlane in his book, *Novel to Film* (1996: 201), invokes the analogy of close reading of literary texts for this kind of detailed examination of specific works. I would agree, but such individual readings in either literature or film rarely offer the kind of generalizable insights into theoretical issues that this book seeks to explore. There is yet another problem with the case-study model for the particular task I have set myself here: in practice, it has tended to privilege or at least give priority (and therefore, implicitly, value) to what is always called the "source" text or the "original." As I examine in the first chapter, the idea of "fidelity" to that prior text is often what drives any directly comparative method of study. Instead, as I argue here, there are many and varied motives behind adaptation and few involve faithfulness. Other earlier adaptations may, in fact, be just as important as contexts for some adaptations as any "original." The "adapted text"—the purely descriptive term I prefer to "source" or "original"—can be plural too, as films like Baz Luhrmann's *Moulin Rouge* (2001) have taught us. And there is yet another possibility: our interest piqued, we may actually read or see that so-called original *after* we have experienced the adaptation, thereby challenging the authority of any notion of priority. Multiple versions exist laterally, not vertically.

If this book is not an analysis of specific examples, it is also not an examination of any specific media. It is not primarily focused on film adaptations of literature for the simple reason that, as I mentioned, many such studies already exist; I do, however, draw upon their insights. It is the very act of adaptation itself that interests me, not necessarily in any specific media or even genre. Videogames, theme park rides, Web sites, graphic novels, song covers, operas, musicals, ballets, and radio and stage plays are thus as important to this theorizing as are the more commonly discussed movies and novels. My working assumption is that common denominators across media and genres can be as revealing as significant differences. Shifting the focus from particular individual media to the broader context of the three major ways we engage with stories (telling, showing, and interacting with them) allows a series of different concerns to come to the fore.

That curious double fact of the popularity and yet consistent scorning of adaptation is where *A Theory of Adaptation* begins its study of adaptations *as adaptations*; that is, not only as autonomous works. Instead, they are examined as deliberate, announced, and extended revisitations of prior works. Because we use the word *adaptation* to refer to both a product and a process of creation and reception, this suggests to me the need for a theoretical perspective that is at once formal and "experiential." In other words, the different media and genres that stories are transcoded to and from in the adapting process are not just formal entities; as Chapter 1 explores, they also represent various ways of engaging audiences. They are, in different ways and to different degrees, all "immersive," but some media and genres are used to *tell* stories (for example, novels, short stories); others *show* them (for instance, all performance media); and still others allow us to interact physically and kinesthetically with them (as in videogames or theme park rides). These three different modes of engagement provide the structure of analysis for this attempt to theorize what might be called the *what, who, why, how, when,* and *where* of adaptation. Think of this as a structure learned from Journalism 101: answering the basic questions is always a good place to start.

To launch this investigation, Chapter 2 revisits medium-specificity debates of earlier adaptation theory from this new perspective of modes of engagement to locate both the limitations and advantages of each mode for different kinds of adaptation. Existing theories of adaptation in particular media, especially literature and film, have come to accept certain basic truisms. However, expanding the scope of study to include all three modes of involvement allows some of those theoretical clichés to be tested against actual adaptation practice. The critical truisms that particularly beg for testing—not to mention debunking—are those concerning how different media can deal with elements like point of view, interiority/exteriority, time, irony, ambiguity, metaphors and symbols, and silences and absences.

Adaptation is not only a formal entity, however; it is also a process. Chapter 3 looks at those much maligned and often ignored figures who do the work of adaptation. Determining precisely who is the adapter, especially in a collaborative creative mode of showing like film, is the first task undertaken; the second is to find out why anyone would agree to adapt a work, knowing their efforts would likely be scorned as secondary and inferior to the adapted text or to the audience's own imagined versions. By way of reply, I explore various economic, legal, pedagogical, political, and personal reasons in an extended analysis of one particular—and surprising—story that was adapted multiple times over a 30-year period by a series of adapters with very different motivations and very different skills and obsessions.

Chapter 4 also concerns the process of adaptation, but shifts the focus to how audiences enjoy and engage with "remediated" stories in all three modes. If we know the adapted work, there will be a constant oscillation between it and the new adaptation we are experiencing; if we do not, we will not experience the work *as an adaptation*. However, as noted, if we happen to read the novel after we see the film adaptation of it, we again feel that oscillation, though this time in reverse. Oscillation is not hierarchical, even if some adaptation theory is. Although all three modes of engagement "immerse" their audiences in their stories, usually only one mode is actually called "interactive"—the one that demands physical participation (usually called "user input") in the story. Because this mode has been least discussed in adaptation studies thus far, it is the main focus of discussion here, for there are significant differences between being told a story and being shown a story, and especially between both of these and the physical act of participating in a story's world.

Neither the product nor the process of adaptation exists in a vacuum: they all have a context—a time and a place, a society and a culture. In Chapter 5, *when* and *where* are the keywords for the exploration of what can happen when stories "travel"—when an adapted text migrates from its context of creation to the adaptation's context of reception. Because adaptation is a form of repetition without replication, change is inevitable, even without any conscious updating or alteration of setting. And with change come corresponding modifications in the political valence and even the meaning of stories. An extended analysis of a selection of the many different adaptations of one particular story—that of a gypsy called Carmen—suggests that, with what I call *transculturation* or *indigenization* across cultures, languages, and history, the meaning and impact of stories can change radically.

Because this study begins with an account of the "familiarity and contempt" usually visited upon adaptations today, it seems fitting that it should end with some final questions about the manifest appeal of adaptations, now and in the past. This book is not, however, a history of adaptation, though it is written with an awareness of the fact that adaptations can and do have different functions in different cultures at different times.

A Theory of Adaptation is quite simply what its title says it is: one single attempt to think through some of the theoretical issues surrounding the ubiquitous phenomenon of adaptation *as adaptation*.

Linda Hutcheon
Toronto

Preface to the Second Edition
Plus ça change … plus ça change!

No, things do *not* stay the same, not always, and certainly not in the last six years since *A Theory of Adaptation* was first published. The proliferation of adaptations has continued apace, of course; our thirst for retelling stories has not been quenched in the least. But what *has* changed is the availability of many new forms and platforms. New digital media have burgeoned in these last years. Now iPads and iPhones have become new sites for adaptive play. YouTube is the placement of choice for many adapters—especially for the parodically inclined. Fan culture has taken imaginative (and economic) possession of the fate of its favorite stories. Social networking has altered forever the communication landscape. But we also witness familiar older films being remediated through computerization techniques. The coexistence of the new and the old, the digital and the analogue, is a *fait accompli*: the question remaining is whether this shift is one of degree or, more radically, of kind (see Jenkins 2006: 257). For adaptation studies, is ours a transitional time or are we facing a totally new world?

I had two main aims in writing *A Theory of Adaptation*. The first was to tackle head-on the subtle and not so subtle denigration of adaptation in our (late-Romantic, capitalist) culture that still tends to value the "original," despite the ubiquity and longevity of adaptation as a mode of retelling our favorite stories. And the second aim was to consider the ever-widening range of forms of adaptations, well beyond the fiction-to-film discussions that dominated the field in its early years. To these ends, in Chapter 2 and again in Chapter 4, in theorizing three possible modes of engagement with adapted stories—telling, showing, and interacting with—I also tried, through the latter, to articulate my sense of something new and different happening in everything from videogames to interactive art installations to hypertext fiction. It is not that reading a print book and watching a film are not active, even immersive, processes. They clearly are. But that "something new and different" was evident even in the grammar to which I had to resort: some adaptational strategies demand that we *show* or *tell* stories, but in others, we *interact with* them. The verbal transitivity of showing and telling had to be replaced by the prepositional engagement of the "with" that signals something as physical and kinetic as it is cognitive and emotional. This is true whether the medium be an iPad adaptation of T.S. Eliot's poem *The Waste Land* or a multi-platform site like *Pottermore*, designed not only as a vehicle for the electronic versions of the Harry Potter novels, but as much much more.

I have chosen *not* to rewrite *A Theory of Adaptation* in the light of these recent changes, but rather to add to it. That "interactive" category has been expanded immensely by the rise of the newer digital media, but in ways that seem to me to be a continuation of the kind of thinking begun in the existing book. And my discussion of the growing role of fan culture in Chapter 4, in the context of "The Pleasures of Adaptation," allows room for the expansion needed to further theorize the explosion of fan participation in adaptation that we have witnessed in the last years. But the lateral (not vertical—that is, evaluational and thus higher-lower) continuum of adaptive relations outlined in the final chapter can and should be rethought and retheorized in the light of the new media.

Enter **Siobhan O'Flynn**, the one who has taught me everything I know about adaptation in the new media. It seemed fitting, therefore, that *she*, not I, should move the field of adaptation studies forward in her usual fearless way. Hence, her Epilogue—which, I can assure you, will not be her last word on this emerging and constantly morphing topic. As both a theorist and a practitioner, she *lives* these immersive practices, and can speak with that double authority to the shift that has altered not only the forms of adaptation but also the economics and even the ethics of the global entertainment and media industries.

What's New about Media Change?

In a word, nothing. In the sixteenth century, Leonardo da Vinci's mural painting of the *Last Supper* was adapted into the form of a Flemish tapestry that hangs in Rome's Vatican Museum. Today, however, "media change" is not just a question of remediation. Digital is more than a platform; it is changing the context in which films, for instance, are made, distributed, and consumed (see Perlmutter 2011). But of particular interest to adaptation studies is the fact that technology is also altering how we actually tell and re-tell our stories, for it challenges the traditional cinematic way of narrating: now, a new compendium of graphic text, still and moving images, sound, *and* a cursor or interactive touch screen is to digital narration what cross-cutting, tracking shots, and closeups are to narration that privileges the moving image and sound. But because of those navigating devices, the new media engage us directly—in an individualized, indeed personalized manner (a point to which I shall return). As Tom Perlmutter, the director of the National Film Board of Canada, recently put it, navigation is to interactivity what montage is to film. This also means that the forward-moving temporal force of film is being replaced by the digital media's interactive, spatial movement.

The conventions of storytelling—and story retelling—are changing daily, in other words. Again, this process of change is not new, but its pace has certainly intensified and quickened and its forms multiplied. Japanese cellphone novels are being adapted to print, often in anime form; the ethical values of the story world of Harry Potter are adapted to the real world of social activism. The Harry Potter Alliance website asks:

Did you ever wish that Harry Potter was real? Well it kind of is.

Just as Dumbledore's Army wakes the world up to Voldemort's return, works for equal rights of house elves and werewolves, and empowers its members, we: Work with partner NGOs in alerting the world to the dangers of global warming, poverty, and genocide. Work with our partners for equal rights regardless of race, gender, and sexuality. Encourage our members to hone the magic of their creativity in endeavoring to make the world a better place. Join our army to make the world a safer, more magical place, and let your voice be heard!

(http://thehpalliance.org/)

Without a crystal ball, it's hard to know whether all this adaptive experimentation means that we are in a transitional phase or whether something has changed definitively. The argument for transition could be made by looking, as Siobhan O'Flynn does, at how the iPad's new interactive and intermedial iBooks both integrate and transform the conventions of the physical book through audio (sound and voice-over) additions as well as by incorporating film animation and touch-screen gaming design. But material books are arguably fighting back, adapting through inversion the visual layering technology possible on digital platforms to the paper page: to create his 2010 book *Tree of Codes,* Jonathan Safran Foer literally cut out most of the words of his favourite book, Bruno Schulz's *Tree of Crocodiles,* creating a physically multilayered, sculptural text that told his own story in the interstices (see Figure 1).

As the author put it: "I started thinking about what books look like, what they will look like, how the form of the book is changing very quickly. If we don't give it a lot of thought, it won't be for the better. There is an alternative to e-books" (quoted in Wagner 2010). But that alternative arguably adapts the layered visuality of a form reminiscent of digital media (specifically, Photoshop). We may well "make sense of novelty through the lens of history," defining "new technologies in terms of older, more familiar ones" (Moore 2010: 181), but that process can also be reversed. The transitional can operate both ways with adaptations.

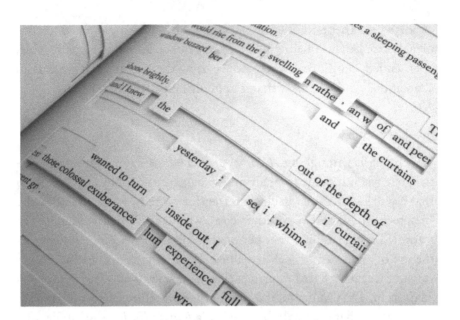

Figure 1 Image from *Tree of Codes* by Jonathan Safran Foer. Reproduced with permission from Visual Edition

That said, in the last six years, what has become evident is that the new entertainment norm, not the exception, is "transmedia" storytelling: "a process where integral elements of a fiction get *dispersed systematically across multiple delivery channels* for the purpose of creating *a unified and coordinated entertainment experience*. Ideally, each medium makes its own *unique contribution* to the unfolding of the story" (Jenkins 2011; emphasis in original). As such it is more likely to target different audiences through different media: "not everyone wants to watch the movie and play the game" (Dena 2009: 162)—but we may want to enter the narrative and its world through some other medium (a graphic novel, for example) or to access backstory or other characters' perspectives. (For more on adaptation in relation to transmedia, see Dena 2009: 147–63.) In marketing terms, "franchise" storytelling was certainly already driving some adaptational practices as I completed this book (see "The Economic Lures" section of Chapter 3), but now, as the Epilogue explores in detail, franchising through transmedia design dominates the marketing strategies of the entertainment industry. And in so doing, it is forcing a rethinking of certain aspects of adaptation theory. For example, when it is not a single, fixed, recognizable story that is being adapted, but rather an on-going, unstable, open-ended "multitext," where do we draw the line at what we call an adaptation? And what is it that is actually being adapted?

Stories vs. Story Worlds

The emphasis throughout *A Theory of Adaptation* is on adapting narrative, but when it came to analyzing videogame adaptations, I realized that it was less the story itself than the story world, or what I called the "heterocosm" (literally, an other cosmos), that was being adapted. In transmedia storytelling, that fictional world is the core, for it becomes the site of multiple possible storylines. The Epilogue argues that this is yet another change that demands the expansion of existing theories of adaptation. The proliferation of franchise storytelling suggests to Clare Parody that what is actually adapted is "a *brand identity*, the intellectual property, advertising language, and presentational devices that cohere, authorize, and market the range of media products that together comprise the franchise experience" (2011: 214). Thematic and narrative persistence is not the name of the new adaptation game; world building is. This also means that theorizing adaptation only in terms of repetition with variation becomes too limiting; what must be added is a way to deal with the range of extensions or expansions of a story world that not only transmedia producers but, as we shall see, fans too have wrought.

It obviously becomes harder and harder to think in terms of "original" or "source" stories or even story worlds when dealing with these kinds of adaptations, because here simultaneity, not priority, reigns. Movie and video game versions, for instance, are conceived and even executed simultaneously; there is no single and prior adapted work. Martin McEachern explains that film crews now work alongside video game artists, who take photographs and record the proportions and textures of sets. They work closely with the film's production designers and the visual effects team "to make sure their game upholds the same production values as the film. ... [I]n this era of cross-platform marketing and convergent technology, major film properties live twice—in the movie theater and in the interactive realm" (2007: 12). But, as the

Epilogue explores, they live in many *other* realms besides these, realms not always under the control of the major studios.

Who Is in Control?

The last decade has witnessed a major democratizing shift in media production—through the sheer (global) reach of the Internet, through software like iMovie and Photoshop, through web platforms like blogs and wikis, and through the ready availability of low-cost (but high quality) recording and editing tools. As O'Flynn argues in the Epilogue, this has had an impact on how adaptations are not only produced and controlled, but also distributed. In this new media environment, "adaptation becomes a strategy of participation. Rather than develop wholly new works, audiences take ownership over existing media, adapting the stories, shows, and films that they most identify with" (Moore 2010: 183). And nowhere has this been more evident than in fan culture. YouTube, Facebook, and Twitter have made it easy to adapt digital content, for that content is not only accessible and repeatable, but also infinitely modifiable. In our capitalist culture, it is no doubt needless to point out that this is not always legal, despite the strong democratizing ethos of the Internet. (See "The Legal Constraints" section of Chapter 3.) The Epilogue analyzes a number of famous cases where copyright law and fan adaptation practices have come into conflict, but it also carefully nuances what is at stake in these struggles by pointing out that media conglomerates paradoxically have an economic interest in fostering fan devotion, while still attempting to retain sole control over the intellectual property that garners them profits.

Fan-generated content has exploded in recent years, and not only online, of course. Yet, when fans can remake their favourite films on minimal budgets ("sweding") and then distribute them on YouTube, who is in control? When they can adapt and thus personalize a video game to suit themselves, should its creators greet this with "cease and desist" letters or with joy at the free publicity? Fan loyalty can obviously translate into sales, but it can also pose a threat to control and ultimately to economic gain. When fans can not only view but remix, interact with, and share content, an argument can be made that individual agency has trumped textual fidelity, and with that, ownership rights. For better or worse, the new media are participatory media.

What Else Has Changed?

The field of adaptation studies itself has grown immensely—and this translates into a considerable change since 2006 when the "fidelity debates" were still ongoing (see Leitch 2008)—that is to say, when adaptations were being judged in terms of quality by how close or far they were from their "original" or "source" texts. One of the reasons for this emphasis was the fact that much of the early work in the field had been based on comparative case studies of particular works, rather than attempting to theorize more broadly the phenomenon of adaptation. With the important work of, first, Robert Stam, Kamilla Elliott, Deborah Cartmell and Imelde Whelehan, and then others such as Julie Sanders, Christine Geraghty, and Thomas Leitch, the critical terrain has changed immensely, though vestiges of fidelity criticism still remain in reviewing practices, especially of films adapted from beloved novels.

Today, if "fidelity" is invoked at all in adaptation studies, it is usually, as in this book (see Chapter 4's "Knowing and Unknowing Audiences"), in the context of fan-culture loyalty rather than as a quality of adaptive strategies. The "success" of an adaptation today, in the age of transmedia, can no longer be determined in relation to its proximity to any single "original," for none may even exist. Perhaps it is time to look instead to such things as popularity, persistence, or even the diversity and extent of dissemination for criteria of success (see Bortolotti and Hutcheon 2007: 450–53). This is how biology thinks about adaptation: in terms of successful replication and change. Perhaps cultural adaptation can be seen to work in similar ways.

If it ever does, it will be because adaptation as a field of study has been expanding its scope in recent years. New journals dedicated to adaptation have appeared, but film and fiction still appear to remain at the top of the list of major academic concerns: the title of *The Journal of Adaptation in Film and Performance* announces its limited focus, as does the "literature on screen" mandate of the more generally-named journal, *Adaptation*. The canonization of literature-to-film adaptation studies persists (see Cartmell and Whelehan 2007; Palmer 2007a and 2007b). Even the move to theorize adaptation in digital media has often been film-oriented (see Constandinides 2010). But new collections of essays have broadened the range of both the theory and practice of adaptation studies to include indigenization across cultures as well as translation across languages (in Laurence Raw, ed., *Translation, Adaptation and Transformation* [2012]; Tricia Hopton, Adam Atkinson, Jane Stadler, and Peta Mitchell, eds., *Pockets of Change: Adaptation and Cultural Transition* [2011]; and to some extent Rachel Carroll, ed., *Adaptation in Contemporary Culture: Textual Infidelities* [2009]). Interdisciplinarity now rules (see Sanders 2011: x). And therefore most new works in the field have not been simple case-study compilations, but rather serious engagements with theoretical issues as well, often within a particular historical period, as in William Verone's *Adaptation and the Avant Garde* (2011). The pedagogical focus of Nassim Balestrini's edited collection, *Adaptation and American Studies: Perspectives on Teaching and Research,* acknowledges the increasingly evident reality of the educational importance and prominence of adaptation today. (See also the textbooks on adaptation by Desmond and Hawkes [2005] and Cahir [2006].) These provide yet further reasons for the addition of the Epilogue here, in order to address not just film but also other new media that are the site of adaptation for an entire new generation of story (re)tellers and story-world makers.

Has anything *not* changed in the last six years? With some regret, I still hear echoes of those all too familiar denigrations of adaptation today in the context of transmedia storytelling where, in O'Flynn's account of the industry debate currently underway, adaptation becomes a "lesser, more simplistic mode of reworking content." Others point to a related and repeated rhetoric of commoditization and commercialization that haunts adaptation discussions of franchise storytelling (Parody 2011: 216). Some acknowledge that video game adaptations of films will probably always be seen as derivative and secondary productions, "beholden to" the prior adapted work (Moore 2010: 185). Yet, in practice, the continuing ubiquity and longevity of adaptational strategies across ever-changing and ever-developing new media suggest a more optimistic future where such dismissive evaluations just might disappear. Just as biology does not evaluate the merit of organisms relative to their ancestors—for all have equal biological validity—so too may all cultural adaptations one day be seen to have equal cultural validity.

ACKNOWLEDGMENTS

My adaptation obsession has driven many of my friends and family members to distraction over the past few years, so I owe apologies as well as thanks to the following: biological consultant and toughest but most inspirational reader Gary Bortolotti; film and Buffy The Vampire Slayer buff and copyeditor extraordinaire Sophie Mayer; inspirational editor and wicked reader William Germano; intrepid and thorough researchers Scott Rayter, Shannon MacRae, Yves St. Cyr, Jessica Li, and Ingrid Delpech; talented adapters Priscilla Galloway and Noel Baker; new media theorist and adapter-survivor Siobhan O'Flynn; legal beagle Stephanie Chong; expert videogame tutor Eric Bortolotti; communications and media expert Lee Easton; opera libretto diva Irene Morra; and engaged and enthusiastic supporting reader Lauren Bortolotti. For making me think first about adaptations—through opera—my gratitude goes to two people in particular: to my collaborator and spouse, Michael Hutcheon, and to my co-instructor and friend, Caryl Clark. Needless to say, any errors, infelicities, and absurdities are mine alone.

Many audiences helped me hone the arguments here by their careful attention, reading suggestions, and astute criticisms. My gratitude therefore to various groups at the University of Toronto, Wilfrid Laurier University, McGill University, York University, the University of Toulouse, the University of Ghent, the University of Syracuse, Pomona College, Stanford University, the University of Virginia, the Johns Hopkins Philological Society, St. Mary's University, Canadian Opera Company's Opera Exchange, the Canadian Association of Comparative Literature, the Rocky Mountain Modern Language Association, and the Modernist Studies Association.

Some of the early attempts to think through the ideas in this book were published as: "From Page to Stage to Screen: The Age of Adaptation," *The University Professor Lecture Series*, ed. Michael Goldberg (Toronto: Faculty of Arts and Science, 2003), 37–54; "Why Adapt?" *Postscript* 23.3 (summer 2004): 5–18 (special issue on adaptation); "On the Art of Adaptation," *Daedalus* (spring 2004): 108–11.

Postscript

For the second edition, two alterations in these original Acknowledgements should be "acknowledged" in turn. The first is to underline my gratitude to Siobhan O'Flynn, mentioned only in passing in the first paragraph, for she now has a much larger role in this book, as the author of its new Epilogue—for the writing of which she has my gratitude and admiration, as well as deep respect. The second is a sadder change, for 2011 marked the death of my brother, Gary Bortolotti, whom I thank first here. Between the publication of the two editions, however, we also had the pleasure of working together on a collaborative paper "On the Origin of Adaptations: Rethinking Fidelity Discourse and 'Success'—Biologically," *New Literary History* 38 2007): 443–58. It is to his memory that I dedicate this revised edition.

BEGINNING TO THEORIZE ADAPTATION:

What? Who? Why? How? Where? When?

[C]inema is still playing second fiddle to literature.

—**Rabindranath Tagore (1929)**

Writing a screenplay based on a great novel [George Eliot's *Daniel Deronda*] is foremost a labor of simplification. I don't mean only the plot, although particularly in the case of a Victorian novel teeming with secondary characters and subplots, severe pruning is required, but also the intellectual content. A film has to convey its message by images and relatively few words; it has little tolerance for complexity or irony or tergiversations. I found the work exceedingly difficult, beyond anything I had anticipated. And, I should add, depressing: I care about words more than images, and yet I was constantly sacrificing words and their connotations. You might tell me that through images film conveys a vast amount of information that words can only attempt to approximate, and you would be right, but approximation is precious in itself, because it bears the author's stamp. All in all, it seemed to me that my screenplay was worth much less than the book, and that the same would be true of the film.

—Novelist John North in Louis Begley's novel, *Shipwreck* (2003)

Familiarity and Contempt

Adaptations are everywhere today: on the television and movie screen, on the musical and dramatic stage, on the Internet, in novels and comic books, in your nearest theme park and video arcade. A certain level of self-consciousness about—and perhaps even acceptance of—their ubiquity is suggested by the fact that films have been made about the process itself, such as Spike Jonze's *Adaptation* or Terry Gilliam's *Lost in La Mancha,* both in 2002. Television series have also explored the act of adaptation, like the eleven-part BRAVO documentary "Page to Screen." Adaptations are obviously not new to our time, however; Shakespeare transferred his culture's stories from page to stage and made them available to a whole new audience. Aeschylus and Racine and Goethe and da Ponte also retold familiar stories in new forms. Adaptations are so much a part of Western culture that they appear to affirm Walter Benjamin's insight that "storytelling is always the art of repeating stories" (1992: 90). The critical pronouncements of T.S. Eliot or Northrop Frye were certainly not needed to convince avid adapters across the centuries of what, for them, has always been a truism: art is derived from other art; stories are born of other stories.

Nevertheless, in both academic criticism and journalistic reviewing, contemporary popular adaptations are most often put down as secondary, derivative, "belated, middlebrow, or culturally inferior" (as noted by Naremore 2002b: 6). This is what Louis Begley's novelist-adapter is expressing in the epigraph; but there are more strong and decidedly moralistic words used to attack film adaptations of literature: "tampering," "interference," "violation" (listed in McFarlane 1996: 12), "betrayal," "deformation," "perversion," "infidelity," and "desecration" (found by Stam 2000: 54). The move from the literary to the filmic or televisual has even been called a move to "a willfully inferior form of cognition" (Newman 1985: 129). Although adaptation's detractors argue that "all the directorial Scheherazades of the world cannot add up to one Dostoevsky" (Peary and Shatzkin 1977: 2), it does seem to be more or less acceptable to adapt *Romeo and Juliet* into a respected high art form, like an opera or a ballet, but not to make it into a movie, especially an updated one like Baz Luhrmann's (1996) *William Shakespeare's Romeo + Juliet*. If an adaptation is perceived as "lowering" a story (according to some imagined hierarchy of medium or genre), response is likely to be negative. Residual suspicion remains even in the admiration expressed for something like Julie Taymor's *Titus* (1999), her critically successful film version of Shakespeare's *Titus Andronicus*. Even in our postmodern age of cultural recycling, something—perhaps the commercial success of adaptations—would appear to make us uneasy.

As early as 1926, Virginia Woolf, commenting on the fledgling art of cinema, deplored the simplification of the literary work that inevitably occurred in its transposition to the new visual medium and called film a "parasite" and literature its "prey" and "victim" (1926: 309). Yet she also foresaw that film had the potential to develop its own independent idiom: "cinema has within its grasp innumerable symbols for emotions that have so far failed to find expression" in words (309). And so it does. In the view of film semiotician Christian Metz, cinema "tells us continuous stories; it 'says' things that could be conveyed also in the language of words; yet it says them differently. There is a reason for the possibility as well as for the necessity of adaptations" (1974: 44). However, the same could be said of adaptations in the form of musicals, operas, ballets, or songs. All these adapters relate stories in their different ways. They use the same tools that storytellers have always used: they actualize or concretize ideas; they make simplifying selections, but also amplify and extrapolate; they make analogies; they critique or show their respect, and so on. But the stories they relate are taken from elsewhere, not invented anew. Like parodies, adaptations have an overt and defining relationship to prior texts, usually revealingly called "sources." Unlike parodies, however, adaptations usually openly announce this relationship. It is the (post-) Romantic valuing of the original creation and of the originating creative genius that is clearly one source of the denigration of adapters and adaptations. Yet this negative view is actually a late addition to Western culture's long and happy history of borrowing and stealing or, more accurately, sharing stories.

For some, as Robert Stam argues, literature will always have axiomatic superiority over any adaptation of it because of its seniority as an art form. But this hierarchy also involves what he calls iconophobia (a suspicion of the visual) and logophilia (love of the word as sacred) (2000: 58). Of course, a negative view of adaptation might simply be the product of thwarted expectations on the part of a fan desiring fidelity to a beloved adapted text or on the part of someone teaching literature and therefore needing proximity to the text and perhaps some entertainment value to do so.

If adaptations are, by this definition, such inferior and secondary creations, why then are they so omnipresent in our culture and, indeed, increasing steadily in numbers? Why, even according to 1992 statistics, are 85 percent of all Oscar-winning Best Pictures adaptations? Why do adaptations make up 95 percent of all the miniseries and 70 percent of all the TV movies of the week that win Emmy Awards? Part of the answer no doubt has to do with the constant appearance of new media and new channels of mass diffusion (Groensteen 1998b: 9). These have clearly fueled an enormous demand for all kinds of stories. Nonetheless, there must be something particularly appealing about adaptations *as adaptations*.

Part of this pleasure, I want to argue, comes simply from repetition with variation, from the comfort of ritual combined with the piquancy of surprise. Recognition and remembrance are part of the pleasure (and risk) of experiencing an adaptation; so too is change. Thematic and narrative persistence combines with material variation (Ropars-Wuilleumier 1998: 131), with the result that adaptations are never simply reproductions that lose the Benjaminian aura. Rather, they carry that aura with them. But as John Ellis suggests, there is something counterintuitive about this desire for persistence within a post-Romantic and capitalist world that values novelty primarily: the "process of adaptation should thus be seen as a massive investment (financial and psychic) in the desire to repeat particular acts of consumption within a form of representation [film, in this case] that discourages such a repetition" (1982: 4–5).

As Ellis' commercial rhetoric suggests, there is an obvious financial appeal to adaptation as well. It is not just at times of economic downturn that adapters turn to safe bets: nineteenth-century Italian composers of that notoriously expensive art form, opera, usually chose to adapt reliable—that is, already financially successful—stage plays or novels in order to avoid financial risks, as well as trouble with the censors (see Trowell 1992: 1198, 1219). Hollywood films of the classical period relied on adaptations from popular novels, what Ellis calls the "tried and tested" (1982: 3), while British television has specialized in adapting the culturally accredited eighteenth- and nineteenth-century novel, or Ellis' "tried and trusted." However, it is not simply a matter of risk-avoidance; there is money to be made. A best-selling book may reach a million readers; a successful Broadway play will be seen by 1 to 8 million people; but a movie or television adaptation will find an audience of many million more (Seger 1992: 5).

The recent phenomenon of films being "musicalized" for the stage is obviously economically driven. The movies of *The Lion King* or *The Producers* offer ready-made name recognition for audiences, thereby relieving some of the anxiety for Broadway producers of expensive musicals. Like sequels and prequels, "director's cut" DVDs and spin-offs, videogame adaptations based on films are yet another way of taking one "property" in a "franchise" and reusing it in another medium. Not only will audiences already familiar with the "franchise" be attracted to the new "repurposing" (Bolter and Grusin 1999: 45), but new consumers will also be created. The multinationals who own film studios today often already own the rights to stories in other media, so they can be recycled for videogames, for example, and then marketed by the television stations they also own (Thompson 2003: 81–82).

Does the manifest commercial success of adaptations help us understand why the 2002 film *The Royal Tenenbaums* (directed by Wes Anderson with a script by Owen Wilson) opens with a book being checked out of a library—the book upon which the film implicitly claims to be based? Echoing movies like David Lean's *Great Expectations* (1946), which begins with a shot of the Dickens novel opened to Chapter 1, scene changes in Anderson's movie are marked by a shot of the Tenenbaums' "book" opened to the next chapter, the first lines of which describe what we then see on screen. Because, to my knowledge, this film is *not* adapted from any literary text, the use of this device is a direct and even parodic recall of its use in earlier films, but with a difference: the authority of literature as an institution and thus also of the act of adapting it seems to be what is being invoked and emphasized. But why would a film want to be seen as an adaptation? And what do we mean by a work being seen *as an adaptation*?

Treating Adaptations *as Adaptations*

To deal with adaptations *as adaptations* is to think of them as, to use Scottish poet and scholar Michael Alexander's great term (Ermarth 2001: 47), inherently "palimpsestuous" works, haunted at all times by their adapted texts. If we know that prior text, we always feel its presence shadowing the one we are experiencing directly. When we call a work an adaptation, we openly announce its overt relationship to another work or works. It is what Gérard Genette would call a text in the "second degree" (1982: 5), created and then received in relation to a prior text. This is why adaptation studies are so often comparative studies (cf. Cardwell 2002: 9). This is not to say that adaptations are not also autonomous works that can be interpreted and valued as such; as many theorists have insisted, they obviously are (see, for example, Bluestone 1957/1971; Ropars 1970). This is one reason why an adaptation has its own aura, its own "presence in time and space, its unique existence at the place where it happens to be" (Benjamin 1968: 214). I take such a position as axiomatic, but not as my theoretical focus. To interpret an adaptation *as an adaptation* is, in a sense, to treat it as what Roland Barthes called, not a "work," but a "text," a plural "stereophony of echoes, citations, references" (1977: 160). Although adaptations are also aesthetic objects in their own right, it is only as inherently double- or multilaminated works that they can be theorized *as adaptations*.

An adaptation's double nature does not mean, however, that proximity or fidelity to the adapted text should be the criterion of judgment or the focus of analysis. For a long time, "fidelity criticism," as it came to be known, was the critical orthodoxy in adaptation studies, especially when dealing with canonical works such as those of Pushkin or Dante. Today that dominance has been challenged from a variety of perspectives (e.g., McFarlane 1996: 194; Cardwell 2002: 19) and with a range of results. And, as George Bluestone pointed out early on, when a film becomes a financial or critical success, the question of its faithfulness is given hardly any thought (1957/1971: 114). My decision not to concentrate on this particular aspect of the relationship between adapted text and adaptation means that there appears to be little need to engage directly in the constant debate over degrees of proximity to the "original" that has generated those many typologies of adaptation processes: borrowing versus intersection versus transformation (Andrew 1980: 10–12); analogy versus commentary versus transposition (Wagner 1975: 222–31); using the source as raw material versus reinterpretation of only the core narrative structure versus a literal translation (Klein and Parker 1981: 10).

Of more interest to me is the fact that the morally loaded discourse of fidelity is based on the implied assumption that adapters aim simply to reproduce the adapted text (e.g., Orr 1984: 73). Adaptation is repetition, but repetition without replication. And there are manifestly many different possible intentions behind the act of adaptation: the urge to consume and erase the memory of the adapted text or to call it into question is as likely as the desire to pay tribute by copying. Adaptations such as film remakes can even be seen as mixed in intent: "contested homage" (Greenberg 1998: 115), Oedipally envious and worshipful at the same time (Horton and McDougal 1998b: 8).

If the idea of fidelity should not frame any theorizing of adaptation today, what should? According to its dictionary meaning, "to adapt" is to adjust, to alter, to make suitable. This can be done in any number of ways. As the next section will explore in more depth, the phenomenon of adaptation can be defined from three distinct but interrelated perspectives, for I take it as no accident that we use the same word—adaptation—to refer to the process and the product.

First, seen as a *formal entity or product*, an adaptation is an announced and extensive transposition of a particular work or works. This "transcoding" can involve a shift of medium (a poem to a film) or genre (an epic to a novel), or a change of frame and therefore context: telling the same story from a different point of view, for instance, can create a manifestly different interpretation. Transposition can also mean a shift in ontology from the real to the fictional, from a historical account or biography to a fictionalized narrative or drama. Sister Helen Prejean's 1994 book, *Dead Man Walking: An Eyewitness Account of the Death Penalty in the United States,* became first a fictionalized film (directed by Tim Robbins, 1995) and then, a few years later, an opera (written by Terrence McNally and Jake Heggie).

Second, as *a process of creation,* the act of adaptation always involves both (re-)interpretation and then (re-)creation; this has been called both appropriation and salvaging, depending on your perspective. For every aggressive appropriator outed by a political opponent, there is a patient salvager. Priscilla Galloway, an adapter of mythic and historical narratives for children and young adults, has said that she is motivated by a desire to preserve stories that are worth knowing but will not necessarily speak to a new audience without creative "reanimation" (2004), and *that* is her task. African film adaptations of traditional oral legends are also seen as a way of preserving a rich heritage in an aural and visual mode (Cham 2005: 300).

Third, seen from the perspective of its *process of reception,* adaptation is a form of intertextuality: we experience adaptations (*as adaptations*) as palimpsests through our memory of other works that resonate through repetition with variation. For the right audience, then, the novelization by Yvonne Navarro of a film like *Hellboy* (2004) may echo not only with Guillermo del Toro's film but also with the Dark Horse Comics series from which the latter was adapted. Paul Anderson's 2002 film *Resident Evil* will be experienced differently by those who have played the videogame of the same name, from which the movie was adapted, than by those who have not.

In short, adaptation can be described as the following:

- An acknowledged transposition of a recognizable other work or works
- A creative *and* an interpretive act of appropriation/salvaging
- An extended intertextual engagement with the adapted work

Therefore, an adaptation is a derivation that is not derivative—a work that is second without being secondary. It is its own palimpsestic thing.

There is some apparent validity to the general statement that adaptation "as a concept can expand or contract. Writ large, adaptation includes almost any act of alteration performed upon specific cultural works of the past and dovetails with a general process of cultural re-creation" (Fischlin and Fortier 2000: 4). But, from a pragmatic point of view, such vast definition would clearly make adaptation rather difficult to theorize. My more restricted double definition of adaptation as process and product is closer to the common usage of the word and is broad enough to allow me to treat not just films and stage productions, but also musical arrangements and song covers, visual art revisitations of prior works and comic book versions of history, poems put to music and remakes of films, and videogames and interactive art. It also permits me to draw distinctions; for instance, allusions to and brief echoes of other works would not qualify as extended engagements, nor do most examples of musical sampling, because they recontextualize only short fragments of music. Plagiarisms are not acknowledged appropriations, and sequels and prequels are not really adaptations either, nor is fan fiction. There is a difference between never wanting a story to end—the reason behind sequels and prequels, according to Marjorie Garber (2003: 73–74)—and wanting to retell the same story over and over in different ways. With adaptations, we seem to desire the repetition as much as the change. Maybe this is why, in the eyes of the law, adaptation is a "derivative work"—that is, one based on one or more preexisting works, but "recast, transformed" (17 USC §101). That seemingly simple definition, however, is also a theoretical can of worms.

Exactly What Gets Adapted? How?

What precisely is "recast" and "transformed"? In law, ideas themselves cannot be copyrighted; only their expression can be defended in court. And herein lies the whole problem. As Kamilla Elliott has astutely noted, adaptation commits the heresy of showing that form (expression) can be separated from content (ideas)—something both mainstream aesthetic and semiotic theories have resisted or denied (2003: 133), even as legal theory has embraced it. The form changes with adaptation (thus evading most legal prosecution); the content persists. But what exactly constitutes that transferred and transmuted "content"?

Many professional reviewers and audience members alike resort to the elusive notion of the "spirit" of a work or an artist that has to be captured and conveyed in the adaptation for it to be a success. The "spirit" of Dickens or Wagner is invoked, often to justify radical changes in the "letter" or form. Sometimes it is "tone" that is deemed central, though rarely defined (e.g., Linden 1971: 158, 163); at other times it is "style" (Seger 1992: 157). But all three are arguably equally subjective and, it would appear, difficult to discuss, much less theorize.

Most theories of adaptation assume, however, that the story is the common denominator, the core of what is transposed across different media and genres, each of which deals with that story in formally different ways and, I would add, through different modes of engagement—narrating, performing, or interacting. In adapting, the story-argument goes, "equivalences" are sought in different sign systems for the various elements of the story: its themes, events, world, characters, motivations, points of view, consequences, contexts, symbols, imagery, and so on. As Millicent Marcus has explained, however, there are two opposing theoretical schools of thought on this point: either a story can exist independently of any embodiment in any particular signifying system or, on the contrary, it cannot be considered separately from its material mode of mediation (1993: 14). What the phenomenon of adaptation suggests, however, is that, although the latter is obviously true for the audience, whose members experience the story in a particular material form, the various elements of the story can be and are considered separately by adapters and by theorists, if only because technical constraints of different media will inevitably highlight different aspects of that story (Gaudreault and Marion 1998: 45).

Themes are perhaps the easiest story elements to see as adaptable across media and even genres or framing contexts. As author Louis Begley said about the themes of his 1996 novel *About Schmidt* when the work was transcribed to the screen by Alexander Payne and Jim Taylor: "I was able to hear them rather like melodies transposed into a different key" (2003: 1). Many Romantic ballets were derived from

Hans Christian Andersen's stories simply, some say, because of their traditional and easily accessible themes, such as quests, magical tasks, disguise and revelation, and innocence versus evil (Mackrell 2004). Composer Alexander Zemlinsky wrote a "symphonic fantasy" adaptation of Andersen's famous "The Little Mermaid" (1836) called *Die Seejungfrau* (1905) that includes musical programmatic descriptions of such elements as the storm and musical leitmotifs that tell the story and its themes of love, pain, and nature, as well as music that evokes emotions and atmosphere befitting the story. A modern manual for adapters explains, however, that themes are, in fact, of most importance to novels and plays; in TV and films, themes must always serve the story action and "reinforce or dimensionalize" it, for in these forms, storyline is supreme—except in European "art" films (Seger 1992: 14).

Characters, too, can obviously be transported from one text to another, and indeed, as Murray Smith has argued, characters are crucial to the rhetorical and aesthetic effects of both narrative and performance texts because they engage receivers' imaginations through what he calls recognition, alignment, and allegiance (1995: 4–6). The theater and the novel are usually considered the forms in which the human subject is central. Psychological development (and thus receiver empathy) is part of the narrative and dramatic arc when characters are the focus of adaptations. Yet, in playing videogame adaptations of films, we can actually "become" one of the characters and act in their fictional world.

The separate units of the story (or the *fabula)* can also be transmediated—just as they can be summarized in digest versions or translated into another language (Hamon 1977: 264). But they may well change—often radically—in the process of adaptation, and not only (but most obviously) in terms of their plot ordering. Pacing can be transformed, time compressed or expanded. Shifts in the focalization or point of view of the adapted story may lead to major differences. When David Lean wrote, directed, and edited the film version of E.M. Forster's 1924 novel *Passage to India* in 1984, he altered the novel's focalization on the two men, Fielding and Aziz, and their crosscultural interrelations. Instead, the film tells Adela's story, adding scenes to establish her character and make it more complex and interesting than it arguably is in the novel. More radically, *Miss Havisham's Fire* (1979/revised 1996), Dominick Argento and John Olon-Scrymgeour's operatic adaptation of Dickens' *Great Expectations* (1860/1861), all but ignored the story of the protagonist Pip to tell that of the eccentric Miss Havisham.

In other cases, it might be the point of departure or conclusion that is totally transfigured in adaptation. For instance, in offering a different ending in the film version of Michael Ondaatje's novel *The English Patient*, Anthony Minghella, in his film script and in his directing, removed the postcolonial politics of the Indian Kip's response to the bombing of Hiroshima, substituting instead another smaller, earlier bomb that kills his co-worker and friend. In other words, a personal crisis is made to replace a political one. As the movie's editor Walter Murch articulated the decision: "The film [unlike the novel] was so much about those five individual people: the Patient, Hana, Kip, Katharine, Caravaggio—that to suddenly open it up near the end and ask the audience to imagine the death of hundreds of thousands of unknown people … . It was too abstract. So the bomb of Hiroshima became the bomb that killed Hardy, someone you knew" (qtd. in Ondaatje 2002: 213). And, in the movie version (but not in the novel), the nurse Hana actually gives her patient the fatal morphine shot at the end, undoubtedly so that she can be seen to merge with his lover Katharine in the patient's memory, as in ours. On the soundtrack, their voices merge as well. The focus of the film is on the doomed love affair alone. This change of ending may not be quite the same as Nahum Tate's making Cordelia survive and marry Edgar in his infamous 1681 version of *King Lear*, but it is a major shift of emphasis nonetheless.

If we move from considering only the medium in this way to considering changes in the more general manner of story presentation, however, other differences in what gets adapted begin to appear. This is because each manner involves a different mode of engagement on the part of both audience and adapter. As we shall see in more detail shortly, being shown a story is not the same as being told it—and neither is the same as participating in it or interacting with it, that is, experiencing a story directly and kinesthetically. With each mode, different things get adapted and in different ways. As my examples so far suggest, to tell a story, as in novels, short stories, and even historical accounts, is to describe, explain, summarize, expand; the narrator has a point of view and great power to leap through time and space and sometimes to venture inside the minds of characters. To show a story, as in movies, ballets, radio and stage plays, musicals and operas, involves a direct aural and usually visual performance experienced in real time.

Although neither telling nor showing renders its audience passive in the least, they also do not engage people as immediately and viscerally as do virtual environments, videogames (played on any platform), or even theme-park rides that are, in their own ways, adaptations or "remediations" (Bolter and Grusin 1999). The interactive, physical nature of this kind of engagement entails changes both in the story and even in the importance of story itself. If a film can be said to have a three-act structure—a beginning in which a conflict is established; a middle in which the implications of the conflict are played out; an end where the conflict is resolved—then a videogame adaptation of a film can be argued to have a different three-act structure. The introductory material, often presented in what are called "movie cut-scenes," is the first act; the second is the core gameplay experience; the third is the climax, again often in filmed cut-scenes (Lindley 2002: 206). Acts one and three obviously do the narrative work—through showing—and set up the story frame, but both are in fact peripheral to the core: the second-act gameplay, with its intensity of cognitive and physical engagement, moves the narrative along through visual spectacle and audio effects (including music) and through problem-solving challenges. As Marie-Laure Ryan has pointed out: "The secret to the narrative success of games is their ability to exploit the most fundamental of the forces that move a plot forward: the solving of problems" (2004c: 349). Story, in this case, is no longer central or at least no longer an end in itself, although it is still present as a means toward a goal (King 2002: 51).

Although there has been a long debate recently about whether interactivity and storytelling are at odds with one another (see Ryan 2001: 244; Ryan 2004c: 337), what is more relevant in a game adaptation is the fact that players can inhabit a known fictional, often striking, visual world of digital animation. Nintendo's 3-D world of *Zelda*, for instance, has been described as "a highly intricate environment, with a complicated economics, an awesome cast of creatures, a broad range of landscapes and indoor scenarios, and an elaborated chemistry, biology, geology and ecology so that its world can almost be studied like an alternative version of nature" (Weinbren 2002: 180). Though *Zelda* is not an adaptation, this description of its world fits so many games that are adaptations. Similarly, Disney World visitors who go on the Aladdin ride can enter and physically navigate a universe originally presented as a linear experience through film.

What gets adapted here is a heterocosm, literally an "other world" or cosmos, complete, of course, with the stuff of a story—settings, characters, events, and situations. To be more precise, it is the *"res extensa"*—to use Descartes' terminology—of that world, its material, physical dimension, which is transposed and then experienced through multisensorial interactivity (Grau 2003: 3). This heterocosm possesses what theorists call "truth-of-coherence" (Ruthven 1979: 11)—here, plausibility and consistency of movement and graphics within the context of the game (Ward 2002: 129)—just as do narrated and performed worlds, but this world also has a particular kind of "truth-of-correspondence"—not to any "real world" but to the universe of a particular adapted text. The videogame of *The Godfather* uses the voices and physical images of some of the film's actors, including Marlon Brando, but the linear structure of the movie is transmuted into that of a flexible game model in which the player becomes a nameless mafia henchman, trying to win the respect of the main characters by taking over businesses, killing people, and so on. In other words, the point of view has been changed from that of the mafia bosses to that of the underlings, who allow us to see familiar scenes from the film's world from a different perspective and possibly create a different resolution.

What videogames, like virtual reality experiments, cannot easily adapt is what novels can portray so well: the *"res cogitans,"* the space of the mind. Even screen and stage media have difficulty with this dimension, because when psychic reality is shown rather than told about, it has to be made manifest in the material realm to be perceived by the audience. However, expanding the idea of what can be adapted to include this idea of a heterocosm or visual world as well as other aspects of the story opens up the possibility of considering, for instance, Aubrey Beardsley's famous illustrations for Oscar Wilde's play *Salomé* as a possible adaptation or even Picasso's cubist recodings of some of the canonical paintings of Velásquez.

Are some kinds of stories and their worlds more easily adaptable than others? Susan Orlean's book, *The Orchid Thief*, proved intractable to screenwriter "Charlie Kaufman" in the movie *Adaptation*. Or did it? Linear realist novels, it would appear, are more easily adapted for the screen than experimental ones, or so we might assume from the evidence: the works of Charles Dickens, Ian Fleming, and Agatha Christie are more often adapted than those of Samuel Beckett, James Joyce, or Robert Coover. "Radical" texts, it is said, are "reduced to a kind of cinematic homogenization" (Axelrod 1996: 204) when they are adapted. But Dickens' novels have been called "theatrical" in their lively dialogue and their individualized, if broadly drawn, characters, complete with idiosyncratic speech patterns. Their strongly pictorial descriptions and potential for scenes of spectacle also make them readily adaptable or at least "adaptogenic" (Groensteen 1998a: 270) to the stage and screen. Historically, it is melodramatic worlds and stories that have lent themselves to adaptation to the form of opera and musical dramas, where music can reinforce the stark emotional oppositions and tensions created by the requisite generic compression (because it takes longer to sing than to speak a line). Today, spectacular special effects films like the various *The Matrix* or *Star Wars* movies are the ones likely to spawn popular videogames whose players can enjoy entering and manipulating the cinematic fantasy world.

Double Vision: Defining Adaptation

Given this complexity of what can be adapted and of the means of adaptation, people keep trying to coin new words to replace the confusing simplicity of the word "adaptation" (e.g., Gaudreault 1998: 268). But most end up admitting defeat: the word has stuck for a reason. Yet, however straightforward the idea of adaptation may appear on the surface, it is actually very difficult to define, in part, as we have seen, because we use the same word for the process and the product. As a product, an adaptation can be given a formal definition, but as a process—of creation and of reception—other aspects have to be considered. This is why those different perspectives touched on earlier are needed to discuss and define adaptation.

Adaptation as Product: Announced, Extensive, Specific Transcoding

As openly acknowledged and extended reworkings of particular other texts, adaptations are often compared to translations. Just as there is no such thing as a literal translation, there can be no literal adaptation. Nevertheless, the study of both has suffered from domination by "normative and source-oriented approaches" (Hermans 1985: 9). Transposition to another medium, or even moving within the same one, always means change or, in the language of the new media, "reformatting." And there will always be both gains and losses (Stam 2000: 62). Although this seems commonsensical enough, it is important to remember that, in most concepts of translation, the source text is granted an axiomatic primacy and authority, and the rhetoric of comparison has most often been that of faithfulness and equivalence. Walter Benjamin did alter this frame of reference when he argued, in "The Task of the Translator," that translation is not a rendering of some fixed nontextual meaning to be copied or paraphrased or reproduced; rather, it is an engagement with the original text that makes us see that text in different ways (1992: 77). Recent translation theory argues that translation involves a transaction between texts and between languages and is thus "an act of both inter-cultural and inter-temporal communication" (Bassnett 2002: 9).

This newer sense of translation comes closer to defining adaptation as well. In many cases, because adaptations are to a different medium, they are re-mediations, that is, specifically translations in the form of intersemiotic transpositions from one sign system (for example, words) to another (for example, images). This is translation but in a very specific sense: as transmutation or transcoding, that is, as necessarily a recoding into a new set of conventions as well as signs. For example, Harold Pinter's screenplay for Karel Reisz's film *The French Lieutenant's Woman* (1981) transposed the narrative of John Fowles' novel (1969) into a totally cinematic code. The novel juxtaposed a modern narrator and a Victorian story; in the equally self-reflexive movie, we have, instead, a

Victorian scenario within a modern film that is itself a movie about the filming of the nineteenth-century story. The self-consciousness of the novel's narrator was translated into cinematic mirroring, as the actors who play the Victorian characters live out the scripted romance in their own lives. The role-playing motif of film acting effectively echoed the hypocrisy and the schizoid morality of the Victorian world of the novel (see Sinyard 1986: 135–40).

The idea of paraphrase (Bluestone 1957/1971: 62) is an alternative frequently offered to this translation analogy. Etymologically, a paraphrase is a mode of telling "beside" (para) and, according to the *Oxford English Dictionary*, one of its first meanings is "a free rendering or amplification of a passage" that is verbal but, by extension, musical as well. John Dryden is quoted as defining paraphrase as "translation with latitude, where the author is kept in view …, but his words are not so strictly followed as his sense; and that too is admitted to be amplified." Perhaps this describes best what scriptwriter Robert Nelson Jacobs and director Lasse Hallstrom did in their 2001 cinematic adaptation of E. Annie Proulx's novel *The Shipping News* (1993). The novel protagonist's psychic world, which is amply explored, thanks to the omniscient narration, is freely rendered in the film by having him think in visualized headlines—a realistic device for a newspaperman. In a sense, even the novel's metaphoric writing style is paraphrased in the recurring visual imagery derived from his fear of drowning. Similarly, Virginia Woolf's densely rich associative language in *Mrs. Dalloway* is rendered or paraphrased in "associative visual imagery" in the 1998 film directed by Marleen Gorris (see Cuddy-Keane 1998: 173–74).

Paraphrase and translation analogies can also be useful in considering what I earlier called the ontological shift that can happen in adaptations of an historical event or an actual person's life into a reimagined, fictional form. The adapted text may be an authoritative historical rendering or a more indefinite archive (see Andrew 2004: 200), and the form can range from "biopics" to "heritage" films, from television docudramas to videogames, such as *JFK Reloaded* (by Traffic Games in Scotland), based on the Kennedy assassination. Sometimes the text being paraphrased or translated is very immediate and available. For example, the German television movie called *Wannseekonferenz* (*The*

Wannsee Conference) was an 85-minute film adaptation scripted from the actual minutes of the 85-minute meeting held in 1942 and chaired by Reinhard Heydrich, the Chief of the German State Police, in which the "Final Solution to the Jewish Question" was decided. In 2001, Loring Mandel did a further adaptation in English for BBC and HBO called *Conspiracy*.

At other times, the adapted text is more complex or even multiple: Sidney Lumet's 1975 film *Dog Day Afternoon* was a fictionalized adaptation of an actual 1972 bank robbery and hostage situation in Brooklyn that was covered live on television and was much discussed in the media. In fact, a *Life* magazine article by P.F. Kluge was the basis of the film's screenplay. But in 2002 artist Pierre Huyghe asked the real robber, John Wojtowicz, to reenact and narrate—in effect, to translate or paraphrase—the original event for his camera. In the process, a second-level adaptation occurred: as the perpetrator relived his own past, what became clear was that he could not do so except through the lenses of the subsequent movie version. In effect, the film became, for him, as much the text to be adapted as was the lived event preserved in either his memory or the media coverage. In ontological shifts, it makes little sense to talk about adaptations as "historically accurate" or "historically inaccurate" in the usual sense. *Schindler's List* is not *Shoah* (see Hansen 2001) in part because it is an adaptation of a novel by Thomas Keneally, which is itself based on survivor testimony. In other words, it is a paraphrase or translation of a *particular* other text, a particular interpretation of history. The seeming simplicity of the familiar label, "based on a true story," is a ruse: in reality, such historical adaptations are as complex as historiography itself.

Adaptation as Process

The Adapter's Creative Interpretation/Interpretive Creation   Early in the film *Adaptation*, screenwriter "Charlie Kaufman" faces an anguished dilemma: he worries about his responsibility as an adapter to an author and a book he respects. As he senses, what is involved in adapting can be a process of appropriation, of taking possession of another's story, and filtering it, in a sense, through one's own sensibility, interests, and talents. Therefore, adapters are first interpreters and then creators. This is one reason why *Morte a Venezia,* Luchino Visconti's 1971 Italian film version of Thomas Mann's 1911 novella *Der Tod in Venedig,* is so different in focus and impact from Benjamin Britten and Myfanwy Piper's English opera *Death in Venice,* which premiered only a few years later in 1973. The other reason, of course, is the adapter's choice of medium. E.H. Gombrich offers a useful analogy when he suggests that if an artist stands before a landscape with a pencil in hand, he or she will "look for those aspects which can be rendered in lines"; if it is a paintbrush that the hand holds, the artist's vision of the very same landscape will be in terms of masses, not lines (1961: 65). Therefore, an adapter coming to a story with the idea of adapting it for a film would be attracted to different aspects of it than an opera librettist would be.

Usually adaptations, especially from long novels, mean that the adapter's job is one of subtraction or contraction; this is called "a surgical art" (Abbott 2002: 108) for a good reason. In adapting Philip Pullman's trilogy of novels, *His Dark Materials,* from 1,300 print pages to two three-hour plays, Nicholas Wright had to cut major characters (for example, the Oxford scientist Mary Malone) and therefore whole worlds they inhabit (for example, the land of the mulefas); he had to speed up the action and involve the Church right from the start. Of course, he also had to find two major narrative climaxes to replace the three of the trilogy. He also found he had to explain certain themes and even plot details, for there was not as much time for the play's audience to piece things together as there was for those reading the novels.

Obviously, not all adaptations involve simply cutting. Short stories, in particular, have often inspired movies; for example, John M. Cunningham's 1947 "The Tin Star" became Fred Zinneman and Carl Forman's 1952 film *High Noon.* Short story adaptations have had to expand their source material considerably. When filmmaker Neil Jordan and Angela Carter adapted Carter's story "The Company of Wolves" in 1984, they added details from two other related tales in Carter's *The Bloody Chamber* (1979): "The Werewolf" and "Wolf-Alice." They took a contemporary prologue from Carter's own earlier radio play adaptation to set up the dream logic of the piece. Screenwriter Noel Baker similarly described his attempt to take "a whisper of a movie idea" and make it into a feature film. He had been asked to adapt not a short story but, in fact, Michael Turner's book *Hard Core Logo* (1993), but this book is a fragmentary narrative about the reunion of a 1980s punk band that is made up of letters, songs, answering machine messages, invoices, photos, hand-written notes, diary entries, contracts, and so on. Baker said that he first felt the challenge of the fragmentation itself and then of the fact that it was "lean and spare, full of gaps and silences, the eloquence of things left unsaid" (1997: 10). In the end, he noted in his diary that this latter point was what made the task more fun, more creative: "Must thank Turner for writing so little yet suggesting so much" (14).

Of course, there is a wide range of reasons why adapters might choose a particular story and then transcode it into a particular medium or genre. As noted earlier, their aim might well be to economically and artistically supplant the prior works. They are just as likely to want to contest the aesthetic or political values of the adapted text as to pay homage. This, of course, is one of the reasons why the rhetoric of "fidelity" is less than adequate to discuss the process of adaptation. Whatever the motive, from the adapter's perspective, adaptation is an act of appropriating or salvaging, and this is always a double process of interpreting and then creating something new.

If this sounds somewhat familiar, there is good reason, given the long history in the West of *imitatio* or *mimesis*—imitation—as what Aristotle saw as part of the instinctive behavior of humans and the source of their pleasure in art (Wittkower 1965: 143). Imitation of great works of art, in particular, was not intended only to capitalize on the prestige and authority of the ancients or even to offer a pedagogical model (as the *Rhetorica ad Herennium* argued [I.ii.3 and IV.i.2]), though it did both. It was also a form of creativity: "*Imitatio* is neither plagiarism nor a flaw in the constitution of Latin literature. It is a dynamic law of its existence" (West and Woodman 1979: ix). Like classical imitation, adaptation also is not slavish copying; it is a process of making the adapted material one's own. In both, the novelty is in what one *does with* the other text. Indeed, for "Longinus," *imitatio* went together with *aemulatio*, linking imitation and creativity (Russell 1979: 10). Perhaps one way to think about unsuccessful adaptations is not in terms of infidelity to a prior text, but in terms of a lack of the creativity and skill to make the text one's own and thus autonomous.

For the reader, spectator, or listener, adaptation *as adaptation* is unavoidably a kind of intertextuality *if the receiver is acquainted with the adapted text.* It is an ongoing dialogical process, as Mikhail Bakhtin would have said, in which we compare the work we already know with the one we are experiencing (Stam 2000: 64). By stressing the relation of individual works to other works and to an entire cultural system, French semiotic and post-structuralist theorizing of intertextuality (e.g., by Barthes 1971/1977; Kristeva 1969/1986) has been important in its challenges to dominant post-Romantic notions of originality, uniqueness, and autonomy. Instead, texts are said to be mosaics of citations that are visible and invisible, heard and silent; they are always already written and read. So, too, are adaptations, but with the added proviso that they are also acknowledged as adaptations *of specific texts.* Often, the audience will recognize that a work is an adaptation of more than one specific text. For instance, when later writers reworked—for radio, stage, and even screen—John Buchan's 1914 novel, *The Thirty-Nine Steps*, they often adapted Alfred Hitchcock's dark and cynical 1935 film adaptation along with the novel (Glancy 2003: 99–100). And films about Dracula today are as often seen as adaptations of other earlier films as they are of Bram Stoker's novel.

The Audience's "Palimpsestuous" Intertextuality   For audiences, such adaptations are obviously "multilaminated"; they are directly and openly connected to recognizable other works, and that connection is part of their formal identity, but also of what we might call their hermeneutic identity. This is what keeps under control the "background noise" (Hinds 1998: 19) of all the other intertextual parallels to the work the audience might make that are due to similar artistic and social conventions, rather than specific works. In all cases, the engagements with these other works in adaptations are extended ones, not passing allusions.

Part of both the pleasure and the frustration of experiencing an adaptation is the familiarity bred through repetition and memory. Depending on our relationship with any of the traditionally choreographed versions of Tchaikovsky's 1877 ballet, *Swan Lake* (and there are many of these, from the Petipa/Ivanov one to its reworkings by Ashton and Dowell), we will be either delighted or irritated by Matthew Bourne's adaptation, with its updating and queer ironizing of the popular classical ballet. His muscular male swans and their homo-erotic, violent, and sexually charged choreography allow, among many other things, the traditional *pas de deux* between the prince and the swan to be a dance of equals—perhaps for the first time. This prince is no athletic assistant to a ballerina star. Not everyone in the audience will enjoy this transgression of and critical commentary upon the sexual politics of the balletic tradition. But no matter what our response, our intertextual expectations about medium and genre, as well as about this specific work, are brought to the forefront of our attention. The same will be true of experiencing the Australian Dance Theatre's version, entitled *Birdbrain* (2001), with its hyperspeed edgy choreography, film clips, and mechanized music. As audience members, we need memory in order to experience difference as well as similarity.

Modes of Engagement

A doubled definition of adaptation as a product (as extensive, particular transcoding) and as a process (as creative reinterpretation and palimpsestic intertextuality) is one way to address the various dimensions of the broader phenomenon of adaptation. An emphasis on process allows us to expand the traditional focus of adaptation studies on medium-specificity and individual comparative case studies in order to consider as well relations among the major modes of engagement: that is, it permits us to think about how adaptations allow people to tell, show, or interact with stories. We can be told or shown a story, each in a range of different media. However, the perspective, and thus the grammar, changes with the third mode of engagement; as audience members, we interact *with* stories in, for instance, the new media, from virtual reality to machinima. All three modes are arguably "immersive," though to different degrees and in different ways: for example, the telling mode (a novel) immerses us through imagination in a fictional world; the showing mode (plays and films) immerses us through the perception of the aural and the visual—the latter in a way related to that of Renaissance perspective painting and Baroque *trompe l'oeil* (Ryan 2001: 3); the participatory

Key Word: immersive

mode (videogames) immerses us physically and kinesthetically. But if all are, in some sense of the word, "immersive," only the last of them is usually called "interactive." Neither the act of looking at and interpreting black marks—words or notes—on a white page nor that of perceiving and interpreting a direct representation of a story on the stage or screen is in any way passive; both are imaginatively, cognitively, and emotionally active. But the move to participatory modes in which we also engage physically with the story and its world—whether it be in a violent action game or a role-playing or puzzle/skill testing one—is not more active but certainly active in a different way.

In the telling mode—in narrative literature, for example—our engagement begins in the realm of imagination, which is simultaneously controlled by the selected, directing words of the text and liberated—that is, unconstrained by the limits of the visual or aural. We can stop reading at any point; we can re-read or skip ahead; we hold the book in our hands and feel, as well as see, how much of the story remains to be read. But with the move to the mode of showing, as in film and stage adaptations, we are caught in an unrelenting, forward-driving story. And we have moved from the imagination to the realm of direct perception—with its mix of both detail and broad focus. The performance mode teaches us that language is not the only way to express meaning or to relate stories. Visual and gestural representations are rich in complex associations; music offers aural "equivalents" for characters' emotions and, in turn, provokes affective responses in the audience; sound, in general, can enhance, reinforce, or even contradict the visual and verbal aspects. On the other hand, however, a *shown* dramatization cannot approximate the complicated verbal play of *told* poetry or the interlinking of description, narration, and explanation that is so easy for prose narrative to accomplish. Telling a story in words, either orally or on paper, is never the same as showing it visually and aurally in any of the many performance media available.

Some theorists argue that, at a basic level, there is no significant difference between a verbal text and visual images, that, as W.J.T. Mitchell outlines this position, "communicative, expressive acts, narration, argument, description, exposition and other so-called 'speech acts' are not medium-specific, are not 'proper' to some medium or another"

(1994: 160). (See also Cohen 1991b.) A consideration of the differences between the modes of engagement of telling and showing, however, suggests quite the contrary: each mode, like each medium, *has* its own specificity, if not its own essence. In other words, no one mode is inherently good at doing one thing and not another; but each has at its disposal different means of expression—media and genres—and so can aim at and achieve certain things better than others.

Consider, for example, the interesting technical task the British novelist E. M. Forster set himself at one point in his 1910 novel *Howards End*: how to represent *in told words* the effect and the meaning of *performed music*—music that his readers would have to imagine, of course, and not hear. He begins the novel's fifth chapter with these words: "It will be generally admitted that Beethoven's Fifth Symphony is the most sublime noise that has ever penetrated into the ear of man" (Forster 1910/1941: 31). Forster goes on to describe the effect on each member of the Schlegel family, whose ears this "sublime noise" penetrates. In a telling mode, a novel can do this: it can take us into the minds and feelings of characters at will. However, the focus of this episode, in which the family attends a symphony concert in Queen's Hall in London together, is specifically on one character, Helen Schlegel—young, newly hurt in love, and therefore someone whose response to the music is intensely personal and deeply tied to her emotional troubles at the time.

As the orchestra plays the third movement, we are told that she hears "a goblin walking quietly over the universe, from end to end" (32). In the first movement, she had heard "heroes and shipwrecks," but here it is terrible goblins she hears, and an "interlude of elephants dancing" (32). These creatures are frightening because of what Helen sees as their casualness: they "observed in passing that there was no such thing as splendour or heroism in the world" (32). Forster continues, telling us that: "Helen could not contradict them, for, once at all events, she had felt the same, and had seen the reliable walls of youth collapse. Panic and emptiness! Panic and emptiness! The goblins were right" (33). Totally moved, not to mention upset, by the end of the piece, she finds she has to leave her family and be alone. As the novel puts it: "The music had summed up to her all that had happened or could happen in her career. She read it as a tangible statement, which could never be superceded" (34). She leaves the hall, taking by mistake the umbrella of a stranger, one Leonard Bast, who will play an important part in the rest of her life and, indeed, in the rest of the novel.

What happens when this told scene is transposed to the showing mode—in this case, to film—in the Merchant/Ivory production adapted by Ruth Prawer Jhabvala? The concert, in a sense, remains, but Helen attends alone. It is not a full orchestral concert this time, but a four-handed piano performance, accompanying a lecture on Beethoven's Fifth Symphony. A few of Forster's own words remain, but very few. Because we can only *see* Helen on film and not get into her head, we can only guess at her thoughts. So in the shown version, it is not she who experiences the "panic and emptiness" of the goblins; it is simply the lecturer who uses this as an image in his explanation of the piece in response to a question from a member of the audience. In fact, Helen, from what we can see, seems rather more bored than upset by the whole experience. We do get to hear the full orchestral version of the symphony on the soundtrack (nondiegetically), but only after she leaves the hall, pursued by the young man whose umbrella she has taken by mistake.

Although Forster uses this scene to tell us about the imaginative and emotional world of Helen Schlegel, the film makes it the occasion to show us Helen meeting Leonard Bast in an appropriately culturally loaded context. In terms of plot action, that is indeed what happens in this scene, and so this is what the film aims to achieve. Interestingly, what the showing mode can do that the telling one cannot is to let us actually *hear* Beethoven's music. We cannot, however, get at the interior of the characters' minds as they listen; they must visibly, physically embody their responses for the camera to record, or they must talk about their reactions. Of course, this film contains lots of performed talk about music, art, and many other things, and not only in this rather overt lecture form.

Interacting with a story is different again from being shown or told it—and not only because of the more immediate kind of immersion it allows. As in a play or film, in virtual reality or a videogame, language alone does not have to conjure up a world; that world is present before our eyes and ears. But in the showing mode we do not physically enter that world and proceed to act within it. Because of its visceral impact, a scripted paintball war game would be considered by some to be a different kind of adaptation of a war story than, say, even the graphic violence of a film like *Saving Private Ryan* (1998). Civil War battle reenactments may involve role-playing, and new narrative media works may require database "combinatorics," but, in both cases, the audience's engagement is different in kind than when we are told or shown the same story.

Stories, however, do not consist only of the material means of their transmission (media) or the rules that structure them (genres). Those means and those rules permit and then channel narrative expectations and communicate narrative meaning *to someone* in *some context*, and they are created *by someone* with that intent. There is, in short, a wider communicative context that any theory of adaptation would do well to consider. That context will change with the mode of presentation or engagement: the telling mode can use a variety of material media, as can the live or mediated showing mode, just as each medium can support a variety of genres. But media distinctions alone will not necessarily allow the kind of differentiations that adaptations call to our attention. For instance, "machinima" is a form of filmmaking that uses computer game technology to make films within the virtual reality of a game engine. As such, it's a hybrid form, but basically the *medium* is electronic. The machinima adaptation of Percy Bysshe Shelley's 1817 poem "Ozymandias" (by Hugh Hancock for Strange Company) is indeed a digitalized visualization of the poem's "story" about a man walking across a solitary desert and finding a ruined statue of a king inscribed with a chillingly ironic message about worldly glory and the power of time. Even if the figure of the man on screen creates suspense by having to wipe the sand off the final line of the inscription ("Look upon my works, ye Mighty, and despair"), we experience little in the digital version of the frisson we feel reading the poem's devastating irony. Considering medium alone would not be useful to getting at the success (or failure) of this adaptation: although this machinima is in a digital medium, it is not interactive. If anything, the act of interpreting what is really a shown story here is even less actively engaging than reading the told version.

This is not to say that we do not engage differently with different media, but the lines of differentiation are not as clear as we might expect. The private and individual experience of reading is, in fact, closer to the private visual and domestic spaces of television, radio, DVD, video, and computer than it is to the public and communal viewing experience in a dark theater of any kind. And when we sit in the dark, quiet and still, being shown real live bodies speaking or singing on stage, our level and kind of engagement are different than when we sit in front of a screen and technology mediates "reality" for us. When we play a first-person shooter videogame and become an active character in a narrative world and viscerally experience the action, our response is different again. Medium alone cannot explain what happens when an interactive videogame is adapted into a museum-displayed digital work of art, for it becomes a way to show, rather than interact with, a story. For instance, in a piece by Israeli American video artist Eddo Stern called *Vietnam Romance* (2003), the viewer finds that the game's enemies have already been taken out by the artist-shooter, leaving us to watch—in other words, to be shown—only a series of empty sets that have been manipulated to recall classic shots from war films, from *M*A*S*H* to *Apocalypse Now*. In reversing the intended outcome by breaking all the rules of game action, the artist has ensured that the audience cannot and does not engage in the same manner as it would with the interactive game. Likewise, Stern's *Fort Paladin: America's Army* presents a scale model of a medieval castle within which a video screen reveals—again—the final results of the artist's mastery of the U.S. military's game used for recruiting, also called *America's Army*. The work and the pleasure of the observing audience here are different from the kinetic and cognitive involvement of the interactive gamer.

Framing Adaptation

Keeping these three modes of engagement—telling, showing, and interacting with stories—in the forefront can allow for certain precisions and distinctions that a focus on medium alone cannot. It also allows for linkages across media that a concentration on medium-specificity can efface, and thus moves us away from just the formal definitions of adaptation to consider the process. These ways of engaging with stories do not, of course, ever take place in a vacuum. We engage in time and space, within a particular society and a general culture. The contexts of creation and reception are material, public, and economic as much as they are cultural, personal, and aesthetic. This explains why, even in today's globalized world, major shifts in a story's context—that is, for example, in a national setting or time period—can change radically how the transposed story is interpreted, ideologically and literally. How do we react today, for instance, when a male director adapts a woman's novel or when an American director adapts a British novel, or both—as in Neil LaBute's film version of A.S. Byatt's 1991 novel, *Possession*? In shifting cultures and therefore sometimes shifting languages, adaptations make alterations that reveal much about the larger contexts of reception and production. Adapters often "indigenize" stories, to use an anthropological term (Friedman 2004). In Germany, for instance, Shakespeare's works were appropriated through Romantic translations and, through an assertion of the Bard's Germanic affinity, used to generate a German national literature. However strange it may seem, this is why the plays of an enemy-culture's major dramatist continued to be performed—with major variations that could be called adaptations—throughout the two World Wars. The National Socialists, in fact, made these works both political, with private values stressed as being subordinated to public ones in the tragedies, and heroic, with leadership themes dominating (Habicht 1989: 110–15).

Even a shift of time frame can reveal much about when a work is created and received. Robert Louis Stevenson's 1886 novel, *The Strange Case of Dr. Jekyll and Mr. Hyde*, has been adapted many times for the stage and for the movie and television screens. (To get a sense of the whole range, see Geduld 1983.) The showing mode entails embodying and enacting, and thereby often ends up spelling out important ambiguities that are central to the told version—especially, in this case, Hyde's undefined and unspecified evil. Because of mode change, these various versions have had to show—and thus to "figure"—that evil physically, and the means they have chosen to do so are revealing of the historical and political moments of their production. In 1920, at the start of Prohibition, we witness a sexual fall through alcohol in John Robertson's silent film; in the 1971 Hammer film, *Dr. Jekyll and Sister Hyde* (directed by Roy Ward Baker), we see instead Britain's confused responses to feminism after the 1960s (see McCracken-Flesher 1994: 183–94). For economic reasons, adapters often rely on selecting works to adapt that are well known and that have proved popular over time; for legal reasons, they often choose works that are no longer copyrighted.

Technology, too, has probably always framed, not to mention driven, adaptation, in that new media have constantly opened the door for new possibilities for all three modes of engagement. Lately, new electronic technologies have made what we might call fidelity to the *imagination*—rather than a more obvious fidelity to *reality*—possible in new ways, well beyond earlier animation techniques and special effects. We can now enter and act within those worlds, through 3-D digital technology. One of the central beliefs of film adaptation theory is that audiences are more demanding of fidelity when dealing with classics, such as the work of Dickens or Austen. But a whole new set of cult popular classics, especially the work of J.R.R. Tolkien, Philip Pullman, and J.K. Rowling, are now being made visible and audible on stage, in the movie theater, on the video and computer screens, and in multiple gaming formats, and their readers are proving to be just as demanding. Although our imaginative visualizations of literary worlds are always highly individual, the variance among readers is likely even greater in fantasy fiction than in realist fiction. What does this mean when these fans see one particular version on screen that comes from the director's imagination rather their own (see Boyum 1985)? The answer(s), of course, can be found in the reviews and the audience reactions to the recent adaptations of *The Lord of the Rings* stories and the Harry Potter novels. Now that I know what an enemy orc or a game of Quidditch (can) look like (from the movies), I suspect I will never be able to recapture my first imagined versions again. Palimpsests make for permanent change.

Nicholas Wright's dramatic adaptation of Pullman's *His Dark Materials* trilogy had to cope with the fact that the books had sold three million copies and had been translated into thirty-six languages. The adapter had to find a way to visualize and then bring to physical life on stage—

without the technological advantages of film—important elements that
the fans would demand be done well: things like the novels' multiple
parallel worlds, the windows cut to move characters into each world,
and especially the wondrous creatures known as "daemons"—animals
of the opposite sex that embody the inner soul of characters. These were
technical issues as well as imaginative ones, because Wright knew the
novels' fans would be a demanding audience. The two plays that were
finally seen in London at the National Theatre in 2003 and revised in
2004 were set within an elaborate "paratextual" context in order to pre-
pare the audience and perhaps forestall any objections: the program was
larger and much more informative than most, offering photos, interviews with the novelist and the adapter, maps, a glossary of places, people, things, and "other beings," and a list of literary intertexts.

As this suggests, a further framing of adaptation across all modes of
engagement is economic. Broadway adapts from Hollywood; novelizations are timed to coincide with the release of a film. November 2001
saw the infamous simultaneous international release of the film and
multiplatform videogame versions of the first installment of the story of
Harry Potter. Book publishers produce new editions of adapted literary
works to coincide with the film version and invariably put photos of the
movie's actors or scenes on the cover. General economic issues, such as
the financing and distribution of different media and art forms, must
be considered in any general theorizing of adaptation. To appeal to a
global market or even a very particular one, a television series or a stage
musical may have to alter the cultural, regional, or historical specifics
of the text being adapted. A bitingly satiric novel of social pretense
and pressure may be transformed into a benign comedy of manners in
which the focus of attention is on the triumph of the individual, as has
happened in most American television and film versions of Thackeray's
Vanity Fair (1848). Videogames derived from popular films and vice
versa are clearly ways to capitalize on a "franchise" and extend its market. But how different is this from Shakespeare's decision to write a
play for his theater based on that familiar story about two teenage lovers or, for that matter, from Charles Gounod's choice to compose what
he hoped would be a hit opera about them? In their different ways,
Giuseppe Verdi and Richard Wagner were both deeply involved in the

financial aspects of their operatic adaptations, yet we tend to reserve our negatively judgmental rhetoric for popular culture, as if it is more tainted with capitalism than is high art.

In beginning to explore this wide range of theoretical issues surrounding adaptation, I have been struck by the unproductive nature of both that negative evaluation of popular cultural adaptations as derivative and secondary and that morally loaded rhetoric of fidelity and infidelity used in comparing adaptations to "source" texts. Like others, I have found myself asking whether we could use any less compromised image to think about adaptation as both process and product. Robert Stam, too, has seen one intriguing possibility in the film *Adaptation,* despite all its ironies; because his focus is specifically on novel to film adaptation, he finds an analogy between these two media and the film's dichotomous screenwriting twins (or split personality). He is also attracted to the metaphor of adaptations as hybrid forms, as "meeting places of different 'species,'" like the orchid (Stam 2005b: 2). For Stam, mutations—filmic adaptations—can help their "source novel 'survive'" (3).

Because my focus is on modes of engagement rather than on two specific media or on "sources," different things have caught my attention. I was struck by the other obvious analogy to adaptation suggested in the film by Darwin's theory of evolution, where genetic adaptation is presented as the biological process by which something is fitted to a given environment. To think of narrative adaptation in terms of a story's fit and its process of mutation or adjustment, through adaptation, to a particular cultural environment is something I find suggestive. Stories also evolve by adaptation and are not immutable over time. Sometimes, like biological adaptation, cultural adaptation involves migration to favorable conditions: stories travel to different cultures and different media. In short, stories adapt just as they are adapted.

In his 1976 book on Darwinian theory called *The Selfish Gene,* Richard Dawkins bravely suggested the existence of a cultural parallel to Darwin's biological theory: "Cultural transmission is analogous to genetic transmission in that, although basically conservative, it can give rise to a form of evolution" (1976/1989: 189). Language, fashions, technology, and the arts, he argued, "all evolve in historical time in a way that looks like highly speeded up genetic evolution, but has really nothing to do with genetic evolution" (190). Nonetheless, he posits the parallel existence of what he calls "memes"—units of cultural transmission or units of imitation—that, like genes, are "replicators" (191–92). But unlike genetic transmission, when memes are transmitted, they always change, for they are subject to "continuous mutation, and also to blending" (195), in part to adapt for survival in the "meme pool." Although Dawkins is thinking about ideas when he writes of memes, stories also are ideas and could be said to function in this same way. Some have great fitness through survival (persistence in a culture) or reproduction (number of adaptations). Adaptation, like evolution, is a transgenerational phenomenon. Some stories obviously have more "stability and penetrance in the cultural environment," as Dawkins would put it (193). Stories do get retold in different ways in new material and cultural environments; like genes, they adapt to those new environments *by virtue of* mutation—in their "offspring" or their adaptations. And the fittest do more than survive; they flourish.

2

WHAT?
(Forms)

As it proved, among my best memories of the filmmaking are the conversations (drunken or otherwise) I had with [director] Fred [Schepisi], in which we both acknowledged, I think, that, different as film directors and novelists are, our abiding obsession was the same: the mysteries of storytelling—of timing, pacing and the exactly judged release of information and emotion.

—Novelist Graham Swift on the adapting of his novel, *Last Orders*

Medium Specificity Revisited

As a creative and interpretive transposition of a recognizable other work or works, adaptation is a kind of extended palimpsest and, at the same time, often a transcoding into a different set of conventions. Sometimes but not always, this transcoding entails a change of medium. Although my main focus is on adaptations' different modes of engagement, the medium—as the material means of expression of an adaptation—is crucially important. But as W.J.T. Mitchell reminds us, "The medium does not lie between sender and receiver; it includes and constitutes them" (2005: 204; see also Williams 1977). My emphasis on adaptation as process (as well as product) means that the social and communication dimensions of media are important too, even when the particular emphasis, as in this chapter, is on form.

When a change of medium does occur in an adaptation, it inevitably invokes that long history of debate about the formal specificity of the arts—and thus of media. This concept received one of its most influential articulations in G.E. Lessing's 1766 "essay on the limits of painting and poetry" called *Laocöon*. As we have also seen, however, adaptation recalls as well, and usually to its disadvantage, that idea of a hierarchy in the arts. And this evaluative framework has had a significant role in this debate about specificity and difference throughout the centuries. Inevitably writers and literary critics hierarchize in their own particular art's favor. But in 1940, the visual art critic Clement Greenberg responded to Irving Babbitt's anti-Romantic *The New Laoköon: An Essay in the Confusion of the Arts* (1910) with "Towards a Newer Laocöon," where he famously argued that each art has its own formal and material specificity and thereby defined modernist art's self-reflexive focus on that very specificity (see Groensteen 1998b: 11). This essay too has had a long history, for it has implicitly informed much of the critical response to new media, such as film: it seems that no art can acquire cultural capital until it has theorized itself as medium-specific with its own formal and signifying possibilities (Naremore 2000b: 6). Witness pronouncements like this: "Each medium, according to the ways in which it exploits, combines, and multiplies the 'familiar' materials of expression—rhythm, movement, gesture, music, speech, image, writing (in anthropological terms our 'first' media)—each medium ... possesses its own communicational energetics" (Gaudreault and Marion 2004: 65).

Adaptations are obviously least involved in these debates when there is no change of medium or mode of engagement: comic strip versions of other comic strips or film remakes do not necessarily raise these particular issues of specificity (Gaudreault 1998: 270) nor do music covers or jazz variations. Heiner Müller's *Hamletmaschine* (1979) may adapt Shakespeare's *Hamlet*, but it is still a stage play, however different. Rather, it is when adaptations make the move across modes of engagement and thus across media, especially in the most common shift, that is, from the printed page to performance in stage and radio plays, dance, opera, musical, film, or television, that they find themselves most enmeshed in the intricacies of the medium-specificity debates; so too when works are adapted from either print or performance to interactive media, with their multiple sensory and semiotic channels (Ryan 2004c: 338). What can one art form or medium do that another cannot, if indeed all the "essential elements of each of the arts" can be determined, as Greenberg insisted (1940/1986: 29)? Lessing had argued that literature was an art of time, whereas painting was an art of space (1766/1984: 77), but performance on stage or screen manages to be both.

Film is usually said to be the most inclusive and synthesizing of performance forms: "A composite language by virtue of its diverse matters of expression—sequential photography, music, phonetic sound and noise—the cinema 'inherits' all the art forms associated with these matters of expression ... —the visuals of photography and painting, the movement of dance, the décor of architecture, and the performance of theater" (Stam 2000: 61; see also Klein 1981: 3). But a dance work, a musical, a television show each has its own composite conventions and, some would say, even its own grammar and syntax that all operate to structure meaning for the perceiving audience. When Paul Karasik and David Mazzucchelli adapted a verbally and narratively complex novel, Paul Auster's *City of Glass* (1985), into a graphic novel (2004), they had to translate the story into what Art Spiegelman calls the "Ur-language of Comics"—"a strict, regular grid of panels" with "the grid as window, as prison door, as city block, as tic-tac-toe board; the grid as a metronome giving measure to the narrative's shifts and fits" (Spiegelman 2004: n.p.). Like all formal conventions, this grid both constrains and enables; it both limits and opens up new possibilities.

The familiar move from telling to showing and, more specifically, from a long and complex novel to any form of performance is usually seen as the most fraught transposition. In director Jonathan Miller's strong words, "most novels are irreversibly damaged by being dramatized as they were written without any sort of performance in mind at all, whereas for plays visible performance is a constitutive part of their identity and translation from stage to screen changes their identity without actually destroying it" (1986: 66). The differences in material scale alone make the novel-to-performance adaptation difficult, but the same is obviously true in reverse. When François Truffaut wrote a "cinéroman" (1977) of his film/screenplay (co-written with Suzanne Schiffman and Michel Fermaud) of his *L'homme qui aimait les femmes*, it was a very short and very un-novelistic book, even with its self-reflexive novel-within-a-novel structure.

On the contrary, a novel, in order to be dramatized, has to be distilled, reduced in size, and thus, inevitably, complexity. Writer and director Todd Williams therefore chose to adapt only the first third of John Irving's *A Widow for One Year* (1998) for his 2004 film called *The Door in the Floor*. Most reviewers saw this cutting as a negative, as subtraction, yet when plots are condensed and concentrated, they can sometimes become more powerful. In 1975, when adapting Thackeray's novel, *The Luck of Barry Lyndon* (1844), Stanley Kubrick tightened up the entire structure of the novel, "giving a hypnotic and fatal linearity to a narrative that in Thackeray's hands was a diffuse picaresque" (Sinyard 1986: 133). Another way to think about this distillation is in terms of narrative redundancy giving way to narrative pertinence, as in some *film noir* adaptations (Cattrysse 1992: 56).

Sometimes even the novelist agrees on the benefits of changes in his or her work. Witness Zadie Smith's response to the cuts made to her lengthy novel, *White Teeth* (2000), for a television adaptation:

> The cuts were necessary to make the fat and messy kid presentable, and at least one of the changes is inspired … . A cut has been made; a motivation inserted, and an artistic clarity is the result. The moment I saw it, I gasped—this section of the novel would have been so improved had I thought of the same strategy … . In a novel, one scrabbles in the dirt for motivation or stretches for decorative

language to hide the lack of it. In film, no such disguise will be toler-
ated by the viewer. When we watch a man do something on screen,
our guts much more than our brains will tell us the truth of the gesture. It cannot be fudged. (2003: 10)

What Smith points to at the end of these remarks is not just the cutting but also the adding in this case, of the motivation necessary in a
naturalistic medium such as film. Of course, film adaptations obviously also add bodies, voices, sound, music, props, costumes, architecture, and so on.

When Raymond Chandler adapted James M. Cain's 1935 novel
Double Indemnity for director Billy Wilder (1944), he may have streamlined the plot and cut expository passages, but he also added more wit
to the dialogue, more cynical self-conscious play, more hard-edged
eroticism, and a moral center. In short, he made it more like his own
fiction than Cain's (Schickel 1992: 52). Additions in performance adaptations might range from this kind of stylistic and even ethical material
to inserting new characters or increasing suspense. Or, in structural
terms, the adapter might impose on a loosely episodic or picaresque
narrative a familiarly patterned plot of rising and falling action, with a
clear beginning, middle, and end; or he or she might even deliberately
substitute a happy ending to mute tragedy or horror, as director Volker
Schlöndorff and screenplay writer Harold Pinter did in their 1990
film adaptation of Margaret Atwood's dark, dystopic narrative, *The
Handmaid's Tale* (1985).

Most of the talk about film adaptation, however, is in negative terms
of loss. Sometimes what is meant is simply a reduction of scope: of
length, of accretion of detail, of commentary (Peary and Shatzkin 1977:
2–8). Ray Bradbury's script for John Huston's 1956 film version of
Melville's *Moby Dick* (1851) might stand as a typical example of the pragmatic necessity of cutting a sprawling novel to make it fit the screen in
terms of time and space, because it usually takes longer to perform an
action than to read a written report of it. But at other times the change is
perceived as less a question of quantity and more one of quality. To
remain with Melville, the morally complicated tale in the novella of *Billy
Budd* is rendered in black and white, both literally and ethically, in
Peter Ustinov's 1962 film version. In this negative discourse of loss,

performance media are said to be incapable of linguistic or narrative subtlety or of representing the psychological or the spiritual. No film, it is said, can be as experimental as James Joyce's *Finnegans Wake*. (For an extended argument on this topic, see S. Smith [1981].)

It is opera, however, that has been singled out as particularly guilty on both the loss of quality and quantity counts, given its extremes of compression; again, it takes much longer to sing than to say a line of text, much less read one. Operatic recycling "denatures" a novel, we are told, "reducing it to a cartoon spray-painted in Day-Glo colors and outlined with a Magic Marker" (Honig 2001: 22). Yet, as we shall see, Benjamin Britten's opera of *Billy Budd* (libretto by E.M. Forster and Eric Crozier) turns out to be considerably more subtle in terms of psychology and style than is Ustinov's film—and, some would even say, Melville's novella. In other words, the customary theoretical generalizations about the specificity of media need to be questioned by looking at actual practice. And this is the main purpose of this chapter on the "what?" of adaptation, or what I am simply going to call its form(s). But first let us look at these formal elements from the point of view of each of the three modes of engagement open to adaptations.

Telling ← → Showing

The most commonly considered adaptations are those that move from the telling to the showing mode, usually from print to performance. But the flourishing "novelization" industry today cannot be ignored. Like the readers of earlier popular "cineromanzi" or "fotoromanzi," the fans of *Star Wars* or *The X-Files* can now read novels developed from the film and television scripts. The problem is, again, one of size or scale. As William Burroughs contentiously puts it: "If you took the actual filmscript of *Jaws* and turn it back into a novel, with no reference to the actual novel and just the filmscript as your given material, you would most likely end up with a very dull novel and also quite a short one" (1991: 76). Film adaptations of almost any medium are themselves open to (re-)novelization today: K.J. Anderson has written a novel adaptation (2004) of James Robinson's 2003 film adaptation of Alan Moore and Kevin O'Neill's continuing comic book series/graphic novel called *The League of Extraordinary Gentlemen*. Of course, he had to keep the changes made by the film adaptation to important elements like the villain and the number of characters, but because the script was so short, Anderson could add descriptions and develop character motivation, and to do so he often returned to the graphic novel.

When we work in the other direction—that is, from the telling to the showing mode, especially from print to performance—a definitional problem potentially arises. In a very real sense, every live staging of a printed play could theoretically be considered an adaptation in its performance. The text of a play does not necessarily tell an actor about such matters as the gestures, expressions, and tones of voice to use in converting words on a page into a convincing performance (J. Miller 1986: 48); it is up to the director and actors to actualize the text and to interpret and then recreate it, thereby in a sense adapting it for the stage. In musical drama, the score too has to be brought to life for the audience and "shown" in actual embodied sound; it cannot remain inert as lifeless black notes on a page. A visual and aural world is physically shown on stage—be it in a play, a musical, an opera, or any other performance piece—created from verbal and notational signs on the page. But most theories draw the line here and claim that only *some* dramatic productions merit the designation of adaptation. Although it is not only stage and film directors like Peter Brook (though he is infamous for doing this) who edit a printed play text heavily, rearrange plot events, reassign lines, or cut characters, radical reinterpretations-in-performance like his usually qualify as adaptations in the sense that they are extended critical and creative engagements with a particular text. The Mabou Mines version (2003) of Henrik Ibsen's 1879 *A Doll's House* by director Lee Breuer was renamed *Doll-House* for a reason: to signal its adaptive status. Because all the men playing in it were shorter than 4 ½ feet tall and the women were much taller, this adaptation/production made an extended and announced visual commentary on the play's infamous sexual politics.

But when most of us consider the move from print to performance, it is usually the common and familiar phenomenon of the adaptation of novels that comes to mind. Novels contain much information that can be rapidly translated into action or gesture on stage or screen or dispensed with altogether, admits novelist and literary critic David

Lodge. In the move from telling to showing, a performance adaptation must dramatize: description, narration, and represented thoughts must be transcoded into speech, actions, sounds, and visual images. Conflicts and ideological differences between characters must be made visible and audible (see Lodge 1993: 196–200). In the process of dramatization there is inevitably a certain amount of re-accentuation and refocusing of themes, characters, and plot.

Because of the required changes, the epistolary novel would seem to present the most obvious difficulties for dramatization. *Les Liaisons dangereuses*, Choderlos de Laclos' episodic novel (1782) written as a series of letters, has nonetheless undergone many adaptations in many different media in recent years. For instance, Christopher Hampton's 1986 play translated the novel's letters into spoken dialogue and, in the process, changed the focus from the extended ironies of a decadent aristocracy to the more intense intellectual battles of two mutually manipulative characters. But when Hampton wrote the screenplay of his own stage work for Stephen Frears' (1988) film, the story became a more straightforward moral one of evil punished. In the hands of filmmaker Miloš Forman (screenplay by Jean-Claude Carrière), the story was transmuted into *Valmont* (1989), which turned out more like a Molière comedy than the Hollywoodized moral tragedy of the film from the year before (Axelrod 1996: 200). In Frears' version, the letter concept was transcoded into a visual, medium-specific motif, that of eavesdropping: keyhole peeping and hiding behind screens. But when Roger Vadim had adapted and updated the novel in 1959, he had used the more literary device of a voice-over narration for some of the letters. The fact that there have also been a television miniseries, an opera, several ballets, and a good number of other stage and screen adaptations of this epistolary novel suggests that formal difficulties in dramatizing are more likely to be seen as challenges than as disincentives for adapters.

When theorists talk of adaptation from print to performance media, the emphasis is usually on the visual, on the move from imagination to actual ocular perception. But the aural is just as important as the visual to this move. First, there are, as Kamilla Elliott reminds us, many words spoken in films (2003: 78); then there are the separate soundtracks that permit elements like voice-overs, music, and noise to intermingle. For the adapter, music in film "functions as an emulsifier that allows you to dissolve a certain emotion and take it in a certain direction," according to sound editor Walter Murch (in Ondaatje 2002: 103). At best, it is "a collector and a channeler of previously created emotion" (in Ondaatje 2002: 122). Soundtracks in movies therefore enhance and direct audience response to characters and action, as they do in videogames, in which music also merges with sound effects both to underscore and to create emotional reactions. Film sound can be used to connect inner and outer states in a less explicit way than do camera associations: John Huston's 1987 adaptation of Joyce's "The Dead" (1914) uses music (the singing of "Lass of Aughrim") and differences in Irish accents (the guests versus the servant Lily) to bring out not just the characters' responses but also the specifically Irish political implications of the story.

In stage musicals, the music has been called "the embodiment of excess": when speaking characters break into song, they imply that "life cannot be contained in its ordinariness, but must spill over into it, and into rhythm, singing and movement" (Tambling 1987: 101). In opera, music is arguably as important a narrating component as are the words; this function is in addition to its manifest affective and even mimetic power. Composer Richard Strauss' infamous ability to make his music pictorially suggestive as well as emotionally powerful comes to mind.

Adapting a novel into a radio play brings the importance of the aural to the fore, for the aural is everything in this case. The issues common to all dramatizations come into play, with distillation uppermost; because each character/voice must be aurally distinguishable, there cannot be too many of them. For this reason, most radio plays concentrate on primary characters alone and therefore simplify the story and time-line, as Lindsay Bell did in her 2001 adaptation of Virginia Woolf's *To the Lighthouse* for the Canadian Broadcasting Corporation. The characters who remain double as storytellers, but many are eliminated to keep the focus on the Ramsay family and Lily Briscoe. The words we hear come from the novel, but they are moved around, recontextualized, and read by different voices. These changes allow the aural version to give a sense of the novel's linguistic texture, its associative range, and its narrative rhythm. Here, as in all radio plays, music and sound effects are added to the verbal text to assist the imagination of the listener. This addition was done particularly effectively in the 1981 BBC 26-part radio adaptation of J.R.R. Tolkien's *The Lord of the Rings* (1954–55), enabling listeners to enter an aural world of fantasy. In some ways, though, radio plays are no different from other performance media: as in any dramatization, with the director's guidance, the performers, who are adapting the script, we might say, must set up the rhythm and tempo and create the psychological/emotional engagement with the audience.

Adaptations for the ballet stage not only add a visual dimension but they also subtract the verbal, even when they retain the musical, as they do specifically when adapted from operas: Tchaikovsky's operatic adaptation of Pushkin's *Pikovaya Dama* (*Queen of Spades*; 1890) was adapted for Les Grands Ballets Canadiens de Montréal by Kim Brandstrup in 2002, but there are many other examples in which the moving body replaces the operatic voice as the primary conveyer of both meaning and emotion through music. The adaptation of a novel or short story to the (spoken) dramatic stage also involves the visual dimension, as well as the verbal; with that added dimension come audience expectations not only about voice but, as in dance, also about appearance, as we move from the imagined and visualized to the directly perceived.

The limitations of the physical stage also add restrictions on the possible action and characterization. All performance media are said to lose internal character motivation in the shift to externalization (Brady 1994: 3), but the stage's material constraints potentially intensify this loss. When Salman Rushdie co-adapted his own verbally and narratively extravagant novel *Midnight's Children* (1981) into a play in 2003, it was met with predictable lamentations from the novel's fans, for the play's manner was as stylized and spare as the novel's was exuberant and complicated. The minimal props and scenery on stage offered a visual contrast to the baroque extravagance of the verbal fireworks of both the novel and the play. Yet there were formal attempts to incorporate the complexity of temporal and ontological states: the stage version used a large diagonally split movie screen at the back to present both historical scenes and magic realist ones.

This use of cinematic techniques points to one of the major advantages films have over stage adaptations of novels: the use of a multitrack medium that, with the aid of the mediating camera, can both direct and expand the possibilities of perception. Yet, that is not how this point is usually made. More often we are told that the camera *limits* what we can see, eliminating the action on the periphery that might have caught our attention when watching a play on stage. Not only is the kind of attention and focus different in a theatrical production but plays also have different conventions than films or television shows. They have a different grammar: cinema's various shots, their linking and editing, have no parallel in a stage play. Film has its own "form-language," to use Béla Balázs' term.

Neither performance medium, however, has an easy time transcoding print texts. Telling is not the same as showing. Both stage and screen adaptations must use what Charles Sanders Peirce called indexical and iconic signs—that is, precise people, places, and things—whereas literature uses symbolic and conventional signs (Giddings, Selby, and Wensley 1990: 6). Graphic novels are perhaps adapted more easily to film for this reason. Frank Miller's *noir*-like series called *Sin City* (1991–92) was made into a visually spectacular surreal movie by Robert Rodriguez (2005) with live actors but digitally created settings that recall those of the comics. But when Dan Clowes' *Ghost World* (1998) was transferred to the screen by director Terry Zwigoff in 2002, fans felt it lost in the process what was considered the perfect, if sickly, analogue for the two punky girls' hyper-self-conscious and cynically ironic lives: the drained-out blue-green tint of the comics' pages.

One reason for this loss may be that conventional as opposed to avant-garde film is resolutely naturalistic in its mode of presentation, or as one theorist puts it more strongly, it gives "an ultra-naturalistic representation at every level from the *mise-en-scène* through to the behavioral stereotypes and codes of acting, linking to a form of montage and camera placement or movement that heightens the illusion of instantaneity" (LeGrice 2002: 232). If those manuals written for screenwriters are to be believed, realist film requires cause-and-effect motivation, basically linear and resolved plot development, and coherent characterization. To return to an example used earlier, when Thomas Mann presents his writer character, Gustav von Aschenbach, in the novella of *Der Tod in Venedig*, he insists on the writer's complex aesthetic and psychological dualities from the start, offering internal motivation that frames reader expectations. When Luchino Visconti transfers this character to the screen in *Morte a Venezia*, he only allows viewers to see his contradictions progressively (Carcaud-Macaire and Clerc 1998: 157, 167). He also makes him into a composer, whose musical creativity is arguably easier or at least more potentially interesting to represent aurally and visually than that of a cerebral and verbal writer.

Avant-garde film, of course, offers other means to the adapter, and interestingly these devices have been exploited most in the transfer of poetic texts to the screen. The available technical possibilities have multiplied from the early, non-avant-garde days of cinema when D.W. Griffith's silent film *Pippa Passes* (1909) could use Robert Browning's poem for the intertitles, to Sandra Lahire's more recent (1991) cinematic response to Sylvia Plath's reading of her poems in *Lady Lazarus*. The poetry, poetic prose, and songs of Leonard Cohen, in particular, have been adapted in modes that vary from photographic montage (Josef Reeve's *Poen* [1967]) to animation (Roselyn Schwartz's *I'm Your Man* [1996]): in each case, the texts are read or sung, and their story elements and even their metaphoric language are translated into evocative visual images.

Poems simply set to music are also adaptations from the telling to the showing mode when they are then performed. In 2005 composer William Bolcolm adapted William Blake's (1789/1794) "Songs of Innocence and Experience" for over 400 musicians and chorus members. But this adaptation is only an amplification of the long *Lieder* tradition of poems set to music and sung to piano or orchestra accompaniment. However, Simon Keenlyside recently adapted even the *Lieder* or song cycle to an even more performative medium when he worked with choreographer Trisha Brown to develop a danced version for himself and three dancers of Franz Schubert's famous cycle of songs called *Winterreise* (1827).

When operas and musicals adapt literary works, the move to the showing from the telling mode has the usual formal consequences, because condensation is crucially necessary for both plays and novels. As Ulrich Weisstein explains, other conventions also lead to modifications in the process of adapting:

Since music lacks the speed and verbal dexterity of language, fewer words are needed in opera than would be required in a play of comparable length. Librettos are usually shorter than the texts of ordinary dramas [not to mention novels] … . Repetitions are frequently called for … . This drastic reduction in the quantity of text, in conjunction with the highly sensual nature of music, necessitates a simplification of both action and characters, the emotions expressed in the closed musical numbers occupying a large segment of the time normally reserved for the dramatic events. (1961: 19)

Characters are defined "succinctly and forthrightly" as a result (Weisstein 1961: 19), but may seem poorly motivated for that reason.

Yet the paring down of the plot can have a coherent and powerful dramatic effect, as in Peter Pears' reduction of Shakespeare's *A Midsummer Night's Dream* to about half its size for Benjamin Britten's operatic adaptation. A musical, which uses dialogue, may keep a literary text's words—as did Richard Nelson in writing the musical stage adaptation of part of Marcel Proust's multivolume (1913–27) *A la recherche du temps perdu* as *My Life with Albertine* (2003; music by Ricky Ian Gordon)—but it may still translate its themes to a different medium. In this adaptation, the stage version uses repetitions of the music itself to make the audience experience directly Proust's theme of time and memory and also makes Marcel a composer and not a writer.

The move from a telling to a showing mode may also mean a change in genre as well as medium, and with that too comes a shift in the expectations of the audience. W.R. Burnett's novel, *The Asphalt Jungle*, has been adapted into a straight crime film of the same name (1950), a western (*Badlanders* [1958]), a caper film (*Cairo* [1963]), and even a "blaxpolition" film (*Cool Breeze* [1972]; see Braudy 1998: 331). The same genre shift can happen with various media within one mode of engagement as well. Richard Loncraine's 1995 updated cinematic version of Shakespeare's *Richard III* has been called a generic mix of the British "heritage film" and the American gangster movie (Loehlin 1997: 72–74), no doubt causing conflicting responses in audiences. When the same playwright's *Romeo and Juliet* was transcoded into Leonard Bernstein's *West Side Story* as both a stage musical (1957) and a film (1961), its generic focus shifted along with the medium, as it did once again when choreographer and hip-hop poet Rennie Harris created his *Rome and Jewel*—a political allegory of power and desire in which Jewel/Juliet is never seen on stage but remains an invisible projection of male desire and male gang politics. These last examples suggest, however, that the formal properties of the different media involved in this one particular mode of showing need to be further distinguished one from the other.

Showing ← → Showing

Stories shown in one performance medium have always been adaptable to other performance media: movies and even movie adaptations become stage musicals (*Mary Poppins* [2004], *The Producers* [2001], *The Lion King* [1997]) and turn back into films again (e.g., *The Little Shop of Horrors* [1986]). A French stage farce, *La cage aux folles,* became a 1978 film (director: Edouard Molinaro), and then had two movie sequels (1980 and 1985) before becoming a Broadway musical in 1983 and then being remade as an American story (*The Birdcage* [1996]). Television skits from *Saturday Night Live* have been adapted to film (*Wayne's World* [1992], *Blues Brothers 2000* [1998]), and films have been made of TV series (*Maverick* [1994], *The Flintstones* [1994], *Mission Impossible* [1996], *I Spy* [2000], *Starsky and Hutch* [2004], and so on). But both film and television are relatively realist media. What happens when a manifestly artificial performance form like an opera or a musical is adapted to the screen?

There seem to be two possible ways to proceed. The artifice can be acknowledged and cinematic realism sacrificed to self-reflexivity, or else the artifice can be "naturalized." An example of the first case is Hans-Jürgen Syberberg's 1982 film of Richard Wagner's *Parsifal* (1872), which uses an anti-naturalistic *mise-en-scène* that is both strikingly theatrical and bravely uncinematic: the director has the characters play out the action in a highly stylized manner and on a set that consists of an enlargement of Wagner's death mask. The opera is filmed in a studio, using rear projections of other works of art as settings. Refusing to direct our eyes by the customary shot/reverse shot structure, the director deliberately moves the camera slowly, using pan and dissolve and echoing the leisurely pace of the continuous music (Syberberg 1982:

45). All but two of the characters are played by nonsinging actors, and the prerecorded music is lip-synched—but never perfectly. Using Brechtian alienation effects, Syberberg refuses to coordinate sound and image. He also casts two actors as Parsifal—a woman (Karin Krick) and a man (Michael Kutter), but retains only one voice (the male one of Rainer Goldberg).

The alternative to this kind of reveling in filmic artifice is the naturalizing that takes place in the 1972 Bob Fosse film version of *Cabaret* (screenplay by Jay Allen with Hugh Wheeler). More naturalistic than either the John van Druten play (*I Am a Camera* [1952]) or the Harold Prince-directed musical (book by Joe Masteroff and John Kander; music by Fred Ebb [1966]), the film allows only one major plot character to sing and that is Sally Bowles—because she is a singer by trade, like the MC—and even then, she only sings at the Kit Kat Klub, where her singing can be realistically explained. The deliberate exception is the politically charged Nazi song, "Tomorrow Belongs to Me": when the chorus joins the Hitler Youth soloist, the orchestration swells to unrealistic proportions (Clark 1991: 54). But the film's other music is played, naturalistically, on a gramophone, on the street by an accordionist, or in a room by a piano player.

Television shares with cinema many of the same naturalistic conventions and therefore the same transcoding issues when it comes to adaptation. However, in a television series, there is more time available and therefore less compression of the adapted text is required. When Tony Kushner adapted his own plays from the 1990s, *Angels in America*, for television in 2003, the running time was approximately the same (six hours) for the series as for the plays, and the verbal text and dramatic scenes were not altered substantially. Mike Nichols, the director, did not therefore have to use filmic techniques for condensation the way the television adaptation of David Lodge's novel, *Nice Work* (1988), had used cross-cutting at the start to convey a lot of visual information quickly. In contrast, the novel had taken its time to describe places and characters and to give biographical information about relationships in order to set up the two very different worlds of the two protagonists; the television version did this very quickly and effectively. The self-conscious, self-reflexive theatricality of Kushner's plays—in their

portrayal of that eerie Angel, for starters—was translated into technological wizardry in the TV version, but when Peter Eötvös composed
an opera based on the plays in 2004, he used different vocal and musical styles plus sound effects to get the same kind of hallucinatory effect.

Less intuitively obvious is the fact that television has also provided
adaptations for the operatic stage, most controversially with *Jerry
Springer—The Opera* (2003) (music by Richard Thomas; libretto by
Stewart Lee). This opera transfigures "trash TV" into a high art form
musically while retaining its coarseness of words and action. In a final
ironic twist, a televised version of the opera adaptation was broadcast
by the BBC in 2005, but not without considerable outrage from the
public who found its anti-Christian allegory inappropriate for an opera
on television!

Films too have been adapted to opera: Robert Altman's 1978 movie,
A Wedding, was "operatized" by Arnold Weinstein and William Bol-
com for the Chicago Lyric Opera in 2004, with Altman directing once
again. In the adaptation, 48 film characters are reduced to 16 singing
parts, and the multiplotted, diffuse, and chaotic (because improvised)
screen story is focused more narrowly. The realistic film's sharp class
satire, the vulgarity of the nouveau riche, the snobbery and hypocrisy
of the blue-bloods, the pieties of both regarding marriage, is attenuated
in the more artificial sung and staged version, perhaps because of the
conventions of operatic comedy: Mozart's class-based comic opera, *Le
Nozze di Figaro* (1786), was clearly the model for this modern marriage
story, and the impact of its mix of comedy of manners and romance
conventions was what likely made for a gentler and more sympathetic
portrayal of the characters than the realist film had allowed.

Hybrid forms that provide sung music for existing films (often silent)
are partial remediations that also function as adaptations. Philip Glass'
Beauty and the Beast (1995) takes the 1946 film by Jean Cocteau and
provides music and new words for live singers, who are never quite in
synch with the film action we watch on screen. Benedict Mason's *Chap-
linoperas* (1988) adapts three Chaplin shorts from 1917, *Easy Street, The
Immigrant*, and *The Adventurer*, by, again, showing the films and adding live sung words and music that this time are synchronized with the
screen action, but often more parodically than realistically.

In a reversal of this adapting relationship between film and musical theater, there is, as we have seen, that strange mixed form that many consider a kind of adaptation: the opera film or "screen opera" (Citron 2000) in which the naturalistic conventions of cinema are used to translate a most unrealistic staged art form. The integrity of both the musical score and the verbal libretto is usually retained, despite the different exigencies of a different medium, even though cuts can be made and parts of the music even recorded at different tempos to accommodate the film director's needs, as happened in Franco Zeffirelli's 1986 film version of Giuseppe Verdi *Otello* (1887). But in film the orchestra disappears into the sound track, and the physical presence of the conductor is lost as the "horizon stabilizing the level of artificiality the audience is asked to accept" (J. Miller 1986: 209). Instead, opera films can be shot on location, even if not necessarily the location intended in the libretto: Don Giovanni's Seville becomes a visually sumptuous Palladian Veneto in Joseph Losey's 1979 film of Mozart's *Don Giovanni* (1787). People appear to sing in the open air, but the sound we actually hear is that of a concert hall or recording studio. Miming, they "sing," but their mouths and throats do not strain in close-up on camera. The embodied drama and intensity of live performance are replaced not by realism so much as by the conventions of cinema's realist acceptability: these close-ups do not risk exposing the very real physicality of singing, including the "quite repulsive detail of dental fillings and wobbling tongues" (J. Miller 1986: 208). Of course, the miniaturization that occurs with video or DVD viewing of these films reverses the effects of this gigantism of the close-up on the big screen.

All the media discussed above are performance media. What all share, therefore, is a showing mode of engagement; where they differ is in the specific constraints and possibilities of each medium's conventions. When Andrew Bovell adapted his own 2001 play, *Speaking in Tongues,* for the cinema (renamed *Lantana* and directed by Ray Lawrence [2001]), he found he had to change the nonrealistic play's plot, based as it was on coincidence, to suit the cinema's naturalistic rules of probability. But when John Guare transposed his 1990 play, *Six Degrees of Separation*, to the screen (1993), he left the text virtually unaltered, but changed the theatrical conceit of the play, in which characters tell the story to the audience, to a cinematic and realist one. He made the audience for the film's story a shifting group of friends who tune in for successive installments at different public gatherings. Not all showing is the same.

Interacting ← → Telling or Showing

The formal and hermeneutic complexity of the relationship between the telling and the showing modes that I have been exploring so far is certainly matched by that of the shift of level and type of engagement from either of these modes to the participatory one. "Deliberate user action," to use Marie-Laure Ryan's term, is what is considered fundamental and "truly distinctive" in digital media (2004c: 338), along with the interface and database (Manovich 2001). But the dice game adaptation of Jane Austen's (1796/1813) novel, *Pride and Prejudice*, arguably involves deliberate user action as well: the winner is the player who gets to the church first in order to marry. Computerized gaming, however, is the most frequent form taken by this particular adapting process. Nika Bertram's novel *Der Kahuna Modus* (2001) has a computer game adaptation (available at http://www.kahunamodus.de/swave.html) that, according to those who play it, changes how we read and interpret the novel. But most videogames have a close, not to say permeable, relationship to film, rather than to prose fiction and not only in the obvious sense of usually sharing a "franchise."

The computer-generated animation movie *Toy Story 2* (1999) opens with a self-reflexive gaming theme that continues throughout. *Buzz Lightyear to the Rescue* is the PlayStation game adaptation both of this film, with Buzz being a character, and of the game in which the opening sequence of the film itself is supposed to be taking place (Ward 2002: 133). The *Die Hard* films (1988, 1990, 1995) spawned the games *Die Hard Trilogy* (1996) and *Die Hard Trilogy 2* (2000), and their narrative provides the frame for the gaming experience. But in the games, there is none of the films' security that the protagonist will prevail; that insecurity or tension is, of course, part of the fun for the player. As with the various forms of hypermedia, it is process, not final or finished product, that is important.

We saw in Chapter 1 that what is often most significant for videogames is the adapted heterocosm, the spectacular world of digital animation that a player enters. Our visceral responses to the immersive experience of both the visual and audio effects (sounds and music) create an "intensity of engagement" (King 2002: 63) unrivaled in most other media.

But interactivity also makes for different formal techniques: the sense of coherence is spatial and is created by the player within a game space that is not just imagined or even just perceived but also actively engaged (Tong and Tan 2002: 107). The heterocosm of film is experienced in a game in a more intense form of "vicarious kinesthesia" and with a feeling of sensory presence (Darley 2000: 152), whether it is the world of *Star Wars* or *The Blair Witch Project*. For this reason, perhaps, the game versions (by 2004, there were five), of the survival horror story, *Silent Hill*, are predicted to be much more nightmarish than anything Christophe Gans' forthcoming film adaptation could manage. In addition, game programming has an even more goal-directed logic than film, with fewer of the gaps that film spectators, like readers, fill in to make meaning. Digital games may draw on televisual, photographic, and cinematic devices, tropes, and associations, but they always have their own logic (King and Krzywinska 2002b: 2).

Equally interactive, though in different ways, are theme parks, where we can walk right into the world of a Disney film, and virtual reality experiences, where our own bodies are made to feel as if they are entering an adapted heterocosm. Much virtual art presents mythic contexts in an illusionistic manner through a polysensory interface (Grau 2003: 350). Less immersive but still more involving than most other media are CD-ROM and Web site kinds of "interactive storytelling." Although users here are actively involved in making plot choices at certain nodal points as they experience the narrative, it is also the case that the way they "navigate through scenery and scenes, 'interact' both with locations and, even more importantly, virtual actors, the perspectives from which they view events, the atmospheres and moods encountered and experienced: everything has to be consciously designed and must adhere to fixed rules. This might also be termed the 'staging of interactivity'" (Wand 2002: 166). This carefully designed electronic staging is best for adapting certain kinds of narrative structures and therefore genres, namely those of thrillers, detective stories, and documentaries.

Throughout this section, in referring to a generic category of form when discussing adaptations and the question of medium specificity, I have obviously been including what Gérard Genette (1979) would separate out as "form" (prose, poetry, images, music, sounds), "genre" (novel, play [comedy, tragedy], opera), and "mode" (narrative, dramatic). My alternate choice of theoretical focus—on the shifts among telling, showing, and interacting modes of engagement—is what has motivated my seeming mixing of categories. To explore the complexities of these shifts in more detail, however, I select several formal areas that either have been the most contested or have spawned the most "givens" or accepted truisms and therefore need challenging. For instance, the teleological historical argument for film as the culminating development of other genres and media, or at least as the most absorptive of media, goes like this: "Historically, the novel succeeded the drama, but absorbed some of its qualities (character, dialogue) while adding possibilities of its own (interior monologue, point of view, reflection, comment, irony). Similarly, film initially followed the basic principles of narrative prose and copied stage drama" while developing its own techniques and forms, as well as its own means of production, distribution, and consumption (Giddings, Selby, and Wensley 1990: ix-x). Of this long list, it is precisely such elements as interior monologue, point of view, reflection, comment, and irony, along with such other issues as ambiguity and time, which have attracted the most attention in the critical and theoretical work on the move from the printed page to any form of performance and from there to the participatory. Therefore, they are my main focus in what follows as I test out some of the most common theoretical truisms or clichés against actual adaptation practice.

Cliché #1: Only the Telling Mode (Especially Prose Fiction) Has the Flexibility to Render Both Intimacy and Distance in Point of View.

As we have seen and as any basic book on storytelling or for that matter any advanced book on narratology will confirm, telling a story is not the same thing as showing a story. But the interrelationships between the novelistic and the cinematic alone suggest that such a simple statement is not without problems. Joseph Conrad, in the preface to *The Nigger of the "Narcissus,"* famously wrote: "My task which I am trying to achieve is, by the power of the written word to make you hear, to make you feel—it is, before all, to make you *see*" (1897/1968: 708). Critics differ on whether the modern novel owes a debt to film or vice versa in its use of multiple points of view, ellipses, fragmentation, and discontinuity (Elliott 2003: 113–14; Wagner 1975: 14–16). Novelist Claude Simon claimed, "I cannot write my novels other than by constantly defining the different positions that the narrator or narrators occupy in space (field of vision, distance, mobility in relation to the scene described—or, if you prefer, in another vocabulary: camera angle, close-up, medium shot, panoramic shot, motionless shot, etc.)" (qtd. in Morrissette 1985: 17).

But the early adaptation theorist, George Bluestone, had argued back in 1957/1971 that film adaptations actually arose when the novel underwent a crisis of identity in the early twentieth century, turning to "the drama of linguistic inadequacy" (11). Because film could represent visual and dramatic narrative so vividly, the novel retreated to interiority (Elliott 2003: 52). This theory makes film adaptations into the revenge of story, abandoned as the novel got all caught up with language. It is as if film versions were the response to that 1927 attempt at literary prognostication, *Scheherazade, or the Future of the English Novel.* Its author, John Carruthers, relegated the high modernists to the trash heap of the future in favor of "a fresh insistence on the story, plot" (1927: 92) by "reincarnations of Scheherazade, the Teller of STORIES" (95). But precisely how would these future Scheherazades tell their stories on film or on stage? Are performance media limited to a third-person point of view? Or can the intimacy of the first-person narrator be achieved in performance? Do techniques like voice-over or a soliloquy work? What about the power of the close-up and its ability to offer "the microdrama of the human countenance" (Bluestone 1957/1971: 27)?

If *Story* (1997), Robert McKee's bible for screenwriters, is to be trusted, films should *never* resort to "literary" devices or their equivalents, such as *deus ex machina* endings or voice-overs: that would be telling not showing. The splendid joke of McKee's "appearance" in the film *Adaptation*, of course, is that the film itself both enacts and explodes his injunction. Linda Seger's popular adaptation manual, *The Art of Adaptation: Turning Fact and Fiction into Film*, calls devices like voice-over disruptive (1992: 25) for they make us focus on the words we are hearing and not on the action we are seeing. It is thus not surprising that Bapsi Sidhwa insisted on voice-overs in the film adaptation of her novel, *Cracking India* (1991), directed by Deepa Mehta (released as *Earth* [1999]), or that this insistence made the director distinctly uneasy (Sidhwa 1999: 21). Clint Eastwood's film of *Million Dollar Baby* (2004)—Paul Haggis' adaptation of F.X. Toole's (Jerry Boyd's pseudonym) *Rope Burns: Stories from the Corner* (2000)—effectively uses voice-over throughout to make one character (Eddie Scrap-Iron Dupris) the moral center of the work. But when Robert Bresson used an off-camera voice to represent the diary entries in his 1950 film adaptation of Georges Bernanos' *Journal d'un curé de campagne* (1936), the critics were immediately divided over its success.

Attempts to use the camera for first-person narration—to let the spectator see only what the protagonist sees—are infrequent. Despite the well-known example of Robert Montgomery's 1946 adaptation of Raymond Chandler's *Lady in the Lake* (1943), in which a camera was positioned on the protagonist's chest, first-person point-of-view films are often called "clumsy, ostentatiously and even pretentiously artistic" (Giddings, Selby, and Wensley 1990: 79). From the other direction, novelizers of films have to decide what point of view to take to replicate the eye of the camera, and their task can be just as difficult. Most films use the camera as a kind of moving third-person narrator to represent the point of view of a variety of characters at different moments (Stam 2000: 72). This is so much the norm that when specific points of view are used, the film stands out, as does Akira Kurosawa's famous *Rashomon* (1950), which provides four different characters' versions of events. When the BBC televised, in a studio, Benjamin Britten's 1951 opera of *Billy Budd* in 1966, the camera made Captain Vere central in a way that librettist E.M. Forster decried (Tambling 1987: 88); however, arguably the opera text itself, in adapting Melville's novel, had already made Vere into a central point-of-view character by having him narrate the beginning and the end of the story on stage.

I have been using the term "point of view," but there is a difference between what characters and therefore what we *see* and what they might actually *know* (Jost 2004: 73). In Anthony Minghella's 1996 film adaptation of Michael Ondaatje's narratively disorienting novel, *The English Patient* (1992), the titular character is the major focalizer: the one who determines what we know. However, in fact our perspective is much broader, thanks to voice-overs and other characters' information, conveyed often through flashbacks (B. Thomas 2000: 222).

In a multitrack medium, everything can convey point of view: camera angle, focal length, music, *mise-en-scène*, performance, or costume (Stam 2005b: 39). What is more important than thinking in terms of first- or third-person narration, argues Robert Stam, is "authorial control of intimacy and distance, the calibration of access to characters' knowledge and consciousness" (2005b: 35). An example is Gustav Hasford's 1983 autobiographical novel, *The Short-Timers*. It is narrated by a character named Joker, a writer for a Marine paper, and the story is told in an episodic, fragmented, disconnected style—ostensibly as an objective correlative to the character's and author's subjective experience of the "insanity" of the war in Vietnam. When Stanley Kubrick and Michael Herr adapted this novel into the film, *Full Metal Jacket* (1987), they substituted a more ironic, distanced journalist's perspective and offered a more self-reflexive showing of the construction of images of war and of war as morally absurd.

In the adaptation from film into videogame too, the use of point of view challenges the truism about prose fiction's unique flexibility. Even without the use of virtual reality, which really is an embodied first-person perspective, computer animation allows for more variety than is usually acknowledged. Games offer either a third-person or a first-person shooter position, with multiplayer options. There are also variants that combine both: we can *act* as first-person shooters, but *see* third-person shooters—from behind the character or avatar. In the first-person role, players do not so much passively watch as have "a proxy view of the gaming world from behind the eyes of their onscreen character" (Bryce and Rutter 2002: 71). This provides a more immediate relationship with the character and a greater immersion in the animated world of the game. Third-person shooter games use prerendered camera angles to direct the attention of the player, much as the camera directs the film spectator's eyes.

However, this cliché about point of view in these different modes of engagement points toward the larger and much-debated issue of the ability of different media to present inner and outer worlds, subjectivity and materiality. Although the discussions of this issue in the critical literature are limited to telling and showing, they may relate as well to the participatory mode, which may not share what film and literature do: "a more or less highly developed use of dialogue, speech, and language" (Morrissette 1985: 13).

Cliché #2: Interiority is the Terrain of the Telling Mode; Exteriority is Best Handled by Showing and Especially by Interactive Modes.

In other words, language, especially literary fiction, with its visualizing, conceptualizing, and intellectualized apprehension, "does" interiority best; the performing arts, with their direct visual and aural perception, and the participatory ones, with their physical immersion, are more suited to representing exteriority. Arguably, modernist fiction exacerbated the division between print literature and cinema, in particular, by giving new significance to the inner life of characters, to psychic complexity, thoughts, and feelings. James Joyce may have claimed that his memory functioned like a "cinematograph," but his classic modernist works have also made him, in some eyes, into the precursor of the new media: "The process of thought itself now constitutes the topic and makes it possible to leave the linear, straightforward world of logic. Joyce … uses the stream of consciousness technique to express the merger of subject and world, of the internal and the external" (Dinkla 2002: 30). And, by this logic, the "rhizomatic networking" of *Finnegans Wake* found a worthy heir in hypertext as a narrative strategy (Dinkla 2002: 31).

That said, there has nonetheless always been a difference between what critics say about Joyce's use of stream of consciousness as cinematic or even new medial and their view that his verbally and structurally complex works are, in fact, unadaptable to the screen (Gibbons 2002: 127). Yet Joseph Strick's film adaptations of Joyce's novels have sought purely cinematic equivalents of such issues as the tension between realism and abstraction by using, in *Ulysses* (1967) for example, a wide-angle lens, associative editing patterns, and a sound design that undermines logic and continuity (Pramaggiore 2001: 56). In short, he refuses the standard Hollywood conventions for representing subjectivity (shot/reverse shot, eye-line match) and uses avant-garde film techniques instead, including experimentations with sound and even trying out screens of total darkness. In his later (1978) adaptation of *Portrait of the Artist as a Young Man*, Strick uses sequential flashbacks and flashforwards to give a sense of Stephen's fractured subjectivity. In the film version of the story, internalized guilt, more than the birth of artistic creativity, becomes the central theme. The director expands on the text's line, "Tear out his eyes / apologise," and selects a visual motif of eyes, in close-up and symbolic montage, to embody and establish this theme in the opening minutes of the film.

Stephen's personal diary has less of a role in the film than in the novel, but in the scenes at the end where it is present, Strick uses voice-over and montage, refusing to let the aural and the visual cohere perfectly until the fourth journal representation as a sign of the diary's "presence"; then, the fifth time the diary is shown, the voice-over gives way to the actual enactment of the scene described (Armour 1981: 284). Presumably the audience has, by this time, been taught and learned this diary-code, even though the voice-over returns at the end just to make sure. It is true that the novel's emphasis on language—Stephen's obsession with words, written and oral—and on the other senses (smells, sounds, sensations) is sacrificed to the visual in the film adaptation. And one result is that the transformation of Stephen into an artist feels unmotivated, but the movie does find visual ways to allow us into Stephen's psyche and imagination.

Nevertheless, despite cinematic attempts like this, *New Yorker* film critic, Pauline Kael, could still confidently assert, "Movies are good at action; they're not good at reflective thought or conceptual thinking. They're good for immediate stimulus" (qtd. in Peary and Shatzkin 1977: 3). She is in good company in this assertion, of course: Bertolt Brecht too claimed that the film demands "external action and not introspective psychology" (1964: 50). Film is not supposed to be good at getting inside a character, for it can only show exteriors and never actually tell what is going on beneath the visible surface. Seger's manual puts it this way: "Material that is internal and psychological, that concentrates on inner thoughts and motivations, will be difficult to express dramatically" (1992: 55). It is decidedly the case that elaborate interior monologues and analyses of inner states are difficult to represent visually in performance, but as Strick shows in *Portrait*, sound and avant-garde film devices can work to signal interiority nonetheless.

Virginia Woolf could not resist attacking the very idea of a film adaptation of *Anna Karenina*, with its heroine presented as a "voluptuous lady in black velvet wearing pearls." She simply refused to recognize her, because she insisted that, as a reader of the novel, she knew Anna "almost entirely by the inside of her mind—her charm, her passion, her despair" (1926: 309). Without that inside information, we would miss the essence of the character. Helen Schlegel's "Panic and emptiness!" moment of terror in *Howards End*, as we saw in Chapter 1, becomes a mere abstract description in a lecture on Beethoven in the Merchant/Ivory film adaptation. Therefore, the argument goes, film can show us characters experiencing and thinking, but can never reveal their experiences or thoughts, except through that "literary" device of the voice-over.

Yet film can and does find cinematic equivalents, as we have seen already. Certain scenes, for example, can be made to take on emblematic value, making what is going on inside a character comprehensible to the spectator. For example, the protagonist in Visconti's *Morte a Venezia*, an aging man, is transformed by a barber through the use of hair dye and cosmetics into a parody of the image of a young man capable of falling in love with a beautiful boy. This scene exists in Mann's novella of *Der Tod in Venedig*, but it has much greater significance and weight in Visconti's film version: given the power of the visual image itself and of Dirk Bogarde's subtle acting, the tension between Aschenbach's anguish and his desire, between his fear and his hope, is made manifest on screen in brutally tight close-up.

External appearances are made to mirror inner truths. In other words, visual and aural correlatives for interior events can be created, and in fact film has at its command many techniques that verbal texts do not. The power of that close-up, for example, to create psychological intimacy is so obvious (think too of Ingmar Bergman's films) that directors can use it for powerful and revealing interior ironies: in the Stephen Frears film adaptation, *Dangerous Liaisons*, described earlier, Valmont watches a woman miscarrying his child in great pain, and the close-up on his face shows his frigid detachment.

Although it is a naturalistic medium in most of its uses, film can also create visual, externalized analogues to subjective elements—fantasy or magic realism—by such techniques as slow motion, rapid cutting, distortional lenses (fish-eye, telephoto), lighting, or the use of various kinds of film stocks (Jinks 1971: 36–37). Stam insists, "As a technology of representation, the cinema is ideally equipped to magically multiply times and spaces; it has the capacity to mingle very diverse temporalities and spatialities" (2005a: 13). Editing becomes what Susan Sontag once called "an equivalent to the magician's sleight of hand" (1999: 256), because unlike theater, film can represent *anything*. Flashbacks and flashforwards can contribute to a sense of unreality, as can sound effects and music, of course. The use of shadow and space in Orson Welles' 1962 adaptation of Franz Kafka's *Der Prozess* (1925) or the deployment of color in Roger Corman's 1964 version of Edgar Allan Poe's *The Masque of the Red Death* (1842) are other good examples of how film can represent the subjective cinematically.

Dream-like states, in fact, have come to have their own visual and auditory conventions in film. It is not for nothing, therefore, that the Dada and surrealist poets saw film as a privileged mode of conveying the unconscious. They were thinking of avant-garde expressionist film, no doubt, with its odd camera angles, unusual lighting, slow motion, and sequences repeated or presented in reverse (Morrissette 1985: 13), but even traditional narrative film has its accepted means of representing interiority, and they are often very sophisticated narratively. The separation of the sound and image tracks, for instance, can allow a character's inner state to be communicated to the audience while remaining unknown to the other characters on the screen. As early as 1916, Hugo Münsterberg had argued that, unlike a stage play, a "photoplay" or film could reproduce mental functions on screen: it "obeys the law of the mind rather than those of the outer world," shaping material to "approximate flashes of memory, imaginative visions, time leaps" (1916/1970: 41). Many years later novelist and filmmaker Alain Robbe-Grillet would corroborate this notion from the reverse angle, arguing that the French New Novelists, as they were known, were not attracted to the objectivity of the camera as an analogy for their work, but rather to its possibilities in the domain of the subjective, of the imaginary (1963: 161).

Lawrence Kramer has argued that it is the music in films that "connects us to the spectacle on screen by invoking a dimension of depth, of interiority, borrowed from the responses of our own bodies as we listen to the insistent production of rhythms, tone colors, and changes in dynamics" (1991: 156). If this is the case for film music on a sound track, how much more so must it be for live opera, for which, it has been argued, music conveys the rhythm of the emotions at the same time as language names them: "The merger of music and words, the temporal and the spatial, the general and the particular, should theoretically result in a more satisfactory image of the mental universe than is furnished by either in isolation" (Weisstein 1961: 18). Although admittedly more often an ideal than a reality, such a merger does allow a consideration of interiority in even this incredibly "stagey" art form.

Characters in an opera or a musical may appear two-dimensional because of that necessary compression of their stories, but their music has been likened to their unverbalized subconscious. The words they sing may *address* the outer world, but their music *represents* their inner lives (Halliwell 1996: 89; Schmidgall 1977: 15; Weisstein 1961: 20). Why? Because the convention of opera is that characters on stage do not hear the music they sing, except when they self-consciously perform what are called "phenomenal songs" (lullabies, toasts, etc.). Only the audience hears the rest of the music; only the audience has access to its level of meaning (Abbate 1991: 119). This is why music can represent interiority. In fact, however, opera also has a fixed convention for representing interiority: the aria. Dramatic action and conversation stop during the aria, and we eavesdrop on a character's moment of introspection and reflection (Weisstein 1961: 18). In "through-composed" operas without arias, such as the music dramas of Richard Wagner, musical repetitions and variations—usually called leitmotifs—can bring to the audience's ears what the characters cannot consciously face. Isolde may sing of her hatred for Tristan in Wagner's work named after the legendary lovers, but she does so to music we already associate with her love for him.

When operas are filmed, as we have seen, the conventions of realism seem to work against even the genre's conventionalized ability to convey interiority. Yet here too ways have been found to do so: Jean-Pierre Ponnelle's 1976 television version of Puccini's 1904 opera, *Madama Butterfly*, visualizes the idea that arias provide the internal thoughts and emotions of characters by not having the singers' lips move during the arias. We hear the arias, but do not see them physically sung. Franco Zeffirelli uses different means to externalize the internal in his 1983 film version of Verdi's opera, *La Traviata* (1853): drawing on the text that the opera had in fact adapted (*La Dame aux camélias* [1848] by Alexandre Dumas, *fils*), he has his Violetta repeatedly look at herself in a mirror. Although this action is cinematically realistic (she is checking to see if she is still beautiful or whether she looks ill), it is also a self-reflexive way of both letting us into her mind and also showing us how she has internalized the objectifying male gaze. The director had already established and underlined the specifically male view of her early in the film by adding the image of a young man's curious and desirous stare. Zeffirelli also allows his camera to get into Violetta's mind in a sense and to show us how she sees her lover, especially when she is ill and feverish (Tambling 1987: 182).

So far, I have been countering one half of the second cliché, suggesting the ability of performance media in the showing mode to "do" interiority, despite assertions to the contrary. However, it is also necessary to examine the other half of the cliché, which claims the reverse, that performance "does" exteriority better than print media. Siegfried Kracauer insisted that filmic adaptations make sense "only when the content of the novel is firmly rooted in objective reality, not in mental or spiritual experience" (in Andrew 1976: 121). So Emile Zola's *L'Assommoir* (1877) would be adaptable; Bernanos' *Le Journal d'un curé de campagne* (1936) would not. Yet Robert Bresson valiantly attempted the latter, as we have seen. But are film adaptations necessarily always better at conveying exteriority than the novels themselves? After all, prose description can go on at some length, but can also select the details that are narratively significant; in a film all the items are concurrently present, of equal weight and thus significance—at least until the camera lingers or lighting cues our eye. Characters may be described once and in significantly selected detail in a novel, but are seen over and over in a movie, so the significant particularities of their appearances are lost with repetition and naturalization. Film is, in editor Walter Murch's terms, a "highly redundant" medium, whereas the novel is characterized by "story abundance," and if this difference is not taken into account by the adapters, it makes for "filmic trouble" (qtd. in Ondaatje 2002: 127). In a novel like *Great Expectations* (1860–61), Dickens was obsessed with both the naturalistic and symbolic value of dress and appearance, but he specifically chose not to describe Jaggers in any detail. Yet, "in the pictorially-naturalistic medium of the film, if we are to see a character, then the character must by necessity be described. But to describe, to visualize the character, destroys the very subtlety with which the novel creates this particular character in the first place" (Giddings, Selby, and Wensley 1990: 81).

With animation in film, video, interactive fiction, or videogames, exterior action is not captured at 24 frames per second by a camera, but is created frame by frame. This is how special effects can be created that make possible comic book adaptations to film—like the recent *Spider-Man* movies. Likewise the supernatural world of wizardry and monsters of the Harry Potter stories can be made visible—and realistic—through computerized media. But just as Eisenstein saw in montage the equivalent of dialectical reasoning, Lev Manovich argues, in "From the Externalization of the Psyche to the Implantation of Technology," that new visual technologies, from Galton's photography to the new media, have indeed been used to externalize and objectify the workings of the mind.

Is this the reason why the animated worlds of videogames can be used to create both interiority and exteriority, the latter either with uncanny naturalistic accuracy or as total fantasy? The use of perspectival space, the precise rendering of surface detail, and the ability to represent movement realistically in games like *Shrek* (2001) all work together to "offer a technological 'appropriation' of the real" (Ward 2002: 132). And although it may be true that the characters or avatars have no real interiority, players do, and in manipulating the avatar's movements, they can attribute their own motives, desires, hopes, and fears in the context of the game, of course, to this character (Weinbren 2002: 186).

Representations of interiority and exteriority obviously involve this spatial dimension and not only in animation; however, the temporal is also relevant to the formal dimension of adaptation: both the time of the content and that of the "narration" (in whatever mode or medium). If Lessing were correct in calling literature an art of time (and painting an art of space), we might expect the telling mode, as in an extended narrative fiction, to be the best at depicting time, thus creating particular problems for adaptation to other modes. Again, however, the truisms of theory need testing against the realities of practice.

Cliché #3: The Showing and Interacting Modes Have Only One Tense: The Present; The Mode of Telling Alone can Show Relations among Past, Present, and Future.

The camera, like the stage, is said to be all presence and immediacy. The same is claimed for electronic technology. Prose fiction alone, by this logic, has the flexibility of time-lines and the ability to shift in a few words to the past or the future, and these abilities are always assumed to have no real equivalents in performance or interactive media. In a realist aesthetic, at any rate, stories in these media take place in the present tense; they are more interested in what is going to happen next than in what has already happened (Bluestone 1957/1971: 50; Seger 1992: 24): "In translating literature into moving pictures, once-upon-a-time collides with here-and-now" (Giddings, Selby, and Wensely 1990: xiii). This is why a film can tolerate less plot "retardation" (Abbott 2002: 109), even for suspense purposes, than can a novel. Yet, unlike the stage, the cinema is indeed capable of flashbacks and flashforwards, and its very immediacy can make the shifts potentially more effective than in prose fiction where the narrating voice stands between the characters immersed in time and the reader. Performance tropes do exist, in other words, to fuse and interrelate past, present, and future.

For instance, literature's "meanwhile," "elsewhere," and "later" find their equivalent in the filmic dissolve, as one image fades in as another fades out and time merges with space in a more immediate way than is possible with words. With the time-lapse dissolve, not only time and space but also cause and effect are synthesized (Morrissette 1985: 18–19). This is one of the ways in which the modernist novel's stream of consciousness and interior monologue became adaptable. Likewise, visual and aural leitmotifs can function in a movie to suggest the past through memory—with the memory of the audience replicating that of the characters, though on another level of narration. Arguably Marcel Proust's externalized internal signs—the Madeleine cookie and the uneven pavement stone that provoke the protagonist's memory in *A la recherche du temps perdu* (1913–27)—prefigure cinema's techniques. And as Stam reminds us, there are in fact many ways in which the past or "pastness" can be represented in film: through décor and costumes, props, music, titles (e.g., London 1712), color (sepia tints), archaic recording devices, and artificially aged or real past footage (2005b: 21).

Another aspect of this temporal truism is that a novel's description of action, setting, or character can be long or short, detailed or vague, and that the reader judges significance from the time spent on it by the narrator. In film, people appear within a setting in action all at once, with no mediating assistance for the spectator. But the kind of shot (long, medium, close-up; angles; reverses), not to mention the duration of the shot, is in fact always dictated by the dramatic importance of what is being filmed, not by any naturalistic timing or pacing of the actual action. The director or editor or camera operator does indeed mediate and not only through the visual. Unlike a live performance on stage that occurs in real time and in which sounds and images are correlated exactly, in a film the relation between sound and image is a constructed one. Visual frames and different soundtracks (dialogue, voice-overs, music, noises) can be combined, as the film editor manipulates time and space relations.

Cinematic adapters, in other words, have at their disposal a veritable wealth of technical possibilities and now learned and accepted conventions to tackle the move from print to screen, even with texts that are temporally complex or resolutely interiorized. However, this does not mean that there will be no problems. Thomas Mann has and takes much time in his novella of *Der Tod in Venedig* to allow a young boy's beauty to insinuate itself into the mind of both his protagonist, Aschenbach, and his reader. In the film adaptation, Visconti has to "throw the image at us, via the handsome Björn Andresen" to get the story going. Rather than gradually learning to see Tadzio through the learned Aschenbach's idealizing (indeed Hellenizing) eyes in the novella, we instead watch him and the boy "exchange lengthy glances, whose sexual explicitness turns Aschenbach into a foolish dirty old man, and the boy into a pretty little tease" (Paul Zimmerman, qtd. in Wagner 1975: 343). Time and timing clearly present a real challenge for the adapter to a different medium.

The stage has different and perhaps more limited means at its disposal for dealing with temporal issues because, as just noted, a live performance takes place in real time. An adaptation has to take into account not only changes in time in the story but also the technicalities of, for example, the time needed to change scenes. Kracauer points out that staged operas have added temporal problems: arias in effect stop time. Not only are arias conventionalized moments of interiority in a seemingly very exteriorized art form, as we have seen, but they also arrest the action: their "sung passions transfigure physical life instead of penetrating it" (Kracauer 1955: 19). For this reason, he argues, "[t]he world of opera is built upon premises which radically defy those of the cinematic approach" (19). The naturalism of television and film may seem alien to the artifice of this sung, staged form, but that has not prevented opera from having a second life in both media, thanks to what are more adaptations than recordings of productions.

Although the opera's drama does indeed go on in real time, its timing is not the timing of the stage play, and the reason is the music (Halliwell 1996: 87–88). As composer Virgil Thomson vividly puts it: "An opera is not a concert in costume. Neither is it just a play with music laid on. It is a dramatic action viewed through poetry and music, animated and controlled by its music, which is continuous. It owes to poetry much of its grandeur, to music all of its pacing" (1982: 6). The pulse of the music, in operas as in musicals, provides another temporal dimension—both an advantage and a constraint—that other art forms do not have. Directors and editors of video versions of operas often derive the pacing of camera shots from the rhythm of the music—including its chord structures and harmonies (see Large 1992: 201).

A special adaptation problem occurs in all media: how to represent or thematize the unfolding of time—something that can be done so easily in prose fiction. Classical films resorted to images of calendar pages turning to cue spectators to time passing. In a novel, characters can *become* bored; we can read of time passing, of mounting boredom, yet not become bored ourselves. In a graphic novel we can actually see this numbing occur, without succumbing to it in our own right. On film, however, the process of becoming bored cannot really be represented so easily, given the amount of screen time in real viewing time it would take to do so naturalistically, as Claude Chabrol discovered when he attempted to dramatize Emma Bovary's boredom in his 1991 film adaptation of Flaubert's *Madame Bovary* (1857). Yet it is also the case that a leap forward (off-screen) is also a cinematic convention that spectators understand. And the repeated breakfast scenes in Orson Welles' *Citizen Kane* (1941) also convey time passing into boredom through the simple act of repetition.

Television adaptations usually have more time at their disposal, of course, and therefore more flexibility. Novels like David Lodge's *Nice Work* (1988) have been made into serials. But this move entails other temporal constraints, such as the need to divide the narrative into a specified number of blocks of equal duration. In the words of Lodge, who wrote the screenplay for his own novel, "No narrative medium is as precisely timed as an episode of a television series. When transmitted, it must fit a preordained slot measured in minutes and even seconds" (1993: 193). Although the writer needs to think about this precise timing, it is the editor, of course, who in the end must achieve it. But this is where another kind of time constraint appears: as a medium television is conventionally faster paced than film, for instance, and an adapter has to take this pace into account even when working with inevitably slower paced literary works. When classic novels are adapted for television, however, a textual resonance of the literary connection is often retained in both action and camera movement, recalling the idea that reading is a more "leisurely, measured and thoughtful pursuit" than television viewing (Cardwell 2002: 112).

The visual and aural immediacy of performance media may indeed create the sense of a continuous present, but time and timing are much more complex than this would suggest in the process of adaptation. The proof is in the parodies. In the 30-second classical movie versions created by animation artist Jennifer Shiman, the stories are deconstructed, reconstructed, and reshown, as acted out by serious, earnest bunny characters. At the other extreme, Douglas Gordon takes popular films and expands them—stretching Hitchcock's *Psycho* (1963) to 24 hours and Ford's *The Searchers* to 5 years (were we to want to play the whole thing). Both artists' parodic adaptations ironically place in the foreground the conventions of the cinematic manipulation of time. The "instantaneity" made technically possible by remote communications systems (telephone, radio, television) is new to the last century, and it is this that makes possible our acceptance of the illusion that a film is happening in the present and that we are present as it happens (LeGrice 2002: 232).

Videogames based on films, of course, go one step further and immerse us in the time and pace of real life while still maintaining this cinematic illusion. But electronic technology in general offers various new adaptation possibilities, not least when it comes to representing the temporal. Lev Manovich argues that in computerized films, for instance, time and memory can actually be spatialized through montage:

> The logic of replacement [of one image by another, filling the screen], characteristic of cinema, gives way to the logic of addition and co-existence. Time becomes spatialised, distributed over the surface of the screen. In spatial montage, nothing is potentially forgotten, nothing is erased. Just as we use computers to accumulate endless texts, messages, notes and data, and just as a person, going through life, accumulates more and more memories, with the past slowly acquiring more weight than the future, so spatial montage can accumulate events and images as it progresses through its narrative. In contrast to the cinema's screen, which primarily functioned as a record of perception, the computer screen functions as a recorder of memory. (2002b: 71)

Whether these possibilities will be exploited extensively by adapters remains to be seen, because most of the films being produced on this model so far are not in fact adaptations at all. The new media, however, are available for use; indeed they offer very suggestive possibilities for adapting temporally and spatially complex works from other media. Hoss Gifford's (Screenbase Media and Canongate Books) production of an interactive Web site (http://hossgifford.com/pi/promo/life_of_ pi.htm), "inspired by" Yann Martel's 2002 novel, *Life of Pi*, selects several scenes from the novel and presents them in a mix of animation and an interactive game, with engaging visual effects. The aural text, both words and sounds, enhances the visuals (in the form of computerized images and words). We experience time passing as in a film, but we also control time in the game parts, making for an intriguing hybrid temporal dimension.

Over the years, point of view, interiority/exteriority, and time have become major contentious issues, as well as a major source of theoretical truisms, about adaptation and medium specificity. But they are joined by another loose grouping of issues around verbal and narrative complexity, and these too need testing against actual practice.

Cliché #4: Only Telling (in Language) Can Do Justice to Such Elements as Ambiguity, Irony, Symbols, Metaphors, Silences, and Absences; These Remain "Untranslatable" in the Showing or Interacting Modes.

In 1898, Henry James published and in 1908 revised what he himself thought of as a "potboiler" called *The Turn of the Screw*. In 1934, Edmund Wilson provoked, even if he did not begin, what has proved to be a seemingly endless scholarly debate about how to interpret this enigmatic text. The fight over this text has always been over its resolute and deliberate ambiguities. Is the story's governess hallucinating the appearance of Quint and Jessel (said to be deceased) because of her own sexual repression? Are the children in the governess' care possessed by something supernatural and malevolent that the governess discovers, or is she herself possessed by some neurotic obsession? *The Turn of the Screw* would seem to be very recalcitrant to adaptation to a performance medium. Yet, it has proved quite the contrary. In one of the many film adaptations of it, Jack Clayton's 1961 *The Innocents* (screenplay by Truman Capote and William Archibald), the spectator is, in fact, given a chance to weigh the evidence for these different possible interpretations of the text's ambiguities. The result is a constant flipping back and forth of our sympathies in response to the governess' imagination. The camera too sometimes alternates point of view, as in the final confrontation between the governess and her charge, Miles (J. Allen 1977: 136). The soundtrack is used not only to suggest interiority but also to reinforce ambiguity: are the eerie sounds we are hearing in the governess' mind, or do they signal supernatural presences? When what we hear does not match what we see, the resulting suggestiveness can be more potent than the actual appearances of the ghosts. But, in the end, James' narrative ambiguity is refused in the naturalistic medium of film, though in an interestingly inclusive way: Quint does exist and possesses Miles, and the governess is herself possessed and in the end also possesses the dead Miles (J. Allen 1977: 140).

When Myfanwy Piper and Benjamin Britten adapted James' story in 1954 to a chamber opera form, they faced an even greater challenge than that of the screenplay writers: how to represent this kind of ambiguity in *live sung stage* action. In fact, however, it is Britten's music that pulls it off. Each of the brief, separate scenes that compose the opera is linked to the one before by a repeated musical theme (with variations), whose intervals rotate in screw-like fashion (Whittall 1992: 847). These children do not *sound* musically like Clayton's "innocents," for even while looking guileless and singing "Tom, Tom, the piper's son," they manage to sound very sinister indeed. Here the ghosts do appear, but their eerie and exotic music makes clear they are from a different realm, even if their malign but seductive power over the children is palpable—and audible. Yet, the novella's famed ambiguity is retained to the very end, as the music underlines the doubt as to the real cause of Miles' death by having the governess' vocal line fade on a chromatic dissonance.

This example seems to contradict Patrick J. Smith's famous pronouncement that in operatic adaptation "any ambiguities or variant readings possible in any of the very great works of art ... must necessarily be omitted or toned down, to the detriment not only of the original but also of the adaptation itself" (1970: 342–43). Verbal and narrative ambiguities do indeed need to be dramatized in performance media, but that task is far from impossible. And something can be gained as well as lost. The visual and aural immediacy of that dramatization cannot be matched even by the prose of someone like Henry James. The price to pay? (There always is a trade-off in adaptation.) When a play or opera is staged, the director and performers make choices that inevitably reduce the "interpretive richness" of the written text (Scholes 1976: 285); in a movie or television adaptation, those choices are final, recorded forever. From a word-oriented writer's point of view, this is a serious limitation, as revealed by Patrick McGrath, who adapted his own novel *Spider* for David Cronenberg's 2002 film:

> The writer of prose fiction, when he first turns his hand to screen-writing, often does so with a condescending air. Surely this can't be so very difficult, he thinks; all that's required is to come up with the bare bones of a story. So he goes to work anticipating a quick job with easy money at the end of it, and possibly a bit of glory. He is soon disabused of these prideful assumptions. It becomes apparent to him that what he has at his disposal is merely an ordered succession of dramatic pictures. With these he must do the work he once did with all the infinite resources of the English language at his back. (2002: R1)

But for visually oriented filmmakers, the opposite is true. They can move from that single-track language to a multitrack medium and thereby not only make meaning possible on many levels but appeal to other physical senses as well.

However, the "infinite resources" of the English—or any other—language include symbols and metaphors, and if these are to be realized in a showing mode in performance media, they could simply be spoken by a character or else they must be physically materialized in an iconic form or otherwise translated into equivalents. Despite the feeling among critics that none of the over 100 adaptations to stage, screen, and radio of Dickens' *Great Expectations* ever managed to achieve the melding of the naturalistic and symbolic in the novel's verbal texture (see, for examples, Bolton 1987: 116–29; Giddings, Selby, and Wensley 1990: 86–87), performance media once again do have their own resources on which to draw. As we have seen, operas and musicals can deploy music to symbolic ends: just as Shakespeare's Othello gradually takes on Iago's imagery, Verdi and Boito's operatic Otello gradually takes on Iago's music (most audibly, its triplets and dotted rhythms), as the protagonist in both the play and the opera is brought down to his antagonist's level. Even in film, with its naturalistic demands, editing can manage to suggest metaphoric comparison by linking disparate images together. The camera can isolate some element of a scene and bestow upon it not only meaning but also symbolic significance by its act of contextualizing. Thomas Hardy's image of his protagonist in *Tess of the D'Urbervilles* (1891) with her "peony lips" is translated by Roman Polanski in his 1979 film *Tess* into an image of Natassia Kinski's full red lips opening to receive a strawberry from Alex (Elliott 2003: 234).

Verbal irony presents a particular challenge for adaptation to performance media, not in dialogue, obviously, but when used in the showing mode. To invoke a work mentioned earlier in another context, William Makepeace Thackeray's 1844 novel, *The Luck of Barry Lyndon*, is presented as intended by its first-person narrator to be the tale of "the triumphs and misfortunes of a sympathetic and resourceful eighteenth-century gentleman," or so we are told. Thanks to Thackeray's deft irony, however, it actually comes across as "the diary of a wicked and self-deceiving brute" (Sinyard 1986: 130). We have already seen that first-person narration is difficult for film, and indeed, Stanley Kubrick's omniscient narratorial camera in his 1975 *Barry Lyndon* rejects intimacy for distance, and what we lose of the sense of the voice of a crass, self-obsessed individual we gain in the feeling of that individual in the context of a snobbish society. The result, however, is that this Barry Lyndon is much more sympathetic than that of Thackeray's novel, despite the movie's use of an ironic voice-over narrator between scenes.

The difficulties of dramatizing such verbal elements as irony, ambiguity, metaphor, or symbolism pale in comparison with the problems faced by the adapter who has to dramatize what is *not* present. Absences and silences in prose narratives almost invariably get made into presences in performance media, or so this aspect of the cliché would have it, thereby losing their power and meaning. But is this necessarily the case? In the next section, I test this truism against an extended example of an adaptational practice that not only addresses this particular point but also engages en route almost all of the issues around mode and medium specificity that this chapter has been addressing. Therefore, it can function as a summary and conclusion.

Learning from Practice

In the late 1940s and early 1950s, Benjamin Britten, with the help of the then-elderly E.M. Forster and the younger, self-defined "man of the theatre," Eric Crozier, adapted for the operatic stage Herman Melville's last, unfinished, and resolutely ambiguous work, *Billy Budd*. Many scholars have written about the problems of the inaccurate and modified editions of the Melville text, but it is of both relevance and interest that Britten's librettists used the 1946 edition by William Plomer, who was the first to talk openly about the homosexual and homosocial themes of the novella. The story is set on a British navy ship in the eighteenth century, just after a series of mutinies that had left the authorities shaken and newly alert; it tells the tale of Billy, the "Handsome Sailor"—presented as a kind of naval stereotype—who is tried and executed for the decidedly provoked killing of the malicious master at arms, John Claggart, who was plotting Billy's own destruction. Although the killing could have been seen as an accident, the sole witness, Captain Vere, chooses not to save the popular and good young man, but rather to give into his professional fears that this act could be seen as the first step to a possible mutiny.

There are obvious difficulties in adapting this story. Most of the critical literature on this particular adaptation has focused on the character of Vere, for in Melville's text he dies shortly after Billy is hanged, whereas in the opera he lives on and in fact narrates the story's frame. This change potentially eliminates two of the immediate problems for the operatic adaptation of the novella: the loss of a narrative voice and the complexity of characterization because of compression, for this character sings of his motivations and worries. The operatic version is framed emotionally and formally by Vere's continuing anguish at his actions or lack thereof and then by his final sense of absolution achieved through Billy's forgiveness and love. Forster said these alterations were undertaken because he wanted to "rescue Vere from Melville" (qtd. in Brett 1984: 135).

But others have been less charitable, if more accurate, in their evaluation of these changes. Robert Martin charges that Vere is changed from the novella's "pompous and pretentious hypocrite" into an "intellectual caught up in a dilemma of conscience" (1986: 52). The effect, for him, is that the opera depoliticizes and de-eroticizes Melville's text, taming his "subversive eros" into a "sentimental and domestic vision" (55). Yet by Eric Crozier's account, the librettists saw themselves as being very faithful to Melville's text and his intentions—at least as interpreted by them, working from Plomer's edition (Crozier 1986: 12, 13, 14, 16, 17, 21). Yet in their alterations of the character of Captain Vere, they ended up changing much: Melville's Vere not only differs in terms of moral character and life expectancy from the opera's character but he is also able to offer rational reasons why Billy has to die: the ship was on a war footing and there was a fear of mutiny. In the opera, mutiny is a threat only *after* Billy, so beloved by the crew, is executed. Vere's motivations in the opera are presented as confused or ambiguous, a decision that has been read as a formal failure (Emslie 1992: 51).

But what if that confusion were intentional? Indeed, what if it were the whole point of the adaptation? Britten was a pacifist and spent the war years just before he wrote this opera in the United States. What if the appeal of the military tale for the opera's multiple creators was, in fact, its very ambivalence, its unfinished and indeterminate nature? The operatic scene that would suggest precisely this kind of reading is one that brings to the fore the questions we are dealing with in this chapter: how to represent in dramatized form such elements as interiority, point of view, and especially ambiguity, equivocation, and, even more radically, absence.

The scene in question comes after Claggart's death and after Billy has been put on trial before a drumhead court of officers that does not include Vere, for the captain must testify as the sole witness to the fatal event. In the section examined here, Vere must inform Billy, who has left the room, of the court's decision: he is to hang from the yardarm for his "crime." In the novella, Vere does so in a scene that is *not* narrated. Melville's garrulous and usually omniscient narrator suddenly changes course and claims, "Beyond the communication of the sentence what took place at this interview was never known" (1891/1958: 337). Nevertheless he remains in character enough to venture what he calls "some conjectures": he speculates that Vere kept nothing from Billy about his own role or motives and that Billy would have accepted his confession in the spirit in which it was tendered. The narrator adds:

Even more may have been. Captain Vere in the end may have developed the passion sometimes latent under an exterior stoical or indifferent. He was old enough to have been Billy's father. The austere devotee of military duty, letting himself melt back into what remains primeval in our formalized humanity, may in the end have caught Billy to his heart even as Abraham may have caught the young Isaac. (337)

It is a challenge, to say the least, to dramatize in an opera a silenced scene or even one left to narratorial conjecture. The narrating figure of the opera version is Vere, not Melville's anonymous and only (obviously) partially omniscient narrator. But the equivocation and ambivalence that Melville achieves by his mix of silence and speculation are indeed recreated in the showing mode—and in a most imaginative way. In the libretto, Vere is said to disappear into the room in which Billy is being kept; there is no further action on stage. Instead, the audience hears only a sequence of 34 clear, triadic chords, each of them harmonizing on a note of the F major triad and each scored differently. The verbal silence and the lack of stage action are accompanied, in other words, by musical sound—but sound with no real melody and no rhythmic variation.

Other showing-mode adaptations of the story have not been this reticent. The Broadway play by Louis O. Coxe and R.H. Chapman, which opened less than a year before the opera, in 1950, dramatizes the narrator's speculations. Billy openly asks Vere to help him understand his sentence. Vere's answer—that the world is full of good and evil and that "most of us find out early and trim to a middle course"—seems enough to bring Billy to understand that "maybe there's a kind of cruelty in people that's just as much a part of them as kindness" (1951: 68). Although critics have argued for years about whether this scene in the novella works or not, what this stage version does is effectively eliminate its ambiguity. The film adaptation of this play mentioned earlier, directed by Peter Ustinov, who also plays Vere, dramatizes the scene as well, though differently. In the film Vere says there is no answer to Billy's question, but then asks the condemned man to hate him as a way of conquering his fear. Billy replies that he is not actually afraid: "I was only doing my duty. You are doing yours." Ustinov accompanies this scene with melodramatic music by Antony Hopkins that could not be more different from the opera's strange and estranging chords.

Britten's silence-substituting music has been interpreted in many different ways. Some readings are resolutely mimetic ones, with critics imagining in the changing chords changes in the emotions of the two men behind the closed door; that is, with critics offering "some conjectures," not unlike those of Melville's narrator. The chords are therefore usually interpreted as articulating the shift from surprise to terror to resignation and composure. Others read the chords thematically as realizing musically the passions involved or as implying a positive or even idealized form of homosexual affection that, at the time, could not be spoken of openly for fear of legal prosecution. For still others the meaning is symbolic or metaphysical. The fact that the chords are heard in two later scenes of the opera determines some of these readings: they are heard right after this scene in the last aria of the condemned man, the piece known as "Billy in the Darbies," at the moment when Billy attains his greatest moral and psychological strength and accepts his death. The chords are heard again in the climax of Vere's Epilogue, as he sings Billy's melody and words (which he could never, realistically, have heard): "But I've sighted a sail in the storm, the far-shining sail, and I'm content." Is the implication of the replaying of some of these chords that Vere's redemption began behind the closed door? If so, did Billy's acceptance and strength begin there as well?

Arnold Whittall points out that composers "often use successions of slow-moving chords ranging widely across the tonal spectrum to represent the sublime, the monumental, but rarely if ever with the complete rejection of melody or significant linear motion involved here" (1990: 157). He goes on to suggest that the harmony may be used here as a way of expressing interiority. If so, this is another example of how music can supplement or replace what is lost when fiction's introspection and reflection are transposed into a performance medium. Thanks in part to the work of Carolyn Abbate (1991), who has brought the insights of literary narratology to musical studies, it has become common to say that the narrator of fiction is replaced by the orchestra in opera. In this scene in *Billy Budd*, the dialectic of chromatic and diatonic chords creates an uneasy, unstable F major tonality that is, to the ears that can hear it, the musical equivalent of Melville's verbal equivocation (see Whittall 1990 for the extended argument). This also suggests that—despite the librettists' visionary *language* suggesting Vere's redemption and peace—the opera's *musical* ending is decidedly more ambiguous and complicated: "It is undoubtedly right that Britten's music should remain perfectly, precariously poised on the knife edge, challenging but not rejecting tonal syntax, challenging but not rejecting the great operatic theme of redemption through love" (Whittall 1990: 170).

The music's ambiguity, however, is mirrored in the very lack of action in the scene being discussed here. This is a supremely un-operatic operatic moment, one in which words and music do *not* interact, in which words do *not* help us interpret what we are hearing in the music. In fact, we are deprived of visual as well as verbal clues. Not surprisingly, audiences are often puzzled by this scene: they think it is a prelude to the encounter between Billy and Vere and so may become restless. They do not feel anything important is happening on stage, and they are right, of course: the action is all off-stage behind that door. But the impact of those chords is such that the un-represented can be made to be more powerful than the represented. It obviously depends on the individual director's ability to provoke our imaginations, to move us to fill in the gap.

Wolfgang Iser's theory of reading—of how readers fill in the narrative gaps that are part of any literary text (1971)—applies here as well (see Abbott 2002: 114–16 on narrative gaps in various media). As we watch and listen, we do not free associate; instead, we fill in the gaps, with the combined guidance of the dramatic set up of the encounter in the previous scene and those 34 chords in their ineffable and suggestive ambiguity.

Billy Budd's infamous closed-door scene is as good an example as any of the complexities involved in the transposition across modes and media. Like realist film, only perhaps more so, staged opera is not self-evidently a medium conducive to representing ambivalence, equivocation, and absence. However, the combination in this scene of a refusal to stage or to verbalize with the addition of the estranging music can render a version of that complexity. And in the process, it can provide an instance of artistic practice that contests a good number of the clichés about the representational inadequacies of the performing media compared to prose fiction. These truisms are usually articulated, it must be said, not by adapters themselves, but by protective literary critics and self-protective writers like Virginia Woolf, writing vividly about her sense of the small worth of film adaptations of fiction: "So we lurch and lumber through the most famous novels of the world. So we spell them out in words of one syllable written, too, in the scrawl of an illiterate schoolboy" (1926: 309). Need we necessarily trust such a view? Should we perhaps listen to the adapter for a change?

3

WHO? WHY?
(Adapters)

Playwrights like to think that they're the sole author of everything that happens on stage. But in this case I knew that I would be sharing the driver's compartment with many others. Like the book-writer of a big musical, or the screenwriter of a film, I would be referring constantly to the designer, the movement director, the composer and every other member of the creative team. I would be working with the producer and the director, both united in the form of Nick Hytner. And I would be working with Philip Pullman.

**—Dramatist Nicholas Wright, about adapting
Philip Pullman's *His Dark Materials* for the stage**

Do other screenwriters feel like this when they're adapting books? I'm aware of needing the approval of the director, producer, and funding bodies, as in getting the script "approved" for production, but this is a practical, political need, not a personal one. Such vanity—not only in wanting the work to measure up to the original creation, but in the desire to measure up to the original creator.

—Screenwriter Noel S. Baker, about adapting
Michael Turner's *Hard Core Logo* for film

Who Is the Adapter?

The answer to this question is simple for Noel Baker. But it is also easy when an author like Alexandre Dumas, *fils* transposes his own novel, *La dame aux camélias* (1848), to the stage (1852). The author and adapter here are one and the same person. The question can sometimes also be answered easily when the author and the adapter differ, as when Helen Edmundson does a stage dramatization (1994) of George Eliot's novel *The Mill on the Floss* (1860). In the case of a musical or an opera adaptation, however, matters become more complicated. Dumas' play was made into the opera *La Traviata* (1853), but was it the librettist, Francesco Maria Piave, who was the adapter, or was it the composer, Giuseppe Verdi? Or must it be both? The complexities of the new media also mean that adaptation there too is a collective process.

Obviously, the move to a performance or interactive mode entails a shift from a solo model of creation to a collaborative one. The transition from the one to the other is often fraught with difficulties: witness Arthur Miller's suit against the Wooster Group for adapting only the basic structure of his play *The Crucible* in their work, *L.S.D.*, in the early 1980s. Given that this group is known for its collaborative and improvisatory ethos and its challenge to theater as individual property, both the ironies and the problems of adaptation as a collaborative practice became evident in this legal encounter (see Savran 1985).

In interactive digital installations and Internet-connected work, a collective model of creation best describes the web of interlinkages that are constantly being reorganized by the various participants both before and during the interaction itself. This fluid collaboration is more like that of an ongoing stage play than a finished product like a film or video. Live stage and radio plays, dance, musicals, operas—all are forms of repeated performances by groups of people, and when they are the site of adaptations from a prior work there is always contention over exactly who of the many artists involved should be called the actual adapter(s).

Film and television are perhaps the most complicated media of all from this point of view. Is the major adapter the often underrated screenwriter who "creates or (creatively adapts) a film's plot, characters, dialogue, and theme" (Corliss 1974: 542)? Although this seems the most obvious answer in one sense—as Noel Baker would agree—it is not the one most people would offer. One of the reasons why not is the possible complexity of a script's "authorship." In Steven Spielberg's 1987 film adaptation of J.G. Ballard's novel, *Empire of the Sun*, the first shooting script/adaptation was written by Tom Stoppard; it was subsequently reworked by Menno Meyjes and changed once again in the editing room (Reynolds 1993b: 7). Who then is the adapter?

The name of the music director/composer does not usually come to mind as a primary adapter, although he or she creates the music that reinforces emotions or provokes reactions in the audience and directs our interpretation of different characters, perhaps solo violins for sweet innocence or a snarling bass clarinet to make us uncomfortable around ambivalent characters. But it is also the case that, although the music is of obvious importance to the success of the adaptation, composers usually work from the script, not from the adapted text, because they have to write music specifically to fit the production's action, timing, and budget. Costume and set designers are other possibilities for the role of adapter, and many admit that they turn to the adapted text, especially if it is a novel, for inspiration; however, what they feel immediately responsible to is the *director*'s interpretation of the *film script* (see the interviews in Giddings, Selby, and Wensley 1990: 110–28, especially). The same sense of responsibility is often felt by cinematographers.

On the question of whether the actors can be considered as adapters, the case is no simpler. As in staged works, the performers are the ones who embody and give material existence to the adaptation. Although clearly having to follow the screenplay, some actors admit that they seek background and inspiration from the adapted text, especially if the characters they are to play are well-known literary ones. But does this make them conscious adapters? Certainly in interviews, novelists often comment on their surprise when actors—through gesture, tone of voice, or facial expression—interpret through incarnating characters in ways the initial creator never envisaged (see Cunningham 2003: 1): actors can bring "their individual sense and senses to the characters and give them those glances and gestures that come from their own imaginations" (Ondaatje 1997: ix). But in a more literal sense, what actors actually adapt in this sense is the screenplay (Stam 2005b: 22).

There is yet another rarely considered candidate for the role of adapter: the film and television editor, whose craft, as Michael Ondaatje has insisted, is "mostly unimagined and certainly overlooked" (2002: xi). As editor Walter Murch puts it, "When it works, film edition—which could just as easily be called 'film construction'—identifies and exploits underlying patterns of sound and image that are not obvious on the surface" (qtd. in Ondaatje 2002: 10). The editor sees and creates the whole in a way no one else does. Yet none of these artists—screenwriter, composer, designer, cinematographer, actor, editor, and the list could go on—is usually considered the primary adapter of a film or television production:

> It is hard for any person who has been on the set of a movie to believe that only one man or woman makes a film. At times a film set resembles a beehive or daily life in Louis XIV's court—every kind of society is witnessed in action, and it seems every trade is busy at work. But as far as the public is concerned, there is always just one Sun-King who is sweepingly credited with responsibility for story, style, design, dramatic tension, taste, and even weather in connection with the finished product. When, of course, there are many hard-won professions at work. (Ondaatje 2002: xi)

That Sun-King, of course, is the director. Peter Wollen has argued that the director as *auteur* is never just another adapter: "The director does not subordinate himself to another author; his source is only a pretext, which provides catalysts, scenes which use his own preoccupations to produce a radically new work" (1969: 113). This is certainly the case with Peter Greenaway's 1991 adaptation of Shakespeare's *The Tempest*, which he renamed *Prospero's Books*, a work clearly marked by his own postmodern aesthetic of self-referentiality and citation. All that this Prospero knows, he has learned from books; therefore, the magic world he creates is a very bookish—and painterly—one. Like Prospero,

Greenaway literally creates his cinematic island world through books, inspired by those of Athanasius Kircher. This is a world that the audience members first hear about orally, then watch being written by a human hand in a visual pun on the idea of "digital," and finally see with their own eyes in digitally enhanced form. Using the Paint Box and Japanese Hi-Vision videotape technologies then available, Greenaway electronically manipulates images, animating the books of the title. But no matter how much he or she is the magus and controller, the director is also a manager, an organizer of other artists upon whom he or she must rely to produce that new work. Performance arts like film are, in fact, resolutely collaborative: as in the building of a Gothic cathedral, there are multiple makers and therefore arguably multiple adapters.

These various adapters, however, stand at different distances from the adapted text. Zadie Smith's response to the televising of her novel *White Teeth* gives a good sense of the complexity of this process: "Telly is watching a creative idea make its excruciatingly slow progress from script-writer to producer to actor to third and second assistant directors to the director himself to the camera man, to that poor maligned fellow who must hold the huge, furry gray Q-tip up in the air if anything is to be heard by anyone. Telly is group responsibility" (2003: 1). There is an increasing distance from the adapted novel as the process moves from the writing of the screenplay to the actual shooting (when the designers, actors, cinematographer, and director move in) and then to the editing when sound and music are added and the entire work as a whole is given shape. The script itself is often changed through interaction with the director and the actors, not to mention the editor. By the end the film may be very far from both the screenplay and the adapted text in focus and emphasis. William Goldman sees the finished film as the studio's adaptation of the editor's adaptation of the director's adaptation of the actors' adaptation of the screenwriter's adaptation of a novel that might itself be an adaptation of narrative or generic conventions (in Landon 1991: 96).

Adaptation for performance on stage can be almost as complex as this process, but without the structuring intervention of the film editor, it is the director who is held even more responsible for the form and impact of the whole. Because, in stage productions as in cinema, the characteristic preoccupations, tastes, and stylistic trademarks of the director are what stand out and become identifiable, perhaps all directors should be considered at least potential adapters. Audiences come to learn that a Harry Kupfer production of an opera is one that self-reflexively places in the foreground the work's underlying violence and sexual tension. The same is true for film, of course: at one point, a Ridley Scott adaptation would have focused on the marginalized and the powerless, and a David Lean version of a classic novel, almost any classic novel, would stress the theme of romantic repression and sexual frustration (Sinyard 1986: 124). In these cases, the directors make the adaptation very much their own work: *Fellini Satyricon* (1969) is 80 percent Fellini and 20 percent Petronius, according to the director himself (qtd. in Dick 1981: 151).

The adapted text, therefore, is not something to be reproduced, but rather something to be interpreted and recreated, often in a new medium. It is what one theorist calls a reservoir of instructions, diegetic, narrative, and axiological, that the adapter can use or ignore (Gardies 1998: 68–71), for the adapter is an interpreter before becoming a creator. But the creative transposition of an adapted work's story and its heterocosm is subject not only to genre and medium demands, as explored in Chapter 2, but also to the temperament and talent of the adapter—and his or her individual intertexts through which are filtered the materials being adapted. French writer Michel Vinaver calls his own adapting process one of substitution—of his intentions for that of the prior text (1998: 84). When film director Bernardo Bertolucci and screenplay writer Gilbert Adair adapted Adair's novel, *The Holy Innocents* (1988), into the film, *The Dreamers* (2004), the romance's gay sex gave way to straight, as Bertolucci's intentions substituted for those of Adair.

The film and the opera made from Thomas Mann's *Der Tod in Venedig* differ for obvious reasons of medium and genre conventions, but they also differ because they are presented by their creators through what we might call different personal artistic filters. Visconti echoes not only Gustav Mahler's music but also paintings by Monet, Guardi, and Carrà, as well as his own film *Senso* (see Carcaud-Macaire and Clerc 1998: 160), thereby creating a lushly sensual visual and aural film world. This has an utterly different impact than does the opera's more intellectualized and verbalized account of the Dionysian body's triumph over the Apollonian control of the mind. But the librettist, Myfanwy Piper, had gone back to Mann's text and been influenced, like him, by both Plato and Nietzsche. In addition, Britten's modern, Balinese-inspired music could hardly be more different from the late Romanticism of the *adagietto* from Mahler's Fifth Symphony, which is used repeatedly in the film version.

Films are like operas in that there are many and varied artists involved in the complex process of their creation. Nevertheless, it is evident from both studio press releases and critical response that the director is ultimately held responsible for the overall vision and therefore for the adaptation *as adaptation*. Yet someone else usually writes the screenplay that begins the process; someone else first interprets the adapted text and paraphrases it for a new medium before the director takes on the task of giving this new text embodied life. For this reason, as in a musical in which the composer and the book-writer share authorship (e.g., Rodgers and Hammerstein), in a film the director and the screenwriter share the primary task of adaptation. The other artists involved may be inspired by the adapted text, but their responsibility is more to the screenplay and thus to the film as an autonomous work of art.

Why Adapt?

Given the large number of adaptations in all media today, many artists appear to have chosen to take on this dual responsibility: to adapt another work and to make of it an autonomous creation. Giacomo Puccini and his librettists were expected to do so in their operas; Marius Petipa was lauded for doing so in his ballets. But when filmmakers and their scriptwriters adapt literary works, in particular, we have seen that a profoundly moralistic rhetoric often greets their endeavors. In Robert Stam's vivid terms: "*Infidelity* resonates with overtones of Victorian prudishness; *betrayal* evokes ethical perfidy; *deformation* implies aesthetic disgust; *violation* calls to mind sexual violence; *vulgarization* conjures up class degradation; and *desecration* intimates a kind of religious sacrilege toward the 'sacred word'" (2000: 54). Like Stam and many others today, I too feel that the time has come to move away from this kind of negative view.

However, there is another even more important question that this use of pejorative terms poses for me: why would anyone willingly enter this moralistic fray and become an adapter? What motivates adapters, knowing that their efforts will be compared to competing imagined versions in people's heads and inevitably be found wanting? Why would they risk censure for monetary opportunism? For example, Jane Campion was attacked for ostensibly giving up her independent feminist and artistic vision to do a traditionally lavish heritage-film adaptation (1996) of Henry James' *Portrait of a Lady* (1881). Like jazz variations, adaptations point to individual creative decisions and actions, yet little of the respect accorded to the jazz improviser is given to most adapters. Need a prospective adapter therefore be a masochist, as well as having all the other qualities said to be ideal: humility, respect, compassion, wit, and a sharp razor (as listed by J.A. Hall 1984: 1 and Sheila Benson in Brady 1994: 2)? In adapting the opera *Aida* for the Broadway stage, Elton John did admit that "the fact that it had already been done by Verdi was playing with fire … . It appealed to my sense of masochism" (qtd. in Witchell 2000: 7).

Over 20 years ago Donald Larsson called for a "*theory* of adaptation based on an accurate history of the motivations and techniques of adaptations" (1982: 69), but few seem to have shared his interest in motivations, except to dismiss them as mercenary and opportunistic. Although the monetary appeal cannot be ignored, perhaps there are a few other attractions.

The Economic Lures

Despite the less moralistic but equally strongly held view among players that a superb computer game cannot be made from an adaptation, videogame adaptations of films proliferate and can be found on many platforms. It is obvious that on one level they are attempts to cash in on the success of certain movies and vice versa, as the popularity on film (2001; 2003) of the *Tomb Raiders* game character, Lara Croft, has shown. However, not all film adaptations of games have had as great commercial or critical success, despite the fact that the same media corporations (e.g., Sony Corporation) control both film (Sony Pictures) and videogame (PlayStation) producers and distributors. We should remind ourselves that games are not alone in this commercial exploitation: films are often made of Pulitzer Prize-winning books like Alice Walker's 1982 *The Color Purple* (in 1985) or Toni Morrison's 1987 *Beloved* (in 1998) in part because, as one handbook for screenwriters claims, "an adaptation is an *original screenplay* and, as such, is the sole property of the screenwriter" and thus a source of financial gain (Brady 1994: xi; his italics).

From another economic angle, expensive collaborative art forms like operas, musicals, and films are going to look for safe bets with a ready audience—and that usually means adaptations. They are also going to seek ways to expand the audience for their "franchise," of course, though they have not been in the habit of thinking about it in quite those terms. Operas are usually commissioned by an opera company well in advance, but a Broadway musical has to survive in a commercial market. Producers raise money from outside investors, readings and workshops are held, out-of-town tryouts follow, and then there are previews before a paying public (see Lachiusa 2002: 15). Films and television series, likewise, have restricted budgets:

> When you are writing a TV script, it is like sitting in a taxi; the meter is always running, and everything has to be paid for. You can always see the price turning over everywhere you go, or the difficulties of performance and production; that is the art of writing for the medium. But the novel has the meter switched off; you can write what you like, have Buenos Aires, have the moon, have whatever you want. That is part of the wonder of the novel, the wonder of being a novelist. (Bradbury 1994: 101)

With film adaptations, the studio system has meant that there have been close allegiances between investment banking and corporate production from the start (Bluestone 1957/1971: 36): the law of the marketplace is at work for both investors and audiences. The star system and all its attendant glamor may not be enough, however, to guarantee a financial or artistic success: witness Guy Ritchie's unsuccessful 2002 remake of Lina Wertmüller's *Swept Away* (1974) as a vehicle for his wife, Madonna.

What does happen as a result of the particular economic structure of the film world—big money = big stars, and big directors—is that the screenwriter becomes a decidedly secondary or tertiary figure, but so does the often unknown writer of the adapted text. Film option fees for novels are small, because so few works are actually made into films. Well-known writers will make lots of money (often millions), however, because studios realize the name alone will sell the movie (Y'Barbo 1998: 378). By contrast, novelizers of films are considered inferior artists by many: working from a script is not seen as the same as inventing and writing a story from one's imagination. Walter Benjamin's judgment on translators echoes commonly held opinions about adapters: "The intention of the poet is spontaneous, primary, graphic; that of the translator is derivative, ultimate, ideational" (1992: 77).

It is no surprise that economic motivation affects all stages of the adaptation process. As comic artist Cameron Stewart has noted, "A lot of comic books are being made to appeal to Hollywood studios— they're being written and illustrated as a film pitch … . They're writing comic books in anticipation of what can be done on a film budget … as a result you get superhero comics that aren't quite as superhero any more" (Lackner 2004: R5). The entertainment industry is just that: an industry. Comic books become live-action movies, televised cartoons, videogames, and even action toys: "The goal is to have the child watching a Batman video while wearing a Batman cape, eating a fast-food meal with a Batman promotional wrapper, and playing with a Batman toy. The goal is literally to engage all of the child's senses" (Bolter and Grusin 1999: 68). This, of course, may give new meaning to the level of engagement I have been calling participatory.

The Legal Constraints

In considering undertaking an adaptation, adapters may find that the financial attractions are more than balanced in some cases by worries about legality. If it is true that adapters are "raiders"—"they don't copy, they steal what they want and leave the rest" (Abbott 2002: 105)— adaptation may have legal consequences. The unlikely survival of F.W. Murnau's adaptation of Bram Stoker's *Dracula* novel is the result of an interesting combination of money and the law. Because he did not want to pay royalties to the English, the German director Murnau made changes to the novel's plot, introducing a love story between the vampire and Mina, cutting the character of Van Helsing, and changing how Dracula dies. However, he was also working with limited means in the economically depressed Germany of 1921–22. Stoker's wife, however, still sued for copyright infringement, and copies of the film in England were ordered to be destroyed. Pirated copies made their way to England and the United States anyway, and German copies continued to circulate, but no "original" or copyrighted print of *Nosferatu* exists for this reason (see Hensley 2002; Roth 1979).

Adaptations are not only *spawned by* the capitalist desire for gain; they are also *controlled by* the same in law, for they constitute a threat to the ownership of cultural and intellectual property. This is why contracts attempt to absolve publishers or studios of any legal consequences of an adaptation. The issues of control and self-protection are foremost from the perspective of those with power; at the other end, there is little of either. As screenwriter Baker puts it:

> The contract lets you know where you the writer stand in brutally frank legal language. You can be fired at any time. You are powerless and for the most part anonymous, unless you also happen to direct, produce, and/or act. Your credit can be taken away from you. Once your work is bought, it's like a house you've designed and sold. The new owners can do whatever they want to it, add mock-Tudor beams, Disneyland castle turrets, plastic fountains, pink flamingoes, garden gnomes, things that satisfy desires and contingencies that have nothing at all to do with you and your original intent for your material. (1997: 15)

There is clearly more than one reason why an adaptation is called, by law, a "derivative" work.

What does the law protect when it comes to adaptations? In U.S. law, literary copyright infringement standards really only cover the literal copying of words, as proved by the unsuccessful suits by the novelists upon whose novels were based such films as *Driving Miss Daisy* (1989) and *Groundhog Day* (1993). A group of dancers and martial artists lost their suit against the makers of the *Mortal Kombat* and *Mortal Kombat II* videogames, even though the company had videotaped their performances and then digitized them for the games' arcade and home video versions. It seems that "substantial similarity" is harder to prove in court than one might think. In the case of a novel adapted to film, the courts study the plot, mood, characters and character development, pace, setting, and sequence of events, but because so much has to be cut from a novel and because so many adapting agents are involved in a collaboratively produced film, the adaptation is rarely ever close enough to warrant prosecution (see Y'Barbo 1998: 368–69). However, if a novelist can argue financial damage through unauthorized or unremunerated appropriation, there is some hope. But on the contrary, often a film version boosts sales of the novel, as publishers know. They even release new editions with photos from the film on the cover. This economic/legal complicity operates in other art forms as well. The 1990's techno adaptation of the "O Fortuna" chorus of Carl Orff's 1936 *Carmina Burana* by the Italian group FCB (called "Excalibur") raised the sales of the Orff recordings considerably (see Hutchings 1997: 391); no legal action was taken.

Parodies have legal access to an additional argument that adaptations cannot really invoke *as adaptations*: the right to comment critically on a prior work. This right was invoked by the publisher of Alice Randall's *The Wind Done Gone* (2000) when sued by the Margaret Mitchell estate for copyright infringement of *Gone with the Wind* (1936). The publisher argued that telling the story of Rhett and Scarlett from the point of view of a mixed-race slave constituted a critical commentary and not illegal copying.

From the perspective of the law, straightforward adaptation is closer to the work of postmodern appropriation artists like Hans Haacke and Sherrie Levine, who take the work of others and "re-function" it either by title changes or recontextualizing. But is this really any different from Claude Monet or Andy Warhol or Pablo Picasso appropriating images from other artists? The law today suggests it might be. In a famous case, Jeff Koons' "String of Puppies" adapted a black-and-white photograph entitled "Puppies" by Art Rogers from a heartwarming note card into the form of a three-dimensional wooden painted sculpture that was similar to, but thanks to considerable irony, different from Rogers' image. In the process Koons made these changes: the people have a distinctly vacant look and have flowers in their hair, and the puppies are blue. And, of course, he showed this piece in the context of his *Banality* series. Not having asked permission to do the adaptation, Koons was sued and used as his defense the parodic argument based on appropriation with "critical purpose" through the concept of "fair use." The court proceedings (see Inde 1998) kept the art as well as the legal world buzzing for years, as the decision favored first one side and then the other (see *Rogers v. Koons*, 960 F.2d 301, 307 [2d Cir.], *cert. denied*, 506 U.S. 934, 121 L. Ed. 2d 278, 113 S. Ct. 365 [1992]).

When it comes to theme parks or even digital media, the law is ever vigilant about ownership: do not try to adapt anything from the Disney domain without permission. On the other hand, there are some companies that allow players to expand their videogames on their own (the first was *Doom* in 1993) and share their new constructions with others through a common library (e.g., *Sims* [2001]). As Lev Manovich shows in "Who Is the Author?" the Open Source model allows infinite modification of a software code because everyone is licensed to change the original. This model clearly offers a new legal model as well, as does the recent development of "Copyleftmedia" and Larry Lessig's *Creative Commons* project in which artists can choose a license that allows them to share their works and others to draw upon a shared artistic community or "commons."

Cultural Capital

There are still other motives for adaptation, however. Given the perceived hierarchy of the arts and therefore media examined in Chapter 1, one way to gain respectability or increase cultural capital is for an adaptation to be upwardly mobile. Film historians argue that this motivation explains the many early cinematic adaptations of Dante and Shakespeare. Today's television adaptations of British eighteenth- and nineteenth-century novels may also want to benefit from their adapted works' cultural cachet. Similarly, in a sort of reverse form of cultural accreditation, classical music performers sometimes aspire to become popular entertainers: Joshua Rifkin's *Baroque Beatles Book* rearranges the famous group's songs for baroque orchestra, including a cantata version of "Help" (see Gendron 2002: 172–73). Related to this desire to shift cultural level is the pedagogical impulse behind much literary adaptation to both film and television. One of the largest markets for these works includes students of literature and their teachers, keen to appeal to the cinematic imaginations of those they teach. Check out the Web sites for just about any film or even stage adaptation that has educational "pretensions" today: there is now a secondary educational industry devoted to helping students and teachers "make the most" of the adaptations.

The existence of the Hollywood Production Code from the 1930s until the 1960s offers a different kind of argument regarding adaptations, cultural capital, and specifically mass audience reception. Even an adaptation of something as classic as *Anna Karenina* would have been suspect under the code's regulations because of its sexual content: seduction, corruption, and illicit love. "A basic premise of the code was that Hollywood did not have the same kind of freedom accorded book authors and Broadway playwrights to produce artistic works. Reformers feared that screening the 'modernism' that pervaded contemporary literature [through adapting it] would be far more corruptive on the mass audience of moviegoers than it was on 'readers'" (Black 1994: 84). Although adaptation remained common nonetheless, the choice of adapted works was more limited.

Personal and Political Motives

It is obvious that adapters must have their own personal reasons for deciding first to do an adaptation and then choosing which adapted work and what medium to do it in. They not only interpret that work but in so doing they also take a position on it. For instance, David Edgar's stage adaptation of Charles Dickens' *Nicholas Nickleby* (1838–39) for the Royal Shakespeare Company in 1980 has been called "a play about Dickens that critiqued his form of social morality, rather than a straight dramatization of the novel" (Innis 1993: 71). Some critics go so far as to insist that a "truly artistic" adaptation absolutely *must* "subvert its original, perform a double and paradoxical job of masking and unveiling its source" (Cohen 1977: 255). In contrast, Merchant/Ivory film adaptations of the novels of E.M. Forster, for example, are intended and received as almost reverential treatments. Sometimes homage is all that is possible—or allowed. In 2005, RTE, Channel 4, Tyrone Productions, and the Irish Film Board sponsored 19 short film adaptations of the work of Samuel Beckett by directors either experienced with or influenced by the playwright. But in the name of fidelity, the Beckett estate would allow no changes to the texts whatsoever.

Some song covers are openly meant as tributes: Holly Cole's *Temptation* is a homage to Tom Waits. Others are meant to critique, however: when a female singer like Tori Amos covers male misogynist songs, the new vocal angle subverts the adapted works' sexist ideology: "'97 Bonnie & Clyde" is a cover of Eminem's song in which a man sings to his child that the two of them (no stepfather, no brothers) are going to the beach, where, we soon learn, he is about to dump the body of her murdered mother. These words are terrifying enough when sung by a male with the cooing of Eminem's little girl's voice sampled in, but when the very same words are sung by the mother, in a baby voice, to the daughter, they become a fiercely condemnatory quoting of the father. In a further adaptation, the daughter of this horror, as a young woman, then sings "Strange Little Girl" by the Stranglers (see Amos and Powers 2005: 288).

There are all kinds of reasons for wanting to adapt, in short. Adaptations of Shakespeare, in particular, may be intended as tributes or as a way to supplant canonical cultural authority. As Marjorie Garber has remarked, Shakespeare is for many adapters "a monument to be toppled" (1987: 7). As proof, witness the screenplay credits of director Franco Zeffirelli's 1966 film version of *The Taming of the Shrew*: "Paul Dehn, Suso Cecchi D'Amico, and Franco Zeffirelli, with acknowledgements to William Shakespeare, without whom they would have been at a loss for words." However, it was not only the Bard who was meant to be ironically displaced here, but also the earlier Mary Pickford and Douglas Fairbanks film of the play. Hence the casting of the very marketable (at the time) pair, Elizabeth Taylor and Richard Burton. In a more subdued vein, Gus Van Sant's 1991 *My Own Private Idaho* has the credit, "Additional dialogue by William Shakespeare." Other adapters prove to have even bolder intentions, however. Rainer Werner Fassbinder's cinematic adaptation of Jean Genet's *Querelle de Brest* (1947) as *Querelle* (1982) was meant by its adapter to be "an unequivocal and single-minded questioning of the piece of literature and its language" (Fassbinder 1992: 168).

An adaptation can obviously be used to engage in a larger social or cultural critique. It can even be used to avoid it, of course: the attempt to sidestep imperialist politics in the 2002 version of A.E.W. Mason's oft-filmed 1902 novel, *The Four Feathers*, by director Shekhar Kapur and scriptwriters Hossein Amini and Michael Schaffer, is, however, much less common these days than are more direct forms of political engagement. Sally Potter's ideological motivation for doing a film version of Virginia Woolf's *Orlando*, as articulated in the introduction to the published screenplay, is different from Woolf's feminist aim, but equally political: Potter wanted to adapt—and therefore inevitably to alter—the text not only to tell a story she loved but also to permit "a more biting and satirical view of the English class system and the colonial attitudes arising from it" (Potter 1994: xi). Postcolonial dramatists and anti-war television producers have likewise used adaptations to articulate their political positions. This kind of political and historical intentionality is now of great interest in academic circles, despite a half-century of critical dismissal of the relevance of artistic intention to interpretation by formalists, New Critics, structuralists, and poststructuralists alike. What still remain suspect are other kinds of more personal and thus idiosyncratic motivations, despite the increased focus on individual agency in feminist, postcolonial, ethnic, and queer studies. Yet a handbook for screenwriters can confidently assert: "If the adapter is not significantly and measurably moved by the novel, for whatever reason, the play will suffer accordingly" (Brady 1994: 10).

Richard Rodgers and Oscar Hammerstein read, were moved by, and then adapted C.Y. Lee's 1957 novel, *The Flower Drum Song*, as a stage musical (1958) and then as a film (1961). The creators' stated progressive, liberal intentions did not prevent their representations of Chinese characters from looking patronizing and inauthentic to writer David Henry Hwang 40 years later. Hwang claimed that he was provoked into writing his own adaptation both by his own "guilty pleasure" (2002: 1) as a young man, enjoying the film because it presented a rarely seen love story between an Asian man and woman, and also by the changes he saw in the cultural issues facing Chinese Americans in the ensuing decades (a shift from intergenerational conflict to assimilation). He kept the general story-line and most of the characters, jettisoned the text, respectfully retained the score, and claimed to return to and thus be "faithful" to the "spirit" of Lee's book. All this information seems to me to be of both interest and importance to our understanding of why and how an adaptation comes into being. Yet in literary studies, this dimension of response has been sidelined. However, adapters' deeply personal as well as culturally and historically conditioned reasons for selecting a certain work to adapt and the particular way to do so should be considered seriously by adaptation theory, even if this means rethinking the role of intentionality in our critical thinking about art in general.

The next section traces the changes in one particular narrative through a series of media and genres as one way to explore precisely all of these economic, legal, cultural, political, and personal complexities of motivation and intention in the process of adaptation. If I may myself adapt a theory from the work done on editing, adaptations are what have been called "fluid texts" that exist in more than one version; they are the "material evidence of *shifting* intentions" (Bryant 2002: 9; his italics). As such, they suggest the need to adopt a form of historical analysis that can accommodate "creative process and the forces that drive textual fluidity" (11).

Learning from Practice

I begin, therefore, with the "why?" question: Why would a whole series of very different twentieth-century European artists all choose to adapt one particular historical narrative: that of 16 Carmelite nuns from Compiègne, France, who faced the guillotine in 1794, just 10 days before the end of the Reign of Terror that followed the French Revolution? On the surface, this is hardly a modernist theme; it does not immediately appear to address anything very obvious in the twentieth-century *zeitgeist*—or at least not in the way that Oscar Wilde's *Salomé* captured the 1890's fearful fascination with the *femme fatale* or Richard Strauss' operatic adaptation of it a few years later translated the *femme fatale* into the terms of the new century, with its obsession with what Freud and Breuer had just labeled as hysteria. In contrast, this is a story about 16 Catholic martyrs who went to the scaffold singing hymns, thereby silencing the mob's heckling by their music and their bravery. As a narrative, their story is certainly interesting, but not so obviously compelling or historically relevant as to have warranted being told and retold in the forms of the novella, film, stage play, and opera over a 30-year period of time.

In the historical account, the Carmelites of Compiègne were forced out of their convent in 1792, after the National Assembly confiscated all ecclesiastical goods and property and first urged and then forced all religious orders to give up what it called their superstition and return to the secular world. The nuns, who had continued to meet in secret to pray as a community, agreed to an act of consecration of their lives for their faith, as suggested by their Prioress, Madame Lidoine. This act, which they repeated daily, later became known as their vow of martyrdom. In June 1794, the nuns were arrested, appeared before the Tribunal, and were sentenced to death as "fanatics"—that is, as religious women, guilty of organizing "counter-revolutionary consultations and assemblies" (Gendre 1999: 277; see also Bush 1999: 201–13; S.M. Murray 1963: 62–65). Radiating joyous anticipation of martyrdom, they mounted the scaffold singing the "Veni Creator" hymn and renewed their vows. The youngest, Sister Constance, went first and Prioress Lidoine last. Constance began singing the "Laudate Dominum omnes gentes" psalm, and as the guillotine literally cut off her voice, the others took up the melody and continued it. The nuns' bodies were thrown into the common pit at Picpus Cemetery; 10 days later the Great Terror ended, as if, some said, in response to the martyrdom of the nuns who had explicitly offered their deaths for their country and their faith. We know all this from the testimony of one sister who survived, Marie de l'Incarnation, who was not with the others in Compiègne, but was in Paris when the arrests occurred. In fear, she then fled to eastern France and much later became the first of the story's many tellers (see Bruno de Jésus-Marie, and Bush's translation and edition of Marie de l'Incarnation).

The Carmelites' story was adapted in 1931 by a young German convert to Catholicism, the Baroness Gertrud von le Fort, who claimed to have discovered it first in a footnote to a religious text she was reading

(S.M. Murray 1963: 66). However, the story was well known in Catholic circles and indeed had come to form part of the mythology around the Revolution and especially the end of the Reign of Terror. This historical account became the frame for the Baroness' story of a fictional character named Blanche de la Force, a pathologically fearful young woman who joins the Carmelite order out of both a religious vocation and a generalized terror of both life and especially death. In the novella, called *Die Letzte am Schafott* (literally, *The Last on the Scaffold*), the writer later claimed that she had wanted to explore two matters: as her eponymous choice of surname for her character suggests, her own fears that her new-found faith would never be up to the kind of test demanded of the nuns and her terror about the rise of totalitarianism in her native country (see Gendre 1994: 283; S.M. Murray 1963: 61; Neuschaffer 1954–55: 35; O'Boyle 1964: 57). Yet history was not simply the backdrop for the story of the fearful young Blanche, as some have suggested (Bush 1999: xv). Instead, it offered the structural, intellectual, and spiritual skeleton on which le Fort could hang Blanche's existential terror. Through it she also could make the link to the (capital T) Terror and thus give historical resonance to an individual psychological response.

Die Letzte am Schafott, later translated into English as *The Song at the Scaffold*, is an epistolary novella, narrated in large part by M. de Villeroi, a French aristocrat who survived the Terror. Haunted by the excesses of the Revolution, he tries to find meaning in the horror of the past. He knows Blanche and her milieu well and so is particularly well positioned to recount her fate with sympathy. He tells of how, outside the convent, which Blanche has entered as a refuge, the forces of Revolution gather and gradually triumph, but inside she feels safe. However, as in the historical account, the nuns are soon cast out of their home, though not before they take a much more dramatic single (not daily repeated) vow of martyrdom; they are urged on this time not by their new Prioress, Madame Lidoine, who is instead absent from the convent at the time, but by Marie de l'Incarnation. In this version Marie is presented as a foil for the frightened Blanche: a natural daughter of a French aristocrat, she is noble in bearing as well as birth, brave, and resolute—a woman much admired by the narrator, and, one senses, by the author herself.

In this novella, Blanche flees the convent after claiming that she too will take the vow. The sisters are arrested in Compiègne while Marie is in Paris, in part to look for Blanche. Despite being the instigator of the vow, Marie is ordered by her spiritual leader not to go back and thus sacrifice herself, but to live on. She witnesses the death of the martyrs, as does the narrator who hears the nuns begin the "Salve Regina"—a hymn sung when a nun is dying—and then the "Veni Creator"; as each woman dies, the sound of the singing becomes quieter. Suddenly, when only one voice is left (that of the oldest nun), Blanche appears and takes up the song. Pale but totally fearless, she sings the rest of the hymn before the mob of women kill her on the spot. The narrator continues the story past this climax though, ending it with the future of Marie, who would write up the nuns' history.

Blanche, however, is the real focus of the story, and Baroness von le Fort later made clear that this character had both personal and political significance for her:

> She never lived in the historical sense, but she took the breath of her trembling being exclusively from my own inner self and she will never be able to be freed from this, her origin. Born out of the deepest horror of a time that in Germany would be overshadowed by the anticipatory forebodings of the history to come, this figure stood before me as the "incarnation of the death anguish of an entire epoch going to its end" (Baroness Gertrud Von Le Fort 1956: 93, my translation).

In the mid-1940s, this version of the tale was adapted by Father Raymond Bruckberger, a "young, ardent, and attractive Dominican" priest who had fought in World War II, had been among the first to rally to the side of Charles de Gaulle, and had been principal chaplain to the Resistance (Speaight 1973: 261). Also seeing the nuns' fate and especially their bravery as allegorical, but this time, of the French Resistance, he wrote a film scenario with the aid of Philippe Agostini. This version of the narrative suppresses much, including the narrator, and changes the emphasis, in part driven by the aesthetic exigencies of the new medium. Because it is intended for the cinema, the scenario is more visual and dramatic; it is based on action, not religious discussion, and reveals a desire for direct camera presentation, rather than narration. For what appear to be complicated interpersonal reasons, there is no copy of this scenario in the public domain, so I rely here on citations and outlines in S.M. Murray (1963: 43–92) and Gendre (1994: 284–86).

Father Bruckberger later claimed to have been attracted to the elements of what he saw as a great classical tragedy in the novella; specifically, he was attracted to what he called the insurmountable conflict between two universes and two irreconcilable mysticisms, that of Carmel and that of the Revolution (1980: 421–22). Nevertheless, when he came to write the scenario, it was the possibilities of spectacular action—and not mysticism—that really attracted him as a potential filmmaker, especially in presenting the scenes of the French Revolution. He cut what he felt were extraneous characters and scenes and freely invented others. But he too kept the focus always on Blanche, who was almost constantly on camera, and thus on her fear of death.

To this end, he made much of a scene that had taken up about ten lines in the novella and actually never took place: the deathbed of the first Prioress, Madame de Croissy. In actual fact, this nun died on the scaffold with the others; in the novella, she is said to be ill when Blanche joins the order and is reputed to be afraid of dying. For this reason she feels a certain sympathy for the always frightened Blanche. Soon after Blanche's arrival in the convent, the Prioress dies a painful death. Blanche, hearing her dying groans, is dismayed that God could let such a holy woman suffer so much. Understandably, the scenario writers could not resist the drama of this scene in their description: the doctor's hurried steps are heard in the hall, the dying woman's cries pierce the silence of the cloister, and Blanche stares at the closed infirmary door with great disquiet. Blanche is summoned to the Prioress' deathbed, but does not understand the confession of her spiritual leader's anguish that she hears. The other nuns are then called in; the Prioress kneels, says farewell and asks them to pray for her, as she humbly admits her fear of death and begs their pardon. This deathbed scene, as we shall see, is the one that changes most in subsequent adaptations.

Looking for someone to write the dialogues for this scenario, in 1947 Bruckberger and Agostini approached first the existentialist novelist, Albert Camus, who reminded them that he himself was not a believer, but suggested that they invite Georges Bernanos to be what in France is called the "dialoguiste" (see Vincendeau 2001: xi). This conservative Catholic writer had returned to France two years before, in 1945, after spending the war years in voluntary exile in Brazil (Béguin 1958: 127; Bush 1985: 2; Gendre 1994: 35). Bernanos was a most appropriate, indeed brilliant, suggestion. Not only was the theme of the story, as developed by both the novella and the scenario, totally consonant with that of his own novels, but Bruckberger had, in fact, himself given Bernanos a copy of the French translation of the novella in 1937 and the novelist had taken it with him to Brazil where he had reread it often (Kestner 1981: 14). But at the moment he was approached to write the film dialogues, the fiercely French, fiercely Royalist, and fiercely political Bernanos was fiercely depressed. Disappointed with the Fourth Republic and the technocratic and materialist society that he felt post-war France had become, he moved to North Africa in disgust. Even more significantly, however, at this moment in 1947, he knew that he was seriously ill—in fact, he was dying from cancer. For details on Bernanos' well-documented reaction to his illness, see Bush (1985: 2), Speaight (1973: 213–47), Béguin (1958: 93–94), S.M. Murray (1963: 17–19), Albouy (1980: 220–30), and Leclerc (1982: 109–71).

The dialogues that Bernanos agreed to write for the film scenario constitute in themselves an adaptation; that is, an appropriation of the story that results in a radically different work. Though of a deeply political and even polemical disposition, he personalizes the story, transforming the political allegory of the film scenario into an interior journey that is both spiritual and psychological, working out through the text his own fear of his coming death and his hopes for religious salvation (Bush 1988: 17).

Bernanos died just after finishing the dialogues; the film's producer decided that the script was unusable for the cinema because it was too long and did not have enough action (O'Boyle 1964: 58). The film, called (in the singular) *Dialogue des Carmélites* was finally made in 1960, but from a decidedly different script that used fewer than half of Bernanos' lines. Albert Béguin, Bernanos' literary executor, found the original manuscript in a trunk after his death and edited it with an eye to publication as a stage play, which he in turn called *Dialogues des Carmélites* (in the plural). The play was published in 1949 and first performed in 1951. Clearly, yet another adapter had come forward, for editors can become adapters if they intervene in a major way, as occurred here; Béguin divided the work into acts, moved dialogue around, added historical decrees and hymns, and summarized mute scenes (Gendre 1999: 286–87; S.M. Murray 1963: 24–42, 125).

Bernanos' own changes to the death scenes in the scenario, however, are revealing in both personal and aesthetic terms. Less interested in external action than in the spiritual and psychological drama of the deathbed, he first makes the ailing Prioress his own age (59) and then calls attention to this added detail by having Blanche's young friend, the novice Constance, comment that, after all, at that age it is about time for one to die. Bernanos also gives to the Prioress a well-documented trait of his own spiritual and psychological makeup: he has her admit that she has meditated on death every hour of her life (Bernanos 1949: 43; see also S.M. Murray 1963: 129). Bernanos' letters and journals, not to mention his novels, are testimony to his life-long obsession with death and to his terror at its always seemingly imminent arrival. His obsession with death is clear from the memories of his friends (see Boly 1960: 15), but his own letters are also painfully explicit (see Béguin 1958: 31).

On her deathbed, Bernanos' Prioress, in great physical pain and equally great psychological and spiritual distress, scandalizes Marie de l'Incarnation by telling her that she feels abandoned by God. She then has a horrific vision of the persecution and destruction of her order. In this version of the story, only Blanche is then called to her side, and it is from her alone that the dying woman begs pardon for her fear. Her face disfigured with pain and despair, the Prioress dies a terrible death, one totally unsuited to her, as Constance later notes, asking whether God made an error in assigning this horrific death to this holy woman. Bernanos then puts in Constance's mouth the words that would mark his greatest thematic change in his adaptation of both the scenario and the novella: the words that express his personal extension of the Catholic doctrine of the Communion of Saints. The logical conclusion of this doctrine, as Father Owen Lee has explained, is the idea that because the Prioress died such a hard death, someone else would have an easy one (1998: 177). In Constance's words: "On ne meurt pas chacun pour soi, mais les uns pour les autres, ou même à la place des autres, qui sait?" (57): "One doesn't die each for oneself, but each for the others, or even one in the place of another, who knows?" The meaning of these words is not clear until the final scene of the play. In that scene, Blanche steps out of the crowd, showing no fear, and goes serenely to her death on the scaffold. Blanche dies easily because she dies the death the Prioress deserved—and gave up for her.

That long and harrowing scene of the holy nun's death has been interpreted as Bernanos' means of coming to terms with his own death and with his fear of physical pain and spiritual desolation. Similarly, the representation of the death of Blanche, in full dignity and without fear for the first time, has been read as his wish-fulfilling projection of his own end. How can such a leap be justified from the textual traces? For one thing, this idea of a mystic exchange of deaths was purely Bernanos' addition. Bernanos scholars, in fact, are insistent that, despite the "debt" to the novella and the scenario, this is a purely Bernanosian text, shot through with all the themes of his entire oeuvre (Aaraas 1988–89: 16; Gendre 1994: 287–88; see also Hell 1978: 244). And they are not wrong, even if their insistence belies a post-Romantic need to assert precedence at all cost. No mere adapter, they suggest, Bernanos is a real creator. French writer Julien Green, called in at one point by the legal authorities to try to sort out the disputes about who "owned" this story, decreed that the invention and the creation of the principal characters belong to the Baroness, but that Bernanos interpreted the tale in his own manner. Because the task of making the characters come alive fell to him, in the arbiter's eyes, he remained the principal author. As Green put it, Bernanos took the scenario and made of it, very legitimately and as one might have expected, pure "Bernanos" (S.M. Murray 1963: 105–6). There is certainly little doubt that his version of the Carmelites' story was very different from what even Father Bruckberger had in mind.

It was Béguin's edition of Bernanos' stage play that the French composer Francis Poulenc saw in Paris, and it moved him deeply. But it was Guido Valcarenghi, of the publishing house of Ricordi, who suggested in 1953 that Poulenc write an opera based on the play. The composer's initial hesitation was based on the fact that there was no love story, and this was to be an opera after all. Poulenc's reluctance was overcome by a feeling that the text was perfect for him as a composer: the rhythm of the language seemed to fit his musical imagination (Poulenc 1954: 213). To most of his friends and acquaintances, however, this religious story would not have seemed at all like ideal Poulenc material. A fashionable and worldly man-about-town, Poulenc had been a member of the irreverent group of young French composers known as "Les Six" and was better known for composing profane than sacred music (see Ivry 1996: 12–34, 110–11). Yet, in 1926, after experiencing a reawakening of his Catholic faith, he composed his *Litanies à la Vierge noire*, in honor of the famous black Virgin whose statue is kept at Rocamadour in France, where he had gone on a pilgrimage after the sudden death of a friend and rival, Pierre-Octave Ferroud (Gagnebin 1987: 33; Ivry 1996: 91–113). From then on, Poulenc would compose both sacred and secular music, often turning to religious themes to commemorate the deaths of friends and acquaintances (Ivry 1996: 162).

According to the ample evidence of his letters, Poulenc's composing of the opera of *Dialogues des Carmélites* was entirely tied up with his hypochondria and nervous collapse caused by his failing relationship with his lover, Lucien Roubert. He came to suspect that he actually needed this anguished emotional climate in order to compose the opera (see his letters to Henri Hell, 14 February 1954 [Poulenc 1991: 216] and to Rose Dercourt-Plaut, 25 December 1955 [237]). But even more important is the fact that just as Poulenc had begun his work on the adaptation with Roubert by his side in 1953, so he wrote the music of the nuns' demise as Roubert met his end, dying of lung disease, with Poulenc by his side in 1955. The mystical exchange of deaths that Bernanos invented was *lived* by Poulenc, or so he believed, writing to a friend that he was haunted by the idea that Roubert had died for him (1991: 232).

However, aesthetic concerns also played their part in this adaptation, along with these intensely personal ones. The shift in medium from play to opera involved making serious cuts to the Bernanos text and therefore to the nuns' story. Despite his rededication to Catholicism, Poulenc chose to cut the play's religious debates, as well as all the class issues raised by the French Revolution. The resulting adaptation process made this into a spare story of individual choice in the face of human mortality. But after all, it was written in existentialist Paris in the 1950s and by a composer caring for a dying lover (Gendre 1994: 73; Ivry 1996: 75–78).

Not surprisingly, then, in the operatic version of the story, the death of the Prioress is the climax of Act I. Poulenc adds powerful music to Bernanos' moving drama, but deliberately keeps the text in the foreground of his audience's attention by very thin scoring, so that every word could be heard and understood (Poulenc 1991: 206). Singer Régine Crespin, who premiered the role of the Prioress at the Metropolitan Opera in 1977, called this a naked death, one experienced in total fear of both the spiritual void and the physical reality of pain. It is a death, she said, that forced her to come to terms with her own mortality (n.d.: 107). It is at one and the same time a normal human death, an extraordinarily intense one, and, for this woman, an utterly inappropriate one. Deathbed scenes are not usually this realistic in opera: they are most often aestheticized and even sanitized (see Hutcheon and Hutcheon 1996: 43–47, 56–57). This death, on the contrary, is horrifically endured, and the Prioress is instructed to sing her part in a very rough manner; the composer even notates her death rattle in the score. The text's words, the bodily sounds of pain, and the stage action as she repeatedly falls back, exhausted, onto her pillow all come together to offer a scene of horror that is intensified by dissonances in the music; that is, by the audible evidence of suffering and, especially, terror. But Poulenc too saw the theme of fear balanced and countered by the theme of the transfer of grace in the exchange of deaths (1954: 213). Perhaps due to this potent (because it is contradictory) combination, the ending of the opera is considerably more moving, in my experience, than that of any of the other versions. Its horrible and haunting power answers that of the Prioress' deathbed scene, just as Blanche's death itself is redeemed by that earlier one.

At the opera's end, beneath the strident funeral march heard as the nuns descend from the carts to approach the scaffold, the musical motif associated with the Prioress' death is heard again, but it is in turn gradually dominated by the nuns' singing of the "Salve Regina" hymn. One after another, the Carmelites march to the guillotine. The sharp and discomfiting sound of the guillotine blade slashes through the music, but each time it does, the defiant nuns sing even louder. Soon, however, the number of voices heard is reduced to a single one, that of Constance, and in the music, that death motif is now suppressed. The scene is now set, both musically and dramatically, for the mystical exchange of deaths: Blanche steps out of the crowd, and as the stage directions announce, her face is free from every vestige of fear. Constance beams and goes happily to her death, as the guillotine silences forever the Prioress' death motif. A "luminous theme" (Lee 1998: 177) associated with the workings of grace in the opera enters the music. Blanche does not finish the "Salve Regina" hymn that Constance had been singing, as might be expected, but in her new solitary strength, she approaches the scaffold singing slowly the last stanza of "Veni Creator"—a song of glory to God, affirming both her life after death and the significance of the nuns' sacrifice in the context of the Communion of Saints. Then the guillotine cuts off her voice as well; silence ensues. The music of the opera as a whole may have been deliberately scored thinly, but in the final moments, Poulenc uses large and lavish orchestral forces to bring home the emotional message of both Blanche's existential choice to die and her redemption in and through death—the death of the Prioress.

Intentionality in Adaptations

The story of these eighteenth-century Carmelite martyrs—an unlikely narrative for an opera of any period, much less the twentieth century—was actually equally unlikely as the adapted subject of a modern novella, film, or play. Or rather, plays in the plural, for there was another (not very successful) one in 1949 by the American Catholic playwright Emmet Lavery, who managed to get the copyright for all dramatized versions, thus almost scuttling both the Bernanos play and the Poulenc opera. In the final wording of the legal agreement, the "authorship" of *Dialogues des Carmélites* is therefore articulated in this bizarrely presented way: "*Les Dialogues des Carmélites* / Opera in three acts and twelve scenes / Based on the text of the play by Georges BERNA- / NOS, inspired by the novella of Gertrud Von Le / Fort and a scenario by Philippe Agostini and of the R.V. [*sic*] Bruckberger, / transposed into an Opera with the authorization of Monsieur Emmet LAVERY" (qtd. in Gendre 1999: 304).

Though tortured, this listing amply demonstrates Millicent Marcus' contention that the adaptive process is a total of the encounters among institutional cultures, signifying systems, and personal motivations (the adapter's "professional agenda at the time of production" [1993: x]). This particular story obviously resonated in complex ways for its various adapters. The motives for choosing the story in each case were also intensely private. The reasons for interpreting it as either a political allegory or a tale of spiritual and psychological redemption were deeply embedded in the individual histories of the adapters, as well as in the political moments in which they were writing. The specific aesthetic form each adaptation took also depended upon the particular abilities and interests of the new creators.

Yet, in academic literary circles, we stopped talking about these dimensions of the creative process some time in the twentieth century. In fact, the very idea of dealing with the creative process began to sound dated in North America shortly after W.K. Wimsatt and Monroe Beardsley's 1946 condemnation of the "intentional fallacy." A few decades later, Roland Barthes effectively entombed intentionality in his famous essay, "The Death of the Author," and Michel Foucault danced on its grave when he shifted critical attention to the anonymity of discourse, making the position of the "author," in his terms, "a particular, vacant space that may in fact be filled by different individuals" (1972: 96).

As H.L. Hix reminds us, in the wittily entitled *Morte d'Author*, Barthes' statement was less an obituary than "the vehicle of a metaphor whose tenor is, roughly, that there is no transcendent figure at the origin of the text's meaning" (1990: 3). What both the New Critics and the poststructuralists alike were protesting, in their very different ways, was having recourse to authorial intent as the *sole* arbiter and guarantee of the meaning and value of a work of art. No one denies that creative artists have intentions; the disagreements have been over how those intentions should be deployed in the interpretation of meaning and the assignment of value. But it has been suggested that much of this debate has really been about critical fashion and academic or cultural politics: in 1990 Annabel Patterson argued that "much of the anti-intentionalism of the past four decades had its origins in local circumstances, in response to change in the cultural environment, and from the force of professional self-interest in the self-propagation of Modernism in the arts and of literary criticism as a professional discipline" (1990: 146). The New Critics broke with the Great Men theory of literature wherein literature's value "lies chiefly in allowing us intimate access to their souls" (Eagleton 1996: 41). Intentions, even if recoverable, therefore, were deemed irrelevant to interpretation. Even the phenomenologically oriented critics of the Geneva school resolutely turned away from biography to trace the registering of human consciousness in the text itself. In focusing primarily on the textual dimension, of course, it is the *critic* who has authority, not the author or the adapter.

The examination of the different versions of the nuns' tale, however, suggests that the political, aesthetic, and autobiographical intentions of the various adapters are potentially relevant to the audience's interpretation. They are often recoverable, and their traces are visible in the text. The political dimension—in, for instance, feminist, queer, postcolonial, race, or ethnic studies—has been rescued. But the general injunction against the personal and aesthetic dimensions of intentionality still holds for the other aspects of the creative process, except in overt genres like confession, autobiography, or *testimonio*. In what some call our "posthumanist" times, with our suspicions of and challenges to notions of coherent subjectivity, what I am proposing may at first appear to be a step backward in theoretical-historical terms. But adaptation teaches that if we cannot talk about the creative process, we cannot fully understand the urge to adapt and therefore perhaps the very process of adaptation. We need to know "why."

In the law, intention or motive determines such factors as the degree of a murder charge (first, second) or the very existence of a libel case. In the arts, by analogy, intention determines matters like why an artist

chooses to adapt a work and how it is to be done. Nevertheless, attention even to this kind of intent is in effect outlawed, for, it has been
argued, considering the artist's life or intentions reduces literature to
autobiography and reading to voyeurism. Yet it is arguably no easier to
separate the creating agent from the creative act than it is to separate
the ethical agent from the ethical act (Hix 1990: 81). *Auteurist* film
critics, musicologists, and art historians usually see little problem with
rooting the authority of meaning and value, not to mention motive, in
artists' personal desires and creative needs, as well as in their conscious
relations to the dominant artistic conventions of their age. Not so for
literary critics, as R.W. Stallman's early articulation of the anathema
against intentionalism makes clear: "Irrelevant to the objective status
of the work of art are criteria which dissolve the work back into the historical or psychological or creative process from which it came" (qtd. in
A. Patterson 1990: 140). In recent years, the historical along with the
political has been rescued, with the help of New Historicist, feminist,
Marxist, and postcolonial theory, and the Lacanians and trauma theorists have redeemed the psychological. However, the creative process
itself in all its dimensions is still taboo or at least still out of critical
fashion, considered too belletristic, journalistic, or simply Romantic.

Nevertheless, as we have seen with the adaptations of the Carmelites' story, adapters usually feel some "equivalence of sensibilities or
form" (Schmidgall 1977: 6) or some "particular affinity with the artistic
temperament or preoccupations" (Sinyard 2000: 147) of the creator of
the work they decide to adapt; they then choose a particular medium
in which to express that coincidence of concern. Of course, the result
may not be as extreme as director David Cronenberg's description of
his film adaptation of J.G. Ballard's *Crash* as "a lovely fusion of me and
Ballard. We're so amazingly in synch" (Cronenberg 1996: vii). But
some connection needs to exist. In the act of adapting, choices are made
based on many factors, as we have seen, including genre or medium
conventions, political engagement, and personal as well as public history. These decisions are made in a creative as well as an interpretive
context that is ideological, social, historical, cultural, personal, and
aesthetic. And that context is made accessible to us later in two ways.
First, the text bears the marks of these choices, marks that betray the

assumptions of the creator—at the very least insofar as those assumptions can be inferred from the text. To return to my example, because the different versions of the Carmelites' story vary more than generic requirements or historical circumstances can explain, the variations function as indicators of the adapter's "voice," what James Phelan calls the "fusion of style, tone, and values" signaled not only by words but also by structural means (1996: 45). Second, and more obvious, is the fact that extratextual statements of intent and motive often do exist to round out our sense of the context of creation. Of course, these statements can and must be confronted with the actual textual results: as many have rightly insisted, intending to do something is not necessarily the same thing as actually achieving it (Nattiez 1990: 99; Wimsatt and Beardsley 1946: 480).

In a later revisiting of his position on intentionality, W.K. Wimsatt wrote:

> An art work is something which emerges from the private, individual, dynamic, and intentionalist realm of its maker's mind and personality; it is in a sense ... made of intentions or intentionalistic material. But at the same time, in the moment it emerges, it enters a public and in a certain sense an objective realm; it claims and gets attention from an audience; it invites and receives discussion, about its meaning and value, in an idiom of inter-subjectivity and conceptualization. (1976: 11–12)

Although Wimsatt meant this to be an argument against taking authorial intent into consideration, I see it rather as exemplifying the need to rethink the function of adapter intention *for the audience* when it comes to understanding both the interpretive and creative dimensions of an adaptation. To use Wimsatt's own terms, in the public realm of "inter-subjectivity," knowledge about the "maker's mind and personality" can actually affect the audience members' interpretation: what they know about artists' desires and motivations, even about their life situations when they are creating, can influence the interpretation of any work's meaning, as well as the response to it. Like the adapter, the audience too interprets in a context. William Bush, a senior scholar of Bernanos' work, writes of being a 23-year-old graduate student studying the play version of *Dialogues des Carmélites*, knowing that it was the writer's "last testament." He asks rhetorically: "How could I not be moved by the fact that he, in the last months before his death in 1948 at age 60, had written those dialogues for a film scenario about 16 nuns who, like him, were consciously preparing to appear before God?" (1999: xiii). Bush read the play as what Ross Chambers would call the testimony of someone "dying as an author" (1998: 23, 85); that is, the text bears witness to his death. It is a last dying gesture. Once known, this fact likely cannot be ignored by any reader.

Music semiotician Jean-Jacques Nattiez insists that an audience's knowledge about the creative process has a real impact upon interpretation, even if we could and should never reduce the explanation of a work to only that aspect (1990: ix). This level of analysis, which he names, borrowing from Etienne Gilson, the "poietic," is defined as "the determination of the conditions that make possible, and that underpin the creation of an artist's (or a producer's or an artisan's) work—thanks to which something now exists which would not have existed except for them" (13). The work of art is not just composed of formal structures, but of the "procedures that have engendered it" (ix) as well. For Nattiez, form results from a process of creation that can be described or reconstituted, at least in part, from textual traces (12). This process offers another context for understanding the motive to adapt. Claude Gendre argues that each new version of the story of the Carmelite martyrs appropriated "aspects of history to suit the author's particular spiritual beliefs" (1999: 274). Although this is demonstrably the case, we have seen that the spiritual is only one element of the context of creation of these works. Other elements play their part as well: the psychological, the political, the personal-historical (the place and time of composition), and the aesthetic (the choice of genre and medium). Armelle Guerne, Bernanos' secretary, claimed that the writer had articulated to her two very different reasons for wanting to write the dialogues for the film scenario: the subject of the Carmelites themselves, to whom he prayed each evening in order not to do something unworthy of them, and the desire to see if he could write for a performance medium (Gendre 1999: 284).

To bring such information into the interpretive and evaluative framework of an adaptation is to displace the adapter/author as "controller" in favor of what Phelan calls a rhetorical attention to "the recursive relationships among authorial agency, textual phenomena, and reader response" (1996: 19). When giving meaning and value to an adaptation *as an adaptation*, audiences operate in a context that includes their knowledge and their own interpretation of the adapted work. That context may also include information about the adapter, thanks to both journalistic curiosity and scholarly digging. In short, it may well matter—to an interpreting audience—whether the artist is working in Germany in 1931 or France in 1945 or Tunisia in 1947 or Paris in 1955, or whether the artist is creating a novella or a scenario or the dialogues for a film or an opera. But it may also matter that each one of the adapters of the Carmelites' historical story had deeply personal motives for being attracted to it. As readers, they interpreted the narrative in their own ways; as creators, they then made it their own.

By their very existence, adaptations remind us there is no such thing as an autonomous text or an original genius that can transcend history, either public or private. They also affirm, however, that this fact is not to be lamented. To use Benjamin's vivid image, "traces of the storyteller cling to the story the way the handprints of the potter cling to the clay vessel" (1968: 91). So too do the traces of the adapting interpreter-creator cling to the adaptation. The process of adapting should make us reconsider our sense of literary critical embarrassment about intention and the more personal and aesthetic dimensions of the creative process. In theoretical-historical terms, our resistance is perfectly understandable, but it has inhibited us from understanding why such a critically denigrated form as adaptation has proved as much of an attraction for artists as for audiences. In *Beginnings: Intention and Method*, Edward Said argues that literature is "an order of repetition, not of originality—but an eccentric order of repetition, not one of sameness" (1985: 12). So too is adaptation. Despite being temporally second, it is both an interpretive and a creative act; it is storytelling as both rereading and rerelating. Any answer to the question, "Why adapt?," needs to take into account the range of responses provided by adapters themselves.

4

HOW?
(Audiences)

Unlike Don Quixote's books, digital media take us to a place where we can act out our fantasies. With a telnet connection or a CD-Rom drive, we can kill our own dragons.

—Janet M. Murray, *Hamlet on the Holodeck*

Movies not only used different materials, they had different cooking times for their great soups, and had to be consumed in public alongside eight hundred other people as opposed to by one solitary diner. A film was closer to the simulated excitement of a soccer stadium while books were a meditative and private act—you sat down to read one or write one and the first thing you did was ignore the rest of the world. Whereas film had various sous-chefs and a studio and a market to deal with. A book could be secret as a canoe trip, the making of a film more like the voyage of *Lord Jim's* Patna—uncertain of ever reaching its destination with a thousand pilgrims on board and led by a morally dubious crew. But somehow, magically, it now and then got to a safe harbour.

—Michael Ondaatje on *The English Patient*, novel and film

The Pleasures of Adaptation

Obviously, the creation and reception of adaptations are inevitably going to be intertwined—and not only in commercial terms. Because audiences react in different ways to different media—thanks to social and material differences, as Ondaatje imaginatively suggests—the possible response of the target audience to a story is always going to be a concern of the adapter(s). Radio, television, and film have radically increased our exposure to stories and therefore, some claim, our ability to comprehend them (K. Thompson 2003: 79). Arguably, these media have also increased our appetite for and delight in stories. But what is the real source of the pleasure derived from experiencing adaptations *as adaptations*?

In Chapter 1, I suggested that the appeal of adaptations for audiences lies in their mixture of repetition and difference, of familiarity and novelty. Novelist Julian Barnes satirizes part of this appeal in *England, England* when his French theorist character describes the joys of a theme park as its "*rivalisation* of reality": "We must demand the replica, since the reality, the truth, the authenticity of the replica is the one we can possess, colonize, reorder, find *jouissance* in" (1998: 35). While parodying various French theorists, Barnes also puts his finger on one of the sources of the pleasure of replication—and adaptation—for audiences. Freudians too might say we repeat as a way of making up for loss, as a means of control, or of coping with privation. But adaptation as repetition is arguably not a postponement of pleasure; it is in itself a pleasure. Think of a child's delight in hearing the same nursery rhymes or reading the same books over and over. Like ritual, this kind of repetition brings comfort, a fuller understanding, and the confidence that comes with the sense of knowing what is about to happen next.

But something else happens with adaptations in particular: there is inevitably difference as well as repetition. Consider the words of librettist, playwright, and adapter for musicals and films, Terrence McNally:

"The triumph of successful operas and musicals is how they reinvent the familiar and make it fresh" (2002: 19). The same could be said of any successful adaptation. To focus on repetition alone, in other words, is to suggest only the potentially conservative element in the audience response to adaptation. Noting that many modern operas (e.g., *The Great Gatsby* [1999]) have been based on novels that had earlier been made into films, Joel Honig has blamed the need for the adapting mediation of film on the opera audience's desire for "warmed-over comfort-food, prepackaged in Hollywood" (2001: 22). But perhaps the real comfort lies in the simple act of almost but not quite repeating, in the revisiting of a theme with variations.

Others argue, instead, that it is a particular kind of story that provides the comfort that explains the popularity of adaptations: the familiar linear and realist story-line "founded upon the principles of narration doubtlessly begun with Aesop, if not Moses, and polished by Walter Scott and Balzac" (Axelrod 1996: 201). Such a story-line has been seen as the appeal of formulaic genres of film adaptation, especially those that use what one critic refers to as Aristotle's notion of plot combined with Joseph Campbell's myth of the hero's quest (Axelrod 1996: 202). Adventure videogames clearly play with this same kind of story structure as well, but we have seen that the story itself is less important than the special effects universe to be entered and experienced or simply the gaming process itself—or at least this seems to be the case for male players.

Girls in the 7- to 12-year-old age range, it would appear, "tend to prefer narrative play and are attracted to narrative complexity" (Laurel 2005). Drawing upon interviews with 1,100 children and questionnaires completed by 10,000 children, Brenda Laurel notes that the vast majority of creators of fan fiction and video are female, suggesting that the fascination with story continues into adulthood. The stories that young women prefer to see adapted into game format, she shows, are those, like *Buffy the Vampire Slayer*, that overlap somewhat with their own lives and their personal issues with parents and siblings and with being accepted at school. Boys of the same age are more likely to be embarrassed by things too close to their own lives and escape instead into superhero exotic action scenarios. It seems that 81 percent of the more violent games are played by males, whereas females prefer role-playing games, like *Sims,* with more social interaction or else games that allow instant immersion in a story-line (e.g., an adaptation like *Nancy Drew*).

Another name for adaptation audiences here is obviously "fans," and the community they constitute is consciously nurtured by adapters, who realize that young women in particular need to be able to "appropriate cultural material to construct personal meaning" (Laurel 2005); this is why the interactive mode can be so attractive to them and why stories, in particular, are central to their pleasure in adaptations. From early childhood onward, as I can testify from experience, girls create imaginative worlds, complete with their own history, geography, people, and rules of behavior, and they inhabit these imaginatively. How different is sending e-mails to game characters, on bulletin boards set up by the adapting companies of course, from making up stories with and for their Barbie dolls? In 2004, Mattel, the Barbie doll's creators, decided to exploit this latter pastime and offered DVDs that are a kind of adaptation, for they bring the "Barbie world" to life "through storytelling," as explained on their Web site (http://www.yenra.com/barbie-dvds/): "Barbie will set the stage and then cue the girls' imaginations to take the story to the next level"—which turns out to be developing "a deeper connection with the Barbie brand." Given this, it is perhaps not surprising that experimental Irish composer Jennifer Walshe was driven to create her musical puppet opera for Barbie and her play friends: as its title (*XXX_LiveNude Girls*) suggests, this work explores the darker side of girls' narrative relationship to their dolls.

Although many of these theories and examples suggest pleasures tainted with a too conservative familiarity, not to mention commodification and commercialization, there are still other reasons for the positive reaction to the repetition with variation that is adaptation: what Leo Braudy, in discussing film remakes, calls "unfinished cultural business" or the "continuing historical relevance (economic, cultural, psychological) of a particular narrative" (1998: 331). Part of this ongoing dialogue with the past, for that is what adaptation means for audiences, creates the doubled pleasure of the palimpsest: more than one text is experienced—and knowingly so. In Tony Richardson's 1963 cinematic adaptation of Henry Fielding's *Tom Jones* (1749), we recognize the novel's manipulating and controlling narrator in the film's disembodied voice-over that ends scenes just in time to prevent indecency or ironically explicates character motivation.

This is the intertextual pleasure in adaptation that some call elitist and that others call enriching. Like classical imitation, adaptation appeals to the "intellectual and aesthetic pleasure" (DuQuesnay 1979: 68) of understanding the interplay between works, of opening up a text's possible meanings to intertextual echoing. The adaptation and the adapted work merge in the audience's understanding of their complex interrelations, as they might in the 1997 BBC television adaptation of *Tom Jones* when we see a character called "Henry Fielding" self-reflexively enacting the narrator's role, but being ironically cut off mid-sentence by the real controlling figure, the director, when he digresses from the story-line selected for that particular filmed version.

In direct contrast to this elitist or enriching appeal of adaptation is the pleasure of accessibility that drives not only adaptation's commercialization but also its role in education. As noted earlier, teachers and their students provide one of the largest audiences for adaptations. Many of us grew up with the *Classics Illustrated* comics or the animated cartoon versions of canonical literature. Today's young people are just as likely to interact with CD-ROM adaptations of either children's or adult literature. In 1992 *Shakespeare: The Animated Tales* offered half-hour versions of the major plays aimed at a 10- to 15-year-old audience and was accompanied by print texts published by Random House that differed, however, from the films. The films obviously made major cuts in the play texts, but retained their language. The style of animation was deliberately not Disney-like. Interestingly the stories seem to have been considered central, and so voice-overs were used to keep the action moving, thereby in a sense translating drama into narrative or showing into telling. There were, however, strong intertextual echoes of other Shakespearean films in the editing and in the appearances of characters and sets, prompting one critic to suggest that the animations prepared students for films of Shakespeare, not for the plays themselves (Osborne 1997: 106).

Adults, of course, often "censor" adaptations, deciding that some are appropriate for children and others not. Or else they change the stories in the process of adapting them to make them appropriate for a different audience. For instance, *Lemony Snicket's A Series of Unfortunate Events* (2004) is a film adaptation of part of three books by Daniel Handler about the Baudelaire orphans. Although the books are aimed at preteens and adolescents, the film wanted and knew it would attract a broader audience and so made the very dark tales considerably brighter, in part by using a narrating Lemony Snicket who can assure younger children that everything will be okay in the end.

Adaptations of books, however, are often considered educationally important for children, for an entertaining film or stage version might give them a taste for reading the book on which it is based. This is what novelist Philip Pullman calls the "worthiness argument" (2004). Although most of the fans of the Harry Potter films will already have read the books, Pullman is not wrong, and this get-them-to-read motivation is what fuels an entire new education industry. The new film adaptation of C.S. Lewis' *The Chronicles of Narnia: The Lion, the Witch and the Wardrobe* is accompanied by elaborate teaching aids, from lesson plans to Web-based packages to material for after-school clubs. Today, hardly a book or a movie aimed at school-aged children does not have its own Web site, complete with advice and materials for teachers.

Novelizations of films, including what are called "junior" novelizations for younger viewers, are also often seen as having a kind of educational—or perhaps simply curiosity—value. If Internet postings are to be believed, fans of films enjoy their novelizations because they provide insights into the characters' thought processes and more details about their background. And, after all, that is what novels have always done well. Web site narratives (e.g., Max Payne) or even films (e.g., *Final Fantasy*) about videogames can offer the same kind of information in a different format. They all increase audience knowledge about and therefore engagement in the "back story" of the adaptation. These various supplements are sometimes released before the films or games and therefore generate anticipation. Not only do these kinds of adaptations provide more details, especially about adapted characters' inner lives, but in the process they also help foster audience/reader identification with those characters. They might also add scenes that do not appear in the screenplay or film versions, perhaps offering a minor character's perspective on the action. The novel often explains plot and motivation elements that remain ambiguous in the film: in Arthur C. Clarke's novelization of *2001: A Space Odyssey* ("based on a screenplay by Stanley Kubrick and Arthur C. Clarke"), the author actually allows us into the consciousness of the computer Hal.

Not everyone approves of novelizations, of course: for many they are simply commercial grabs, unmitigated commodifications, or inflationary recyclings. As we have seen, gamers are equally suspicious of games with direct successful movie links, seeing them as "transparent attempts to cash in on successful movie franchises with products that lack much in the way of compelling gameplay of their own" (King and Krzywinska 2002b: 7). But economic diversification is the name of the game: to use White Wolf Publishing as one example, its pen-and-paper role-playing games have been licensed to videogames, television series, action figures, comic books, interactive media events, arcade games, and even professional wrestlers. Although all of these different incarnations feed audience curiosity and fan instincts, not all are fully adaptations as defined here and as explored further in the concluding chapter. All, however, make money; audiences exist or can be created for them all.

Adaptations have come under the scrutiny not only of money makers but also of the censors, for they too have audiences in mind. This was certainly true in earlier centuries for dramatic and operatic adaptations for the stage. We have also seen that the Hollywood Production Code (1930–66), drafted by Father Daniel Lord, S.J., and sponsored by Will Hayes of the Motion Picture Producers and Distributors of America, decreed that movies must not lower the audience's moral standards by showing any sympathetic representations of evil, crime, or sin. Sinclair Lewis, Ernest Hemingway, William Faulkner, John Dos Passos—all were deemed capable of corrupting the movie-going mass audience. Instead, it was decided, people should see edifying religious dramas and patriotic stories. When Hemingway's *A Farewell to Arms* was adapted to the screen in 1929, it was already a hit on Broadway and a publishing success. But this was a story about an illegitimate birth, illicit love, and an army desertion, and it was a critique of war. It portrayed the Italian army anything but favorably. Needless to say, many compromises needed to be made before *A Farewell to Arms* could come to the screen, including so many changes to the plot and the character motivation that Hemingway refused to endorse it.

Closely related to these moral and educational concerns for audiences is the idea that television adaptations of literature, in particular, can act as substitute vehicles for bringing literature to a larger public, cutting away the class differences inherent in access to literacy and literature. But this does not always work in practice: the BBC's *A TV Dante* (1990), co-directed by Peter Greenaway and artist Tom Philips, is a case in point. Although television implies an address to a mass audience, this show remained "recondite," incomprehensible without explanatory notes (Taylor 2004: 147). The other major danger involved in the motivation to adapt for a wider audience is that a certain responsibility is placed on the adapters to make the "substitute" experience "as good as, or better than (even if different from) that of reading original works" (Wober 1980: 10). Would this experience be the same, however, for the audience that knows the adapted text as it is for the one that does not? How, in short, are adaptations appreciated *as adaptations*?

Knowing and Unknowing Audiences

When either the voice-over narrator or the protagonist of Sally Potter's film, *Orlando* (1994), addresses the audience, a kind of negotiation is set up between Virginia Woolf's text and our knowledge of it and its garrulous narrating biographer (Shaughnessy 1996: 50). If we know the adapted text, I prefer to call us "knowing," rather than the more common descriptors of learned or competent (Conte 1986: 25). The term "knowing" suggests being savvy and street-smart, as well as knowledgeable, and undercuts some of the elitist associations of the other terms in favor of a more democratizing kind of straightforward awareness of the adaptation's enriching, palimpsestic doubleness. If we do not know that what we are experiencing actually *is* an adaptation or if we are not familiar with the particular work that it adapts, we simply experience the adaptation as we would any other work. To experience it *as an adaptation*, however, as we have seen, we need to recognize it as such and to know its adapted text, thus allowing the latter to oscillate in our memories with what we are experiencing. In the process we inevitably fill in any gaps in the adaptation with information from the adapted text. Indeed, adapters rely on this ability to fill in the gaps when moving from the discursive expansion of telling to the performative time and space limitations of showing. Sometimes they rely too much, and the resulting adaptation makes no sense without reference to and foreknowledge of the adapted text. For an adaptation to be successful in its own right, it must be so for both knowing and unknowing audiences.

If we know the basic story outline of Shakespeare's play *A Midsummer Night's Dream*, for instance, we are likely to fill in the gaps necessitated by the distillation of the plot in the opera or ballet versions. When the complication of music is added, it certainly seems to help if the story is a familiar one. As Terrence McNally puts it, "Music adds such an enormously new dimension to a piece, it's enough for any audience (or critic) to absorb at one hearing. If the characters and situation are familiar, listeners can relax and let the music take them somewhere new and wonderful" (2002: 24). Nevertheless, it is probably easier for an adapter to forge a relationship with an audience that is not overly burdened with affection or nostalgia for the adapted text. Without foreknowledge, we are more likely to greet a film version simply as a new film, not as an adaptation at all. The director, therefore, will have greater freedom—and control.

Known adaptations obviously function similarly to genres: they set up audience expectations (Culler 1975: 136) through a set of norms that guide our encounter with the adapting work we are experiencing. Unlike plagiarism or even parody, adaptation usually signals its identity overtly: often for legal reasons, a work is openly announced to be "based on" or "adapted from" a specific prior work or works. If we know the work(s) in question, we become a knowing audience, and part of what hermeneutic theory calls our "horizon of expectation" involves that adapted text. What is intriguing is that, afterward, we often come to see the prior adapted work very differently as we compare it to the result of the adapter's creative and interpretive act. In the move from print to performance, in particular, characters (hobbits) and places (Middle Earth) become incarnate in a way that conditions how we imagine them in a literary work like Tolkien's *Lord of the Rings* when we return to reread it. Our imaginations are permanently colonized by the visual and aural world of the films. But what if we have never read the novels upon which they are based? Do the novels then effectively become the derivative and belated works, the ones we then experience second and secondarily? For unknowing audiences, adaptations have a way of upending sacrosanct elements like priority and originality.

If the adapted work is a canonical one, we may not actually have direct experience of it, but may rely on "a generally circulated cultural memory" (Ellis 1982: 3). Either way, we tend to experience the adaptation through the lenses of the adapted work, as a kind of palimpsest. It is said that producer David Selznick did not worry about adhering to the details of the novel *Jane Eyre* (1847) when adapting it in the 1940s because an audience survey determined that few had read it; however, he did worry about the details of *Gone with the Wind* (1939) and *Rebecca* (1940), because the novels had been recent best-sellers (in Naremore 2000b: 11–12). The disappointment of the fans of the DC comic book *Catwoman* was clear in the responses to Pitof's 2004 film, which kept only the name and added a new cast of characters in a new setting. Critics tended to blame the screenwriters (John Brancato, Michael Ferris, John Rogers, and Theresa Rebeck), calling them the "committee, the gang of four" who "declawed the poor creature" (Groen 2004: R1).

Knowing audiences have expectations—and demands. It may be less, as Béla Balázs tried to insist, that "a masterpiece is a work whose subject ideally suits its medium" and therefore cannot be adapted (qtd. in Andrew 1976: 87) than a case of a "masterpiece" being a work a particular audience cherishes and resists seeing changed. Different adaptations solicit different audiences or fan communities: Harry Potter fans may not be Tolkien fans. When a film or musical announces itself as an adaptation of a particular work, those who like that work turn out for the adaptation, often to discover that only the name remains and that there is little resemblance to anything treasured and thus expected. Here is an early (1928) description of the problems with this process from the other end:

A favorite money-saving habit is to make a picture that is very like a well-known popular novel or play, and then grow timorous at this similarity when the picture is almost completed, and buy the story which was used as a model. The title of the bought and popular tale is then used, but it usually happens that the similarity is not really so great as the nervous producer, haunted by dreams of plagiarism suits, first thought. (Bauer 1928: 294)

The more rabid the fans, the more disappointed they can potentially be, however. As Christopher Columbus, director of *Harry Potter and the Philosopher's Stone* (2001) put it: "People would have crucified me if I hadn't been faithful to the books" (qtd. in Whipp 2002: H4).

There are also other dimensions to this "knowingness" of the audience of adaptation, in addition to the awareness of the specific adapted text(s). One such dimension is treated in detail in the next chapter, and that is context—in cultural, social, intellectual, and aesthetic terms. But this dimension overlaps with another kind of knowing; that is, about what Chapter 2 called the form of the adaptation and therefore the expectations created by it. In terms of genre switching in adaptation, we need only think of the different implied "pacts" made with the reader of autobiography and the reader of comics or graphic novels. Philippe Lejeune's idea of the "autobiographical pact" between reader and author is that we accept that an autobiography is a retrospective narrative by a real person about his or her own life (1975: 14). This pact undergoes an odd twist when Harvey Pekar's own blue-collar life stories become the *American Splendor* comic books drawn by R. Crumb and others and from there get adapted to the stage and screen. In terms of medium, musicals and operas both offer "drama unfolding through song" (Lachiusa 2002: 14), but they have different artistic traditions and, often, different audiences. As musical composer Michael John Lachiusa put it, the musical genre is "the child of European opera tradition transplanted to America" (14), mixing high-brow and low-brow because of its cross-fertilization with ethnic immigrant theater, music, and dance (see Most 2004).

Medium change therefore involves the same kinds of expectation shifts. For example, the 2002 film version of Oscar Wilde's play, *The Importance of Being Earnest*, directed and adapted by Oliver Parker, exchanges the restricted drawing-room sets of the staged version for the streets of London and a grand country estate. Why? Because movie audiences expect the film to have local color and to be shot on location, with characters moving through real space. After several decades, British televised versions of classic novels now generate in their viewers expectations about style, "sumptuous, beautiful, pictorial images, strung together smoothly, slowly and carefully" (Cardwell 2002: 80). These expectations are not really dictated by the adapted literary texts, but rather by the television medium's desire to signal "artistry" through specifically cinematic markers of "quality": "the use of long-take, extreme long shots of grand buildings ... [,] the preference for slow, smooth tracking shots ... [,] their use of a certain type of elegant, decorous or wistful orchestral music on their soundtracks" (Cardwell 2002: 80). The institutionalization of a medium, in other words, can in itself create expectations: a movie of an opera may be allowed to differ from the staged version simply because of the audience's knowledge of its popular or mass dissemination (Leicester 1994: 247).

Readers obviously have different expectations than do spectators at a play or film or interactive participants in the new media. Showing is as different from telling as it is from interacting with a story. But even within one of these modes—especially showing—there are, as we have already seen, important distinctions to be made. Knowing stage audiences have different expectations and demands than knowing film or television audiences, as the hybrid case of Ingmar Bergman's *Magic Flute* reveals. The Swedish Radio commissioned this "production" of Mozart's opera, which became an "adaptation," for its golden jubilee. It was shown on television on New Year's Day 1975 in Sweden and later released as a film. It is a self-reflexive presentation of a staged production in a studio reconstruction of the famous eighteenth-century Drottningholm Theatre. The camera records not only the stage action but also the audience responses and the actors' activities backstage. Arguably, fans of the opera, watching either on TV or on film, might respond differently from others, as they watch their own rapt attention and enjoyment being represented by the filmed audience. Swedes who watched it on television as a family show may have been pleased with the charm and humor of the opera itself and of the film of it. Fans of Bergman's other films might have been disappointed at this existentialist director's rather sunny version of Mozart's most metaphysical opera, despite its clear citation of earlier Bergman motifs (Tambling 1987: 132–34). All "screen operas," however, have different viewing conditions and expectations than either staged operas or normal films, thanks to the guiding and controlling role of the camera and the differences in scale and level of distance/proximity (Citron 2000: 12–13).

Interactive art forms too involve distinct sets of expectations—at least for knowing audiences. To an audience mostly trained on private or public computers in the form of ATMs or information kiosks, being faced with an interactive electronic installation work in a public space like a museum may cause confusion and even alarm. Artist Ken Feingold admitted he was unhappy about how people engaged with one of his computerized works in a gallery because he had to accept that they expected "unambiguous" interaction: "It actually disappointed me tremendously, as I expected the audience, and the audience turned participants, to bring to interactive works the same capacity for abstraction, metaphor and ambiguity that is well-deployed and comfortable when viewing painting, or other artworks" (2002: 124). Audiences need to learn—that is, to be taught—how to be knowing audiences in terms of medium. The expectations of videogame players, on the contrary, certainly include being made participants, being allowed to enter the narrative and visual world of, usually, a film, and being able to enact its logic both physically and cognitively.

Differently knowing audiences bring different information to their interpretations of adaptations. For example, film buffs likely see new movies through the lenses of other ones. Watching Kenneth Branagh's 1989 film adaptation of *Henry V*, they are probably going to see it as much as an adaptation of Laurence Olivier's famous 1944 film as one of Shakespeare's plays, translating the early version's shining clean world, with its self-conscious and stylized theatricalism, into the dank and dirty one of filmic realism. From the dark days of the end of World War II to the time of post-Falklands postimperialism, the message to British audiences changed, or so the differing vision of the two adapting actor-directors would suggest. Similarly, audiences that are well versed in British cinema might argue that Sally Potter's *Orlando* (1994) was adapting *that* tradition—the films of Derek Jarman, Peter Green-away, and David Lean—as much as Virginia Woolf's literary work. Potter self-reflexively—and yet still realistically—suggests as much by having Orlando's daughter (not a son, as in the book) take a film camera in hand at the end and become both subject and object. There is yet another way of reading this scene: this female child may not possess any property (the purpose of having a son in the novel), but she, like Potter and her generation of female filmmakers, does possess the power of the male gaze that women were said to have lost with the medium of film (see Mulvey 1975). And, as Sophie Mayer (2005: 173–86) has explored at length, the filming girl and her film together solicit a female gaze from the audience: changing the adapted text here leads to a change in the adapting medium, defying audience expectations.

Similarly, although it is an American film, Philip Kaufman's adaptation of Milan Kundera's Czech novel, translated as *The Unbearable Lightness of Being* (1988) (screenplay by Jean-Claude Carrière), is arguably a response to Czech New Wave cinema as much as to the novel itself. But only a film expert might understand that level of intertextual reference. Or, to use a more straightforward example, how would we respond to an adaptation in the form of a contemporary musical, if we had only ever seen on the musical stage nineteenth-century European operas? What would we make of the amplified voices, the hyperactive choreography, the scaled-down musical resources? Genre and media "literacy," as it is often called, can be crucial to the understanding of adaptations *as adaptations*.

There are still other aspects to this knowingness to be considered in theorizing about the product and process of adaptation. If the audience knows that a certain director or actor has made other films of a particular kind, that intertextual knowledge too might well impinge on their interpretation of the adaptation they are watching. It can also make for amusing in-jokes and ironies. In the novelization of *Spider-Man* by Peter David (2002), Mary Jane finds Harry reading *Interview with a Vampire*. She tells him she has not read it, but she saw the movie and the little girl in it "creeped" her out. The joke here is that Mary Jane is played in the film by Kirsten Dunst, who played that creepy little girl, Claudia, in the movie adaptation of Anne Rice's novel. Sometimes, of course, an audience member may know too much: as an instance, Alan Sinyard found himself irritated, while watching the film *Morte a Venezia*, by Visconti's use of Mahler's *adagietto* from the Fifth Symphony, instead of the more obvious and appropriate choice of the Ninth Symphony, which is about death. His argument was that in moving from tragedy to triumph, the Fifth offers musical associations that run "contrary to the drift of the film": "Its inappropriateness is crippling to a film that prides itself on its cultural refinement" (1986: 129), he asserted.

But what if we do not know Mahler's music this well? What if we see a film or play a game without even knowing the work from which it is adapted or even that such a work exists? What if we are utterly new to the artistic conventions of the adaptation, say, of opera? What if we are unknowing audiences, in other words? I have been arguing that, in these instances, we simply experience the work without the palimpsestic doubleness that comes with knowing. From one perspective, this is a loss. From another, it is simply experiencing the work for itself, and all agree that even adaptations must stand on their own. After all, it was only in France that *films noirs* were actually seen *as adaptations* (of *romans noirs*; Cattrysse 1992: 58). If we do not know Pushkin's *Eugene Onegin* (1878), we cannot be bothered by the fact that it satirizes what Tchaikovsky's 1881 opera adaptation of it offers seriously as deep emotions. But if we do ... .

Failure in conveying vision or tone in adaptations of classic works of science fiction seems particularly problematic for fans. The 2004 film of Isaac Asimov's *I, Robot* (1950) by director Alex Proyas and screenwriter Michael Cassutt came under just such attack, but it is only one example of many. The more popular and beloved the novel, the more likely the discontent: witness the negative fan reaction to Paul Verhoeven's 1997 adaptation (screenplay by Edward Neumeier) of Robert A. Heinlein's *Starship Troopers* (1959). Science fiction, however, may be particularly difficult to adapt. As Cassutt has suggested, things of the future in the earlier written narrative are now often things of the past, so setting, characters, and action inevitably have to shift and change (2004). As an adapter himself, he says that he would prefer the opening credits to warn the audience of the inevitable changes. Instead of "based on," they could read "suggested by" or "freely adapted from" to forestall the objections of knowing audiences.

Of course, all these complications of possible reception mean that adapters must satisfy the expectations and demands of both the knowing and the unknowing audience. But there are still other differences in audience experience that adaptations bring to our attention, and these involve such factors as the differences caused by the various media's diverse modes of audience involvement and of their degrees and kinds of immersion.

Modes of Engagement Revisited

As shown in Chapter 2, telling, showing, and interacting with stories differ in the kind and manner of engagement of the reader (spectator, player). Adapters know this; so too do those who market adaptations. The relatively small "graduate" audience who bought most of the 10,000 hardback copies of Malcolm Bradbury's 1975 ironic campus novel, *The History Man*, was not the same in size or makeup as the 10 million viewers of the BBC television adaptation a few years later (Bradbury 1994: 99). When television buys the rights for this kind of fiction, it knows it can build upon a "preconstructed and preselected audience" (Elsaesser 1994: 93), but that it must also expand that audience considerably and must use all the available persuasive means at its disposal to do so.

Even within a single mode of engagement, however, there are once again major distinctions to be made, especially with performance media. When director Peter Brook filmed Peter Weiss' baroquely entitled play *Die Verfolgung und Ermordung Jean Paul Marats, dargestellt durch die Schauspielgruppe des Hospizes zu Charenton unter Anleitung des Herrn de Sade* (1964) as the more simply named *Marat/Sade* (1966), he sought a totally cinematic translation of what he had previously done on stage, knowing that spectators of live drama are free to choose at any moment, in any scene, what to look at, whereas with the film he would only be able to show one thing at a time with the camera— what *he* wanted to show. He attempted to break down this limitation by deploying three or four cameras, using twists, advances, and retreats and "trying to behave like what goes on in a spectator's head and simulate his experience" (Brook 1987: 189–90). But even this camera work, he realized, would not do what a stage production does: engage the viewer's *imagination* in a way that film, because of its realism, cannot. Noting the "excessive importance of an image, which is intrusive and whose details stay in the frame long after their need is over," Brook finally accepted that the reality of the image is what gives to film "its power and its limitation" (1987: 192). Or, as another critic has put the difference: "In theatre, the conflict of the hard, undeniable presence of actors together with the conventional artifice of scenery and stage required a suspension of disbelief. On the other hand, narrative cinema, with its flow of action, naturalistic acting, and photographic realism, increasingly involved not so much a suspension as a suppression of disbelief" (LeGrice 2002: 230). A young friend recently admitted to me that, although he loves adaptations, he cannot bear going to stage play versions: they seem so "stagey" and unrealistic to him because he is part of a generation raised on film and television, with their conventions of naturalism and immediacy. Curiously, the three-dimensional world of the stage is far less engaging for him than the two-dimensional screen world.

The human-computer interface offers yet another kind of engagement in a feedback loop between our body and its extensions—the monitor, the keyboard, the joystick, and the mouse, and the processing computer. Katherine Hayles describes this relationship in this way: "We are the medium and the medium is us" (2001: 37). Shelley Jackson's 1995 interactive art work called *Patchwork Girl* is an adaptation of both L. Frank Baum's *Patchwork Girl of Oz* (1913) and Mary Shelley's *Frankenstein* (1818/1831), and it involves us, through our clicking of the mouse, in the kind of activity that is like sewing a patchwork quilt from different fragments of cloth. Our physical acts also allow us to simulate the acts of two female figures: "the heroine Mary Shelley (a fictional counterpart of the author of *Frankenstein*), who assembles a female monster by sewing together body parts collected from different women; and the author, Shelley Jackson, who constructs a narrative identity for the monster from the stories of these women" (Ryan 2005: 524). The creating of mixed media hypertexts like *Patchwork Girl* is the direct result of cutting and suturing, just as is monster-making in the novel:

> The first page to come up on screen is the image of a woman pieced together and crossed by a dotted line. The next link is a title page with collaborative authors: Mary Shelley, Shelley Jackson, and presumably the monster herself. Links from its table of contents take you to rearrangements of the first image … [from which] various sequences of narrative and metafictional texts follow. (LeClair 2000/2003: 8)

Each mode of engagement therefore also involves what we might call a different "mental act" for its audience, and this too is something that the adapter must take into account in transcoding. Different modes, like different media, act dissimilarly on our consciousness (M. Marcus 1993: 17). Telling requires of its audience conceptual work; showing calls on its perceptual decoding abilities. In the first, we imagine and visualize a world from black marks on white pages as we read; in the second, our imaginations are preempted as we perceive and then give meaning to a world of images, sounds, and words seen and heard on the stage or screen. Kamilla Elliott calls this a reciprocal relationship between mental imaging and mental verbalizing (2003: 210–12), but more than words are at stake here. Psychoanalytic film theorists argue that audiences are more deeply involved consciously and unconsciously when watching a movie because of the processes of identification, projection, and integration (M. Marcus 1993: 18). In playing a videogame, of course, we are involved even more directly, physically and mentally, as we concentrate intensely and respond physiologically. Each of these different modes demands of its audiences, in turn, its own decoding processes. In reading, we gather details of narrative, character, context, and the like gradually and sequentially; in seeing a film or play or musical, we perceive multiple objects, relations, and significant signs simultaneously, even if the script or music or soundtrack is resolutely linear. In interactive media, both the simultaneity of film and the sequentiality of texted narrative come together in the game world and its rules/conventions.

Bruce Morrissette noted another important aspect of the mode of engagement involved in audience response when he posed what he thought of as a rhetorical question: "Has the novel ever evoked, even in its most intense action sequence, the physical empathy affecting the muscles, the glands, the pulse, and breathing rate that chase, suspense, and other extremely dynamic sequences in film bring about in most, if not all, viewers?" (1985: 26). But what about the *frisson* of which opera lovers speak, when the hair on the back of the neck stands up in ecstatic response to a soprano's high note? Has any film or novel ever managed *that*? And none of the telling or performing media can likely beat the degree of the active physical involvement of interactive art and especially videogames. The *Die Hard* films (1988, 1989, 1995), no matter how intense their "extremely dynamic sequences," would find it hard to beat the game versions' participatory excitement, intense concentration, engagement of kinesthetic skills, competitive energy, and provoking of often involuntary physical reactions (see Bryce and Rutter 2002: 78).

Part of this difference in physical response is a result of a difference in the audience's experience of space and time in each of these modes. When playing a computer game, we may be part of a multiplayer group, but we play, often at home, as solitary individuals, much as we read. We often have a dedicated space where we can concentrate and will not be bothered. We are alone with our computer, sitting close to the screen so that the game's world takes up our visual field, and the sound (thanks to earphones, often) dominates all, immersing us completely. This kind of gaming is a private mode; although gaming with a group of friends or in arcades is more public, it is still individualized.

With performance media, on the contrary, we frequently sit in the dark in a collectivity and respond to what we are all seeing and hearing (being shown) at the same time. Walter Benjamin saw this as a mass response, the opposite of the contemplative individual response to viewing a painting (1968: 231). Peter Brook agreed, arguing that film in particular engulfs its audience with the image in all its immediacy: "When the image is there in all its power, at the precise moment when it is being received, one can neither think, nor feel, nor imagine anything else" (1987: 190). The theater audience, in contrast, is more distanced from the action; indeed it is at a fixed distance physically, even if actors can create intimacy through their "presence." Brook noted that "the degree of involvement is always varying ... . This is why theatre permits one to experience something in an incredibly powerful way, and at the same time to retain a certain freedom. This double illusion is the very foundation both of the theatre experience and of dramatic form. The cinema follows this principle with their close-up and the long shot, but the effect is very different" (190)—in part because of the difference between live and mediated action. For this reason, Christian Metz sees the film viewer as an isolated and distanced voyeur with no relation to the actors whom he or she regards with "unauthorized sco-pophilia" (1974: 185). In film, of course, our distance from the characters whose story we watch changes, depending on camera angle and type of shot. But in first-person new media art, we actually become the character and travel through an animated version of their world. Space is now something to navigate interactively: "being there" is as important to the pleasure of gaming as is "doing things" (Ryan 2001: 309).

Television too presents spatial challenges for the adapter: like the film spectator, the TV viewer does not share a space with the dramatic events the way a theater audience does, but is "reduced to a pair of eyes" (J. Miller 1986: 207) that look at a *picture* of actual objects that represent a world, rather than at the objects themselves (as on stage). And, like film, television is a representational and realist medium: "A television or film screen provides a window onto a world that is supposed to extend beyond the visible screen, and has the optics of reality. The audience sitting in the theatre knows perfectly well that however realistic the world on the stage appears to be it does not extend beyond the proscenium arch" (J. Miller 1986: 206). When films were watched in the once customary dark, silent, large movie theaters, with "intense light beams … projected from behind toward luminous surfaces in front" (Flitterman-Lewis 1992: 217), there was a cocoon-like feeling of both anonymous collectivity and immersive enclosure that we cannot experience watching film DVDs at home on the television set.

It is not only space, however, but also time that is experienced differently by audiences in the various media; this difference creates new problems for adaptations across media. The much-discussed "present-ness" of television (Cardwell 2002: 83–92), for instance, is both real and yet belied by the fact that, as we watch it at home, we are interrupted by advertisements, by family members and friends, and by telephone calls in a way that we rarely are when watching a film in a cinema or a musical in a theater (at least if all the cell phones are actually turned off). But the privacy and domesticity of TV when we are watching film videos or DVDs are related to those of reading and game playing. In all these modes, we control how much we experience and when. Most obviously, readers are always in control of the process of solitary reading. But novels take time and often lots of it to consume; films must be shorter, in part because of the audience's inability to halt the process, except by leaving the theater.

Artist Stan Douglas rather sadistically plays with precisely this idea of time and the movie audience's entrapment in his 16-mm film installation called *Journey into Fear* (2001). As its title suggests, it is an adaptation, not only of the 1940 Eric Ambler novel but also of the 1942 and 1975 film adaptations and of Melville's *The Confidence Man* (1857) too, in fact. The viewer is caught watching an unending loop of film that works through all possible permutations of dialogue dubbed and synched to talking heads. There is no escape, no exit for 157 hours from this particular "journey into fear." What these distinctions among media and modes point to is an obvious difference in how we become immersed in an adapted story—physically, intellectually, and psychologically.

Kinds and Degrees of Immersion

In Chapter 1, I suggested that all three modes of engagement can be considered immersive: the act of reading a print text immerses us through imagination in another world, seeing a play or film immerses us visually and aurally, and interacting with a story in a videogame or in a theme park adds a physical, enacted dimension. In each there is a sense of being "transported" (Gerrig 1993: 12), in psychological and emotional terms. The recent advent of interactive electronic media has engendered more talk about the desirability of this immersive experience. Yet surely the experimentation undertaken decades ago with works like the early 3-D films and "Aromarama," when perfumes and other odors were dispersed in cinemas to match the content of the screen images, betrays an even earlier desire for at least physical immersion. With that desire, however, comes a certain suspicion that intense engagement of any kind will limit the critical sense: "Movies don't help you to develop independence of mind," according to Pauline Kael (qtd.

in Peary and Shatzkin 1977: 3). Nor do videogames, say others (Grau 2003: 10). But each medium and each mode of engagement brings with it not only different possible kinds (imaginative, visual, physical) and degrees of immersion, identification, and distance but also different critical traditions that have valued one extreme or the other.

Reader-response theory, which flourished in Europe and North America in the 1980s, may be partly responsible for the change in the way we think about reception in the mode of telling. Thanks to the work of theorists like Wolfgang Iser, Stanley Fish, and Michael Riffaterre, readers are no longer considered passive recipients of textual meaning but active contributors to the aesthetic process, working with the text to decode signs and then to create meaning. To these theorists, it was not simply the "ambiguities and semantic resistances" of a difficult modernist writer like Joyce that demanded "a restless, active reader" (Dinkla 2002: 30); for them, *all* readers are engaged in the active making of textual meaning. Stage audiences, argued theater semioticians in the same years, are an active dimension of the meaning-making of any play, not only in their interpretive work but also in their physical and emotional responses at the time of viewing. Stage conventions distance audiences, even as the live presence of actors on stage makes for more intense identification. In operas and musicals, the unrealistic conventions of singing act to distance us, but the music counters that by provoking identification and a strong affective response. Clearly the adapter working from one mode to another has to take into account these different ways of involving the audience.

This may be no easy task, however, thanks to other critical traditions. When adapting to film, should an adapter believe the theory that the spectator is going to be self-consciously "*all-perceiving*" and all-powerful (Metz 1974: 173–74) or the rather different view that the spectator will always be in collusion, desiring "magic transport" and so resisting "recognition of the artifice in favor of immersion in the illusion" (LeGrice 2002: 230)? Can this involvement be controlled by camera movement, for instance? Take any one of the "heritage" British adaptations for film or television of a classic novel like Jane Austen's *Pride and Prejudice*. Their common long takes, combined with beautiful images, might well "elicit a contemplative appreciative gaze, giving us time both to look and to experience emotion" along with the character whose eyes the camera follows (Cardwell 2002: 141).

Given that the influential early media guru, Marshall McLuhan, felt that "hot media" like television were "low in participation" and "cool media" like literature were "high in participation or completion by the audience" (1996: 162), we can only imagine what he would have made of this description of the audience experience in the scenario for first-person shooters in a certain kind of videogame: "You find yourself, usually unintentionally, in a strange, hostile place, unarmed and vulnerable … . You must explore the place to find weapons and other useful items, moving through the many game arenas or levels on some form of quest. In the process you must fight and/or avoid many enemies or monsters" (Morris 2002: 82–83). We move—and control our own movement—through a 3-D fictional world, with a sense of embodiment in the game space, a heterocosm we may already know in a non-animated version through the film from which the game is adapted. Our primary identification is directly through "the constant first-person point of view, the player's own sense of agency and experience of interactivity" (Morris 2002: 89). The player becomes at once protagonist and director in a way no performance spectator or reader ever can (Grau 2003: 8–9; Tong and Tan 2002: 101). Instead of just interpreting, the player intervenes in a kind of "frenetic virtual world" (Mactavish 2002: 34). Interactivity brings a greater degree of immersion, both mentally and physically, in the here and now. Response must be rapid: successful hand-eye coordination and puzzle solving involve learned skills and moves (King and Krzywinska 2002a: 22–23). And players play to win. The aim of any game is to keep the player on the verge of mastery but also on the verge of losing control, just like the avatars or characters *in* the game (Weinbren 2002: 183).

In videogames, therefore, there are aural (music, sound effects), visual, and kinesthetic provocations to response in the active gaming portion that make the mode of engagement one of real participation and thus the degree of immersion intense: we feel physically present in the mediated environment, rather than in our real world (Ryan 2001: 66). Anything that reminds us that we are only gaming destroys this illusion, for immersion in this mode relies on the transparency of the medium; effective games, like theme parks and rituals, must eschew the metafictional or the self-reflexive (Ryan 2001: 284). In the cinematic cut-scenes that frame the gaming, the narrative is both set up and brought to closure, but in them the player is transformed into a spectator, with all the formal and interpretive expectations of any film viewer (Howells 2002: 118). This bringing together of showing and interacting challenges any neat compartmentalization of modes of engagement, but the videogame player has more of an active role in shaping the story than does the audience for a film, play, or even novel (Mactavish 2002: 33). Multiplayer role-playing games involve participants in still other ways through player interaction. Tolkien's novels spawned *Dungeons and Dragons* board and computer games, which in turn became MUDs, narrative worlds in which participants can insert themselves. The programming system allows users in different places to communicate within the same virtual space, becoming characters and creating a collective narrative.

Similar things can happen in interactive fiction. Here too the viewer is not a voyeur and is connected to the story more than by means of emotional identification with a character, as in the telling and showing modes. Instead, "[t]he former audience is lifted out of their seat of distanced contemplation and placed in the limelight of subjective physical involvement: addressed as a storyboard controller, co-author, actor or self-performer" (Zapp 2002: 77). We can now become active participants in a heterocosm—either a fantastic or a realistic one (Ryan 2005: 527). Back in 1926 Virginia Woolf had seen that were it possible to capture the "exactitude of reality and its surprising power of suggestion,"

> we should see violent changes of emotion produced by their collision. The most fantastic contrasts could be flashed before us with a speed which the writer can only toil after in vain; the dream architecture of arches and battlements, of cascades falling and fountains rising, which sometimes visits us in sleep or shapes itself in half-darkened rooms, could be realized before our waking eyes. No fantasy could be too far-fetched or insubstantial. The past could be unrolled, distances annihilated. (1926: 309–10)

She was, of course, writing about cinema, however, and not interactive fiction.

Although again less immersive than videogames, what has been called "expanded cinema" using "multimedia data, visualization and manipulation" (Blunck 2002: 54) does allow members of the audience to become an integral part of the experience by controlling the way in which the story unfolds. If we think back to how important the soliciting of audience participation was for those classical theoreticians of rhetoric or for oral storytellers, we might get a clearer sense of how the audience can figure in the thinking of the adapter working in these emergent forms called "interactive storytelling" that are made possible by broadband and virtual technologies: "Interactive stories are certainly ideal for people who like things like thinking about how to resolve a conflict (in thrillers or courtroom films, for instance), or for people who are not just good listeners, but also like posing investigative questions" (Wand 2002: 177). Audiences have to learn new navigational strategies and accept a new and altered relationship with the creator of the work; in return they are given new kinds of encounters with virtual and fictional worlds that might inspire technological awe as much as increased physical and cognitive immersion. But someone creates those encounter possibilities beforehand. Hypertext fiction, for example, like *afternoon*, a story (1987) by Michael Joyce, one of the founding writers of this mode, offers the reader a variety of narrative threads to choose from, but all have been written by the author in advance. The form may be reader controlled, but the content is not. This is "selective interactivity" (Ryan 2001: 206), and the text is as much a database to be searched as a world in which to be immersed (Ryan 2004c: 342)—which may explain why there have been so few adaptations to or from this medium.

For this and other reasons, the new media are not without their detractors, who often suggest that it may not only be the difficulty of access or mastery that prevents adapters from rushing to use these new forms to attract new audiences. Paul Willeman has articulated many of the ideological arguments against these interactive forms. He points out that their mode of address—imperative or vocative (file, cut, paste, move)—is conducive to "authoritarian and advertising discourses," belying that rhetoric of immersion and freedom: in actual fact, he says we can only obey or ignore orders (2002: 15). He sees this as a reduction in the scope of action "which now has to be conducted according to rigorously policed protocols, by a trivialization of the fields where interaction is encouraged, such as games and bulletin boards, and by increasing isolation of the allegedly interacting individuals" (14–15). The so-called interactivity allowed—that is, with specific, preformatted templates—is less truly interactive, he argues, than other representational media "from religious rituals to painting, novels and cinema" (14). According to this argument, pen and paper and the call and response of gospel and jazz music are more interactive than the electronic media today that only "allow" audiences to interact with the story.

Nevertheless, there are manifest differences in the kind and degree of immersion in the three modes of engagement. The sorts of changes and interventions by users/audiences differ. We may be as much controlled as controllers, but we are still immersed differently in a world with which we interact than with one we are either told about or shown. Think of the difference between simply sitting in a theater and seeing the film of *Pirates of the Caribbean* and going on either the original theme park ride from which the movie is adapted or DisneyQuest's interactive version of it at Disney World. As we plunge into the dark, in both versions, we are told that "Dead men tell no tales!" Neither do rides like this, at least not in the conventional narrative sense: enacting or participating replaces telling. Because people go to theme parks in groups and want to share experiences, the designers of the indoor interactive version have created what they call a virtual reality "overwhelming immersive experience on the high seas" (Schell and Shocket 2001) through a simple physical interface. One person steers at a real helm and controls the direction of the "trip"; three others man six cannons. Together they try to defeat virtual enemy pirate ships and sea monsters while collecting and defending as much gold as they can in 5 minutes. The designers admit to controlling the pace to make sure that, in the space of 5 minutes, excitement will grow to a climax. The wraparound 3-D screens and surround sound, plus the motion platform of the boat, guarantee a sensory experience of considerable intensity that no videogame, much less novel or film can match.

Knowing or unknowing, we experience adaptations across media differently than we do adaptations within the same medium. But even in the latter case, adaptation *as adaptation* involves, for its knowing audience, an interpretive doubling, a conceptual flipping back and forth between the work we know and the work we are experiencing. As if this were not complex enough, the context in which we experience the adaptation—cultural, social, historical—is another important factor in the meaning and significance we grant to this ubiquitous palimpsestic form. When Peter Brooks and Jean-Claude Carrière adapted the *Mahabharata* in 1975, they not only moved from storytelling to film but also from an Indian into a French context. In the process, they realized that they needed some way to bridge cultures and chose to add a French narrator to connect the two worlds. They were not alone in facing this kind of challenge.

5

WHERE? WHEN?
(Contexts)

The History Man is a story about the dying of the liberationist culture of the Sixties, the fading of the era of student revolution, and the book was set, appropriately, in 1972. It was published in 1975, just, as it were, on the cusp between the end of the Sixties radical culture and the emergence of the Seventies—a very contemporary work. But by the time it appeared on British television in 1981, Mrs. Thatcher had been elected to office. We were in the era of Thatcherismus, of the new conservatism. Under Thatcherismus, the entire cultural and political attitude toward the Sixties had been transformed; it was an adversary that had to be overcome. So where the novel version of *The History Man* in 1975 was a kind of half-tragic and half-ironic version of a generation that was dying, the television version of *The History Man* is really a commentary from a later era on what was wrong with an earlier one. So the values of the story, the myth and meaning of the story, had also been adapted in the process of translation from novel to screen.

—Malcolm Bradbury, on the adaptation of his novel

The Vastness of Context

As Malcolm Bradbury suggests, even without any temporal updating or any alterations to national or cultural setting, it can take very little time for context to change how a story is received. Not only what is (re)accentuated but more importantly how a story can be (re)interpreted can alter radically. An adaptation, like the work it adapts, is always framed in a context—a time and a place, a society and a culture; it does not exist in a vacuum. Fashions, not to mention value systems, are context-dependent. Many adapters deal with this reality of reception by updating the time of the story in an attempt to find contemporary resonance for their audiences: when *Here Comes Mr. Jordan* (1941) was remade in 1978 as *Heaven Can Wait*, relevant anti-nuclear and environmental themes of the day were inserted (Seger 1992: 65).

I have been arguing that adaptation—that is, as a *product*—has a kind of "theme and variation" formal structure or repetition with difference. This means not only that change is inevitable but that there will also be multiple possible causes of change in the *process* of adapting made by the demands of form, the individual adapter, the particular audience, and now the contexts of reception and creation. This context is vast and variegated. It includes, for instance, material considerations:

> Just as a painting changes when it is moved from the Eastern [*sic*] end of a church and placed in an art gallery, so a play by Shakespeare, or an opera by Mozart, changes its character according to the physical format in which it is presented. A play that started its theatrical life on the unfurnished platform of the Globe and then went on to be pictorially represented in the Victorian theater, with further alterations in physical format when thrust on to the apron stages that developed after the 1950s, has undergone changes that are just as far reaching as the ones that result from reinterpretations of the spoken lines. (J. Miller 1986: 60)

Likewise, the materiality involved in the adaptation's medium and mode of engagement—the kind of print in a book, the size of the television screen, the particular platform upon which a game is played—is part of the context of reception and often of creation as well. Max Horkheimer and Theodor Adorno famously argued, in *Dialectic of Enlightenment,* that the sound film had blurred the difference between reality and its representation, leaving "no room for imagination or reflection on the part of the audience" (1947/1972: 126). But even they would not have predicted the ontologically bizarre phenomenon of Reality TV. With its mix of fact and fiction, a show like *Survivor* is arguably an adaptation not only of "reality" but also of the ethos, as well as the story of Robinson Crusoe (Stam 2005: 99).

What I am calling context also includes elements of presentation and reception, such as the amount and kind of "hype" an adaptation gets: its advertising, press coverage, and reviews. The celebrity status of the director or stars is also an important element of its reception context. Jonathan Demme's 1998 film adaptation of Toni Morrison's novel, *Beloved* (1987), starred Oprah Winfrey; just as significantly for another arts community, however, *Margaret Garner* (2005), the opera adaptation of part of the novel by Morrison (music by Richard Danielpour) was the vehicle for two major African American singers, Denyce Graves and Jessye Norman. It is not that the larger social and racial issues are *not* also part of the audience's context here, but the fact that they are incarnated in the particular stars conditions the work's meaning and impact.

As this example might suggest, the time is clearly right, in the United States, as elsewhere, for adaptations of works on the timely topic of race. Readiness to reception and to production can depend on the "rightness" of the historical moment. In Italy, for instance, during the Libyan War (1911–12), film adaptations of epics like *El Cid* and *Gerusalemma liberata* abounded—apt expressions of Italy's nationalist-imperialist ambitions. Because epic adaptations continued to flourish through the Fascist years, it is not too surprising that there was an anti-adaptation move by the postwar neo-realists (M. Marcus 1993: 5). It may be no accident, some argue, that "heritage cinema" adaptations flourished in Thatcher's aesthetically and ideologically conservative

Britain (Vincendeau 2001: xix). This wider context of creation and reception must therefore be of interest to any theory of adaptation that defines the term as process, as well as product.

Whether an adapted story is told, shown, or interacted with, it always happens in a particular time and space in a society. Therefore, the videogame adaptation of *The Godfather* will be experienced differently today by an Italian American player than by a Korean one. And adapters know this and take it into consideration. Byron's fragment of a vampire tale was expanded by his doctor, John Polidori, into *The Vampyre* in 1819, and within a year the story had been adapted into a three-act melodrama (by Pierre Carmouche, Achille Jouffrey, and Charles Nodier). But the French adapters changed the Byronic Lord Ruthven's vampiric lust into the passion of a dedicated womanizer. In the same year (1820), this play was adapted, not simply translated, for the English stage by James Robinson Planché; in this national context, the villain was made sympathetic for British audiences because, even though his vampirism was made into the curse for his crimes, he has appropriate moral qualms about his bloody deeds. When both Peter Joseph von Lindpaintner and Heinrich August Marschner created their different German Romantic opera adaptations of the vampire's story, the demonic returned—and so on, throughout the many cinematic adaptations of the last century undertaken by adapters of many different national cultures.

Nations and media are not the only relevant contexts to be considered. Time, often very short stretches of it, can change the context even within the same place and culture. In 1815, Franz Schubert adapted—in this case, set to music for piano and solo voice—a well-known earlier (1782) ballad by Goethe, "Erlkönig" (though the song was not published until 1821). Richard Taruskin sees Schubert's *Lied* as decidedly different in musical emphasis and significance from the other adaptation done three years later (1818) by Carl Loewe. These Romantic composers were contemporaries and thus shared much of the general national musical ideology that had led to the development of the *Lied* genre, especially the link between personal expression and the collective ("das Volk"). But Loewe's setting reveals, among many other things, his "greater nature mysticism" (Taruskin 2005: 3.158), a difference that is not only individual but also reflects subtle changes that Taruskin sees happening in German culture at large. To move to an example closer to home, after Bruce Springsteen's celebratory rock song "Born in the USA" was appropriated by the American Right, he chose to rerecord it alone, on a dark stage, with only an acoustic guitar. His self-cover became an adaptation in that the new context of protest transformed the piece into a somber dirge. Time too changes meaning and always has.

Time also has the ability to make us forget, of course, but we may not ever have known things like details from a temporal context that could be relevant to issues of power. Michael Radford's 2005 film adaptation of *The Merchant of Venice* historicizes, through visual imagery, things of which Shakespeare's audiences (or today's) might or might not have been aware. By having his Venetian Jews wear identifying red hats and his prostitutes appear bare-breasted—as both had to by law at the time of the play's setting—the director makes this a play *about* both anti-Semitism and the role of women. The camera narrates and interprets for us as we move through the labyrinthine streets and canals of historical Venice, watching Antonio spit at Shylock as he passes him on the Rialto bridge.

Transcultural Adaptation

Where is as important a question to ask about adaptation, however, as *when*. Adapting from one culture to another is nothing new: the Romans adapted Greek theater, after all. But what has been called "cultural globalization" (Cuddy-Keane 2003: 544) has increased the attention paid to such transfers in recent years. Often, a change of language is involved; almost always, there is a change of place or time period. Akira Kurosawa's *Throne of Blood* (1957) is a famous Japanese film adaptation and major cultural transposition of *Macbeth*, for instance, just as *The Magnificent Seven* (1960) is a Hollywood remake of Kurosawa's *Seven Samurai* (1954). Almost always, there is an accompanying shift in the political valence from the adapted text to the "transculturated" adaptation. Context conditions meaning, in short.

It seems logical that time and place shifts should bring about alterations in cultural associations; however, there is no guarantee that adapters will necessarily take into account cultural changes that may have occurred over time. When Alain Boublil, Richard Maltby, Jr., and Claude-Michel Schönberg brought Giacomo Puccini's early twentieth-century operatic story of American sexual imperialism in Japan (*Madama Butterfly* [1904]) into the 1970s world of American political imperialism in Vietnam in *Miss Saigon*, they left intact what was, by the musical's premiere in 1989, a dated and much contested stereotype of the Asian woman.

Sometimes, as we saw in an earlier chapter, changes are made to avoid legal repercussions. F.W. Murnau's 1922 *Nosferatu* changed Bram Stoker's *Dracula* in terms of time (dating it back 50 years), place (moving it from Transylvania to Germany and from London to Bremen), and even names (Dracula became Count Orlock). Today those changes would likely be enough to escape copyright infringement suits, but they were not sufficient at the time. Most often adaptations are not back-dated but rather are updated to shorten the gap between works created earlier and contemporary audiences: in adapting Shakespeare's *Romeo and Juliet*, Franco Zeffirelli made his lovers' affection more physical and cut out parts that slowed down the action to satisfy what he perceived as the demands of his film audience in 1968. By 1996, when Baz Luhrmann adapted the same play, the young audience targeted was one attuned to MTV music videos and Hollywood action movies, and this change motivated his gangland setting and frenetic pace. In other words, the reception context determined the changes in setting and style. Just as the psychological novel of the eighteenth century (Sterne) is not like that of the twentieth (Proust), adaptations of the same play that are even decades apart can and should differ: cultures change over time. In the name of relevance, adapters seek the "right" resetting or recontextualizing. This too is a form of transculturation.

For Hollywood, however, transculturating usually means Americanizing a work: the Canadian novel, *Shoeless Joe* (1982) by W.P. Kinsella, may have been named after an American figure, but Phil Robinson's 1989 film of it, *Field of Dreams*, was even more focused south of the 49th parallel. Similarly the characters in A.S. Byatt's very bookish English novel *Possession* (1990) were changed to give American audiences someone to identify with in Neil LaBute's 2002 cinematic adaptation:

the novel's quiet, articulate British Roland became the film's brash and sardonic American Roland. Because Hollywood films are increasingly being made for international audiences, the adaptation might end up not only altering characters' nationalities, but on the contrary, actually deemphasizing any national, regional, or historical specificities.

What happens when a film like the very Italian *Profumo di donna* (1974) is adapted into *Scent of a Woman* a decade later or when *Le Retour de Martin Guerre* (1982) becomes the American Civil War story, *Sommersby* (1993)? David Edelstein argues that the pace gets changed; the life is "streamlined out of the narrative" as temporal tricks and any possible plot ambiguities are eliminated. In addition family values have to be respected while at the same time the story must be "dopily" over-romanticized (2001: 20). Obviously no fan of Americanizations, Edelstein asserts, "It would be terrific to report that Hollywood does not, contrary to popular belief, have a coarsening effect on the foreign properties it remakes. Terrific, but wrong. In this area, as in few others, studios live up to their reputation as titanic forces of philistinism" (3). But wit aside, is Hollywood really alone in this kind of changing? When, in 2005, French director Jacques Audiard adapted James Toback's *Fingers* (1978) into *The Beat That My Heart Skipped*, the dark tale of psychic contradictions against a backdrop of 1970s New York became a more realistic but considerably less anguished story set in twenty-first-century Paris. Context can modify meaning, no matter where or when.

Transcultural adaptations often mean changes in racial and gender politics. Sometimes adapters purge an earlier text of elements that their particular cultures in time or place might find difficult or controversial; at other times, the adaptation "de-represses" an earlier adapted text's politics (Stam 2005b: 42–44). Even within a single culture, the changes can be so great that they can in fact be considered transcultural, on a micro- rather than macrolevel. In the same society, political issues can change with time, as we have seen in the example of David Henry Hwang's new version of Richard Rodgers and Oscar Hammerstein's *Flower Drum Song*. Perhaps not surprisingly, Shakespeare's *The Taming of the Shrew* has been adapted time and time again for the movie and television screen—but differently each time—from the suffragette years of the early twentieth century right up to the 1980s feminist backlash. Similarly it has been argued that Bram Stoker's *Dracula* deployed a myth about the sacred role of women that was particularly appropriate to his time, but that myth seems to be one that can be adapted readily to a new social reality with each of its frequent adaptations (McDonald 1993: 102).

Of course, the politics of transcultural adaptations can shift in unpredictable directions too. When Arthur Schnitzler's sexually and dramatically radical 1900 play *Der Reigen* (or *La Ronde*) was transculturated into Eric Bentley's *Round Two* (1990), there was no banning and no obscenity trial, despite the translation of the straight Austrian sex into the gay American context (see Schechter 1986: 8). Once again, this same temporally induced deradicalizing shift can happen with adaptations within the same culture: the 1928 edgy comedy called *The Front Page* and written by Ben Hecht and Charles MacArthur was adapted often to film, but the best-known adaptation is likely the 1940 *His Girl Friday* (director Howard Hawks; script by Charles Lederer). Although the male ace reporter was transformed into a woman, the gain in women's visibility was matched by the loss of that edge to sentimentality. In 2003, John Guare adapted the play and the film together into a new play, *His Girl Friday*, which added lines from the play that the somewhat sanitizing film had removed, but somehow the new play managed to be even less edgy than the film had been.

Indigenization

As we have seen in Chapter 3, the adapter works in one context, but the meaning he or she establishes within that frame of reference can change over time. Alexandre Dumas, *fils*, adapted the true story of his relationship with his former beloved, Alphonsine Duplessis, into a novel (1848) and then a play (1852) called *La Dame aux camélias*. What began as a warning about the "pernicious threat of prostitution to decent bourgeois family life in Paris in the middle of the nineteenth century" (Redmond 1989: 72) changed considerably with each subsequent adaptation. Giuseppe Verdi's operatic version, *La Traviata* (1853), scandalized audiences, in part because it made its courtesan heroine sympathetic—not a surprising shift, given Verdi's relationship at the time with an unmarried mother, the singer Giuseppina Strepponi. The

1936 Greta Garbo film *Camille*, however, traded on its star's glamor to allow the love story to overtake any social argument. But when Pam Gems adapted the film back to the stage in her 1985 *Camille* for the Royal Shakespeare Company, politics returned, but a different politics this time. The feminist writer introduced themes that the earlier works by men had silenced: sexual and physical abuse and abortion. This is adaptation: repetition without replication.

The context of reception, however, is just as important as the context of creation when it comes to adapting. Imagine an audience watching any of the new adaptations of *Othello* during the O.J. Simpson trial: the fall of a hero, the theme of spousal abuse, and the issue of racial difference would inevitably take on a different inflection and even force than Shakespeare could ever have imagined. Contemporary events or dominant images condition our perception as well as interpretation, as they do those of the adapter. There is a kind of dialogue between the society in which the works, both the adapted text and adaptation, are produced and that in which they are received, and both are in dialogue with the works themselves. Economic and legal considerations play a part in these contexts, as do evolving technologies, as we have seen. So too do things like religion. Canadian First Nations playwright Tomson Highway has spoken revealingly of the adaptation of his plays to the Japanese stage. In North American stage productions of *Dry Lips Oughta Move to Kapuskasing* (1987), one actor plays a trinity of female goddesses (Aphrodite, Pregnant Earth Mother, and Athena) in an echo of Christian imagery; in contrast, when the play was transculturated to polytheistic Japan, three women were used and dance and silence replaced dialogue as the major modes of communication.

As this example suggests, performance media present the greatest challenges for adaptations across cultures and not only because of the presence of paying audiences—on site and ready to respond with incomprehension or anger. Adapting across cultures is not simply a matter of translating words. For audiences experiencing an adaptation in the showing or interacting modes of engagement, cultural and social meaning has to be conveyed and adapted to a new environment through what Patrice Pavis calls the "language-body" (1989: 30). The intercultural, he says, is the "intergestural": the visual is as important as the aural. In transfers from a telling to a performance mode, differences of philosophy, religion, national culture, gender, or race can create gaps that need filling by dramaturgical considerations that are as likely to be kinetic and physical as linguistic. Facial expressions, dress, and gestures take their place along with architecture and sets to convey cultural information that is both verisimilar and an "index of the ideologies, values, and conventions by which we order experience and predicate activity" (Klein 1981: 4).

When stories travel—as they do when they are adapted in this way across media, time, and place—they end up bringing together what Edward Said called different "processes of representation and institutionalization" (1983: 226). According to Said, ideas or theories that travel involve four elements: a set of initial circumstances, a distance traversed, a set of conditions of acceptance (or resistance), and a transformation of the idea in its new time and place (1983: 226–27). Adaptations too constitute transformations of previous works in new contexts. Local particularities become transplanted to new ground, and something new and hybrid results.

Susan Stanford Friedman has used the anthropological term "indigenization" to refer to this kind of intercultural encounter and accommodation (2004). In political discourse, indigenization is used within a national setting to refer to the forming of a national discourse different from the dominant; in a religious context, as in mission church discourse, it refers to a nativized church and a recontextualized Christianity. But the advantage of the more general anthropological usage in thinking about adaptation is that it implies agency: people pick and choose what they want to transplant to their own soil. Adapters of traveling stories exert power over what they adapt.

For most of us there are two small devices that enable ease of travel—the adapter plug and the electrical converter—and for me these offer the best (punning) metaphor I can think of to explain how this aspect of adaptation works. Power comes in different forms, in addition to AC/DC and 120v/220v, of course, and it can be adapted *for use* in different contexts (different countries); the adapter plug and the converter allow the transformation of power to a useable form for a particular place or context. This is how indigenization functions as well.

The cultural power that has accrued to the works of Shakespeare can be adapted and adopted by the British in the name of patriotism and national culture. But for Americans, Australians, New Zealanders, Indians, South Africans, or Canadians, that power must be adapted into differently historically colonized contexts before being transformed into something new. And neither of these kinds of adaptation will resemble the Chinese indigenization in which Shakespeare's work is transformed through cultural transcoding into a "celebration of individuality, the awakening of self-consciousness and competitive individualism, a moral principle against obscurantism, and the concepts of freedom, equality, and universal love" (Zhang 1996: 242)—in short, the ideology and values of a democratic society offered in opposition or contrast to those of a totalitarian state.

Indigenizing can lead to strangely hybrid works. The 2003 American musical adaptation of the thirteenth-century Chinese play, *The Orphan of Zhao*, ended up being a kind of "country and eastern" in both form and content. Director Chen Shi-Zheng asked David Greenspan to write new English dialogue and the eclectic songwriter Stephin Merritt to compose the lyrics and music, to be played on an autoharp and two Chinese instruments, the *jinghu* and the *pipa*. Sometimes conventions clash rather than merge, however. When *King Lear* was adapted to the Indian performance tradition of *kathakali*, a classical improvised dance form, two reciters offered part of the verbal text, but in this new aesthetic context, it was the conventions of the dance form that were significant, not the story in itself. Neither novelty nor naturalism has importance in this dance tradition. The adapters, Australian playwright and director David McRovie and actor-dancer Annette Leday, knew these conventions, but it seems not all of their audience did, leaving mystification and not fascination as the result.

In contrast, Gustave Flaubert's *Madame Bovary* (1857) was reworked more successfully by Ketan Mehta in Hindi as *Maya Memsaab* (1992). This story seemed to translate more effectively across cultures because Emma's novel-inspired romanticism found an analogue in the illusions provoked by Bombay musicals. Framed in an investigation over whether the protagonist was a murder victim or a suicide, Mehta's adaptation is a mixture of mystery, erotic film, and musical (for the fantasy and dream parts). Except for the latter parts, the rest is relatively realistically presented, transcoding well Flaubert's own mix of the romantic and realist (see Stam 2000: 63; 2005a: 183).

Adapters across cultures probably cannot avoid thinking about power. Muhammad 'Uthmān Jalāl's *al-Shaykh Matlūf* is an 1873 Egyptian adaptation of Molière's seventeenth-century French play *Tartuffe*, which freely translated characters and customs as well as language (dialects) into Egyptian contexts. This work is a deliberate and deliberately selective borrowing from the West, a canonical European work fully indigenized into Arabic culture (Bardenstein 1989: 150). A different power differential between colonized and colonizer, however, often plays a role in the adapting process. As mentioned at the end of Chapter 4, Jean-Claude Carrière, who adapted *Mahabharata* for the screen, recognized the "possibility of unconscious colonization by way of vocabulary, since the action of translating Indian words translates our relationship to an entire civilization. To say that we could find an equivalent for every Indian word implies that French culture can in a word appropriate the most profoundly reflected notions of Indian thought" (1985: 14).

Some adaptations tackle the politics of empire from a decidedly postcolonial perspective, thereby changing the context of the adapted work considerably. Patricia Rozema's 1999 film adaptation of Jane Austen's *Mansfield Park* (1814) adds both a feminist and a postcolonial critique of slavery. Similarly, Mira Nair's 2004 version of *Vanity Fair* (1848; script by Julian Fellowes) picks up on the fact that the novel's author, Thackeray, was born in Calcutta to highlight India as the source of a character's wealth. In other words, these adaptations offer a modern rereading of the past that not everyone has found acceptable. For Kamilla Elliott,

> Film adapters build on a hypercorrect historical material realism to usher in a host of anachronistic ideological "corrections" of novels. Quite inconsistently, while adaptations pursue a hyperfidelity to nineteenth-century material culture, they reject and correct Victorian psychology, ethics, and politics. When filmmakers set modern politically correct views against historically correct backdrops, the effect is to authorize these modern ideologies as historically authentic. (2003: 177)

This rereading of the past is obviously not the same as adapting Austen's *Pride and Prejudice* (1813) to Bollywood conventions and a contemporary setting and calling it *Bride and Prejudice*, as did Gurinder Chadha (2004). The postcolonial adaptations are, by definition, willful reinterpretations for a different context, even if the historical accuracy of the time and setting is retained. In other words, this is not unlike a writer and director in 2004 adding women to an adaptation of Plato's famous dialogue on the topic of love, the *Symposium*, because he or she feels that in the twenty-first century women too have important perspectives to offer on the subject. So, in Michael Wirth's film version, Aristophanes and Eryximachus are allowed to cross gender lines.

With indigenizing come accusations of a failure of political nerve or even of less "correctly" changing the politics of adapted works. Steven Spielberg was said to have "repatriarchized" Alice Walker's feminist 1982 novel in his 1985 film of *The Color Purple*. John Ford was accused of shying away from the "socialist drift of the Steinbeck novel" in his 1940 adaptation of *The Grapes of Wrath* (1939; Stam 2000: 73). The possible number and kind of complexities when adapting across cultures are such that another "learning from practice" exercise seems in order in the next section. I have once again chosen an adapted text that has had multiple adaptations across time and place, as well as across medium and genre. It is also a story whose political meaning has changed with those context shifts: it is the story of a woman named Carmen.

Learning from Practice

Why Carmen?

Other viable candidates for this exercise clearly exist, the vampire narrative and *Hamlet* foremost among them. They too revolve around a single protean figure, culturally stereotyped yet retrofitted in ideological terms for adaptation to different times and places. But the narrative of the gypsy woman, Carmen, adds to these significant characteristics a confusing range of political reinterpretations right from the start: is she a dangerous *femme fatale* or an admirable independent woman? These conflicting stereotypes, I argue, have made for the story's continuing

fascination for adapters and audiences alike (see Collier 1994; Maingueneau 1984). As Susan McClary explains, the power of her story lies not
in its "ability to inspire consensus, but rather in its success at provoking
and sustaining debate along the central fault lines of nineteenth- and
twentieth-century culture" (1992: 129). Whether the adaptation por-
trays Carmen as victim or victimizer, in short, depends on the politics
of the particular contexts of creation and reception.

On the surface, this story would not seem to be a prime candidate
for multiple adaptations. It does not appear to be an accepted classic
with some universal truth at its core; it does not in any obvious way
manage to transcend its time and place of creation. The narrative about
the misbegotten love of a gypsy woman and a Spanish-Basque soldier is
very nineteenth century and very French, even if it is about gypsies and
Spain. In 1845, Prosper Mérimée wrote a novella version of a story he
had heard from a friend; within a year Marius Petipa had choreographed
a concert ballet from it (*Carmen and Her Bullfighter*). But it was not until
30 years later that Georges Bizet adapted it into an opera, and the rest
is history—or, as one critic has wittily put it, the rest is discourse: "To a
degree unparalleled by any other opera, *Carmen* has become a *discourse*,
a multiply-authored, historically developing tangle of bits and pieces
from Bizet, Mérimée, high-art criticism, the folk imagination and the
movies: of stock images of Spain, opera, melodrama, *femmes fatales* and
doomed lovers, and heaven knows what else" (Leicester 1994: 250). If
we needed proof of her iconic status, the 2002 "Carmen Conference"
at the University of Newcastle upon Tyne would have offered it, in its
examination of some of the 77 film adaptations of this story—a sampling of both affirmations and contestations of received notions of gender and ethnicity that constitute the appeal of *Carmen*.

The Carmen Story—and Stereotype

Prosper Mérimée traveled to Spain in the 1830s and wrote about his
voyages in the *Revue de Paris*. In the December 29, 1833 issue, he
told of a young woman he called "Carmencita" who served him fresh
water and gazpacho by the side of a road. She was one of the bewitch-
ing Spanish sorceresses, the "sorcières espagnoles" of the title of his
article. In 1840, a friend, Mme Eugénie de Montijo, told him the

story of a brigand who killed his mistress; in 1844, he wrote to her that he had just read George Borrow's *The Zincali* (1841) and *The Bible in Spain* (1843). In 1845, in the travel biweekly specializing in exotic Third World travel journals, the *Revue des deux mondes* (October 1), Mérimée brought these various influences together to tell the Spanish story of a fierce and jealous bandit and his devious and dangerous fortune-telling gypsy woman. But the narrative frame is scholarly, controlled, and complete with footnotes, as if the foreign world here is a threat to be contained. So too is Carmen.

The fictional narrator is a pedantic French scholar, and it is he who first describes Carmen: she is smoking, an act that is definitely transgressive, even for a tobacco factory worker—indeed, smoking was an identifying signal used by French prostitutes. She is beautiful but not conventionally so; her eyes are fierce and voluptuous. He thinks she might be Moorish, but that is because he cannot bring himself to say "Jewish"; she enlightens him as to her gypsy blood. This woman is a thief and perhaps a murderer; she is petulant and demanding. We later read a second description of Carmen from Don José, the man who loved and killed her. In his eyes, she is sexy, scandalously so in dress and behavior; she has a sharp tongue; she is a liar but she is paradoxically honest in paying her "debts"; and she is extravagant and capricious. Where the narrator called her a sorceress, her lover calls her diabolical. It is her fault that he is jealous; it is her fault that he must kill her.

There is a third view of Carmen in Mérimée's story: that of the author himself. In later years, he added to the text an ethnographic treatise on gypsies, in which the race is presented as animalistic, unprincipled, and unattractive in all respects. In this view it becomes the gypsies' fault that Carmen must die. This orientalized construction of the European "other" is typical of the time and place: Victor Hugo, Théophile Gautier, Alexandre Dumas, and Gustave Flaubert all had traveled to Spain and had exoticized it as oriental in their writings. For each, the Spanish gypsy was like the Jew: both domestic and yet foreign, the other on nearby, if not home, turf.

Bizet's librettists, Henri Meilhac and the Jewish Ludovic Halévy, would have been sensitive to these associations and eager, given the expensive performance medium that is opera, to call up the positive rather than the negative ones. An *opéra comique*, this first version of *Carmen* consisted of alternating spoken dialogue and song; characters break into song, often at moments of emotional excess. But the bourgeois family audience of the theater known as the Opéra Comique in 1875 Paris was not ready for such excess—or for a woman dying on the stage, killed by her jealous lover. The popular failure of the opera is said to have hastened Bizet's death. Ernest Guiraud prepared a more conventionally operatic version with recitatives for the Vienna opening the next year, adding a chorus and a ballet with music from other works by Bizet. Both versions are decidedly products of the French musical as well as social culture, however.

What is striking is that neither operatic Carmen is the vicious and devious woman of Mérimée's text. The three narrative voices disappear as we move from a telling mode to a showing one. We see and hear Carmen, unmediated by overt male intervention; she speaks/sings for herself. But the librettists too clearly felt some need to contain Carmen: they invented Micäela as a maternally approved rival for Don José's affection and as a pure and innocent foil for Carmen. The opera's gypsy, however, is not a thief, though she is a smuggler; she has not been previously married, and above all, she is independent and feisty. In short, she has been somewhat sanitized for the family-oriented Opéra Comique audience. Halévy admitted that she was a "softer, tamer Carmen," writing to the anxious co-director Adolphe de Leuven that the gypsies would all be made into "comedians" and Carmen's death would be "glossed over"—"in a holiday atmosphere, with a parade, a ballet, a joyful fanfare" (1905/1987: 36). He was not lying, but the contrast between her death and that festive atmosphere actually makes her murder all the more chilling.

Taking only one part of Carmen's story from Mérimée (the Don José part), the librettists made her into a liberated woman, who takes her future into her own hands as only men were allowed to do at the time. This independence is obviously what has attracted modern adapters and audiences alike. But the context of creation was nineteenth-century France, and there such independence was deemed something diabolical to be curbed. Don José repeatedly asks: "Tu est le diable, Carmen?" Fate was called upon to take care of this "problem": dramatized in Carmen's reading of the cards and rendered audible as a motif in her music, Carmen's fate is to die for her independence in love and life. The opera's shortening and condensing of the novella's plot mean that detail and subtlety are lost, but what is gained is a sense of fated inevitability as the compressed plot hurries to its end.

There is yet another reason why the opera's Carmen differs from that of the novella: she sings. But it is as much how and what she sings as the fact of her vocalizing that make the difference. Just as Mérimée's Carmen was linguistically talented, so Bizet's is a musical virtuoso, but she is also as unpredictable in her music as she is in her behavior. Deemed a triple alien—by her gender, her race, and her class—Carmen proudly sings her identity as other. As McClary has shown, her slippery chromatic music, most of it to sensuous dance tunes, signals her sexuality; ethnic markers of orientalized Spanish music, which differs from the European norm, point us to her racial background; and her most famous songs are based on popular Paris cabaret versions of Spanish and Cuban dance music, the music of the night life of the lower classes (1992: 26–52).

It is this operatic Carmen who would become the stereotype—and the challenge—for interpreters and therefore adapters from then on. For Catherine Clément, in her controversial feminist study *Opera, or the Undoing of Woman*, Carmen is "somewhat whore, somewhat Jewess, somewhat Arab, entirely illegal, always on the margins of life" (1989: 49) and that otherness is what makes her great. But she is also "the image, foreseen and doomed, of a woman who refuses masculine yokes and who must pay for it with her life" (1989: 48). Carmen must die because she acts like a man—or as a feminist *avant la lettre*. For Mario Praz, in contrast, Carmen stands for a "diabolical feminine fascination" that causes men to lose all control and all regard for their social position (1970: 207). In the same vein, Michel Leiris sees Don José as "the wretch whom she has forced to desert" and whom she ridicules "until he kills her": "a bloodthirsty goddess ... the lovely Carmencita, before being murdered, is indeed a murderess" (1963: 54). The battle lines are as clear as the double stereotype: *femme fatale* or liberated woman?

Indigenizing Carmen

Carmen has been called a nomadic, mobile work, one that is an example of geographic and social "transculturality" (Bertrand 1983: 104). The story has certainly circulated widely and displayed a decidedly dynamic and fluid rather than static and fixed meaning. Different cultures at different moments have indigenized this traveling story in their own ways. Depending on the mode and medium selected, of course, different aspects of that story are foregrounded. Paintings of Carmen—such as those of Franz von Stuck in the early twentieth century—inevitably de-narrativize somewhat in adapting, but retain as a result a strong sense of the body and personality of the character. Instrumental adaptations of Bizet's opera music sometimes retain the narrative line, but more often do not, as in Pablo de Sarasate's 1883 *Carmen Fantasy*. Sometimes the plot, in being updated, puts a strain on the very definition of adaptation developed here. Jean-Luc Godard's self-reflexive film *Prénom Carmen* (1983) substitutes Beethoven string quartets for Bizet's music and turns Carmen into a bank-robbing terrorist who knows of her operatic namesake only through the American film *Carmen Jones*. Yet the opera is more than just another intertext; from the film's title on, it haunts the work as a palimpsest.

There are as many ways to indigenize a story as there are ways to tell or show it again. To give a sense of the kind of range in this particular case, I divide the transformations into three dichotomous types: (1) historicizing/dehistoricizing, (2) racializing/deracializing, and (3) embodying/disembodying.

Historicizings/Dehistoricizings   Given that the opera *Carmen*, although it is French, is about a gypsy woman in nineteenth-century Spain, its story would seem to be a difficult one to dehistoricize (or to "de-ethnicize"). But adaptations have aimed at doing so and have managed to achieve precisely such a feat. On stage in 1981 and in 1983 on the screen, Peter Brook presented his pared-down adaptation, *La Tragédie de Carmen*. He reworked the libretto with Jean-Claude Carrière and rearranged Bizet's score, with the aid of Marius Constant, recontextualizing tunes so that we interpret them differently, hearing them in their new contexts. He removed his Carmen from her social contexts—she is neither a tobacco factory worker nor a smuggler. An austere, round, dusty space replaced particularized Spanish sets. He also stripped away the trappings of the *opéra comique* genre, cutting out characters, eliminating the chorus, and excising a variety of comic and exotic details, thereby reducing the work to one act, lasting just over 80 minutes. Four characters remain in what is now a tragedy of four people in two love triangles; two speaking actors supply the rest of the altered narrative action. In Brook's view:

> Carmen has ... the greatest marriage—perhaps of all the operas—between being musically marvelous and having absolutely true human content. These two go hand in hand. The opera is totally accessible. Being in the theater, I'm most interested in what can speak most directly to the most widely assorted people. The music can appeal to anyone without any difficulty, any effort. There are no cultural barriers. (Qtd. in Loney 1983: 12)

For Brook, this spare version captures the universalized story of fate—the human condition: for this adapter, *Carmen* is not about sexual politics, ethnic otherness, or historical specificity.

The contrast with Neapolitan director Francesco Rosi's filmed adaptation of the opera (1984) could not be more striking. Rosi replaces this idea of universalized fate with specific issues of power and human responsibility; instead of removing the social and historical context, he places the story's nineteenth-century Spanish ethnic and class realities in the foreground. Known as a director with a strong interest in social issues, Rosi was attracted to the culture of southern Spain in which the opera is set in part because of its resemblances to his own southern Italian background, with its related poverty, machismo, earthiness, and fondness for song and dance (Citron 2000: 164). This story was not a cultural cliché for him; it was real. So his Carmen is no *femme fatale*, but an uninhibited and life-affirming woman who is in control of her own fate. There is nothing sinister about her sexuality here; it is fully enjoyed. Filming on location and researching everything historical carefully in advance, Rosi places her in the real material culture of Spain, including the oldest Spanish bullring in Ronda; with her, we move right into the tobacco factory and witness working women at their jobs, their babies by their sides. From the start, he plunges the spectator into a nineteenth-century, hispanized, ethnic world that is not so much picturesque as dark and menacing.

In short, Rosi did not update or rewrite anything; instead, he rehistoricized and in the process "re-ethnicized" the opera, removing the nineteenth-century French context of creation and substituting for it a nineteenth-century Spanish one. In the process, he implicitly played his version of an independent Carmen against the other stereotype of the dangerous seductress. His protagonist does not make a dashing star entrance; we almost miss her as she emerges from the group of workers. In fact, the camera is focused more on an old man, Enrique El Cojio, who is dancing with the women. Rosi uses medium-high-angle traveling shots in which the camera pans (pointedly following the binoculars—and the gaze—of the military commander) to show Carmen moving within a bustling social context: this Carmen is obviously part of a community (Leicester 1994: 269, n.42). But that means that her independence has limits: just as the old man catches our eye before Carmen does and indeed literally leads us, along with the village men, to find her, so Don José controls—or desires to control—the free woman who in fact exerts control over him through her sexuality. He makes her pay for her defiance, aided and abetted by a particular culture's celebration of machismo (in the film's opening bullfight) and its religious cult of women's suffering (the macabre Mater Dolorosa procession of penitents that follows it).

Traveling stories, then, are told—and shown—differently at different times in different places. The very French and very nineteenth-century *Carmen* has been indigenized in radically diverse ways in different contexts of adaptation. But ethnic and national historical identities are not the only variants on this theme. Carmen is not only Spanish; she is a gypsy.

Racializings/Deracializings Nietzsche famously declared that the source of *Carmen*'s cheerfulness was "African"—a "southern, brown, burnt sensibility" (1888/1967: 158); the music's "subtlety belongs to a race, not to an individual" (157), he asserted. The racial identity of Carmen the gypsy was clearly central to Mérimée's ethnographic portrait, but it was arguably just as important to Bizet's equally orientalized version. When Oscar Hammerstein II adapted the opera in its original *opéra comique* version as *Carmen Jones* for the Broadway musical stage in 1943 and later for the screen (1954; directed by Otto Preminger, screenplay by Harry Kleiner), race was on his mind as well. His intentions were progressive, even if they might sound patronizing and essentializing today: "The nearest thing in our modern American life to an equivalent of the gypsies in Spain is the Negro. Like the gypsy, he expresses his feelings simply, honestly, graphically. Also as with the gypsy there is rhythm in his body, and music in his heart" (1945: xviii). The music of Spain, he continued, in a Nietzschean vein, had been influenced by the "Moors from Africa." Indigenizing *Carmen* in the United States meant changing genres—from elitist European opera to populist American musical. More surprisingly, in this case it meant changing race, for not only was this Carmen African American, but the entire cast was as well. We need to remind ourselves that this was a time when the mainstream stage and screen were not necessarily open to black performers, though all-black theater for black audiences flourished. This adaptation was made before the Civil Rights movement, though after *Showboat* (1927) and *Porgy and Bess* (1935). On the other hand, what might have been even less acceptable at that moment than blacks on the American Broadway stage would have been the presentation of a mixed-race love relationship on stage—for that was what Carmen's story originally had been, in part, about.

As James Baldwin pointed out in his attack on the film version of *Carmen Jones*, making everyone black removed Carmen's otherness, as a gypsy among Spaniards, and placed the focus on sexual rather than racial politics. Yet Baldwin noted, it also managed to reinforce African American stereotypes of female promiscuity, male violence, rural ignorance, and athletic prowess (1955/1975: 91). Not only was this adaptation a translation—into what he called "Negro speech"—but it was also a transculturation at the same time. Carmen's famous Habañera became "Dat's Love": "If I love you dat's de end of you!" In the process, the flighty "oiseau rebelle" (rebellious bird) became the earthy "baby dat grows up wild." Although the operatic Carmen accepts her fate as she reads it in the cards, with an aria that opens "En vain" (in vain), the musical's heroine faces death boldly, calling it "dat ol' boy" and declaring defiantly that she wants to live life to the full "up to de day I die." And she does. The racial politics become even more complicated, however, because Dorothy Dandridge's singing voice belongs to a white mezzo-soprano, the young Marilyn Horne.

Not only the language is transformed in this adaptation, however. *Carmen Jones* is reset during the Second World War in the southern United States. The soldier Don José becomes Joe, a serviceman who wants to be a pilot; this Carmen works making parachutes, not cigars or cigarettes. The toreador Escamillo translates as Husky Miller, boxing champion; Lillas Pastia's gypsy cabaret is transformed into Billy Pastor's juke joint. When Joe goes AWOL, he hides in a Chicago hotel room as Carmen goes out to the pawn shop to get money to support them; mad with jealousy, Joe feels emasculated and dependent, reflecting, it has been argued, "wartime and postwar anxieties about the decay of masculine power and authority when women are allowed to work" (Leicester 1994: 250). In Americanizing and updating the story of Carmen, *Carmen Jones* indigenizes it in radical ways. Although Bizet's family felt the adaptation was irreverent and managed to get it banned in France (Collier 1994: 1), it likely would not have spoken to a European audience at any rate, or at least not in the same way as it did to Americans in the middle of the twentieth century. When Joe sings at the end, after murdering Carmen, "String me high on a tree / so that soon I'll be / with my darling, my baby, my Carmen," the inevitable echoes of lynchings and other forms of racial violence would have resonated with the U.S. audience.

Because of its gypsy protagonist, then, *Carmen* is an opera that has frequently attracted racialized adaptations, even if not this extreme. In 2000, director Mark Dornford-May and conductor Charles Hazlewood first presented their pared-down version of the opera's story at the South African Academy of Performing Arts in Cape Town. Set totally among the gypsies of Seville this time, it was updated to the 1970s, but the dialogue was in the Xhosa language and the singing in English (in Rory Bremner's translation). Using both amateur and professional black performers and a small stage band, the production was praised for its energy, its earthiness, and thus its assumed proximity to the spirit that Bizet was trying to capture with his music (see, e.g., P. Citron 2002: R3). A film version, *U-Carmen e-Khayelitsha*, again in

Xhosa, is set this time in a modern-day South African township with its particular issues and problems (e.g., smuggling is transculturated into drug trafficking). This film opened first in the township in which it was filmed before going on to win the Golden Bear Award at the 2005 Berlin International Film Festival.

The 2001 film *Karmen Geï* similarly retains the opera's basic plot, but this version chooses to forego Bizet's score in favor of indigenous Senegalese music and choreography. Here, the toreador Escamillo becomes the singer-bard Massigi. Director Joseph Gaï Ramaka moves to this particular African urban environment the theme of "love and freedom" or the conflict between that freedom and the laws and conventions that inevitably constrain that desire (as he explains at http://www.newsreel. org/films/karmen.htm). Freedom necessarily has a political dimension in this African context, and the film opens in a women's prison. But Ramaka changes the sexual politics (Karmen is bisexual) more radically than he does the racial politics. And in this realistic film, almost all singing is "motivated" as "phenomenal song": that is, it is part of a performed show or is done in a club. The exception is Karmen's seductive Habañera, which is sung twice only to Lamine/Don José—when she first seduces him and just before he kills her. Here the words from the opera are pointedly translated into the African language, not the French of some of the dialogue. As in *Carmen Jones*, the whole cast is black, so racial distinctions and conflicts that exist in the opera are not replicated here either.

These various indigenizings, with their all-black casting, are appropriations that in effect deracialize some of the opera's tensions. But changes in time and place have other political repercussions. MTV's 2001 *Carmen: A Hip-Hopera* is as much an adaptation of *Carmen Jones* as of *Carmen*. With a mostly black cast (Carmen is played by Beyoncé Knowles of the pop band Destiny's Child) and a black director (Robert Townsend), this adaptation uses bits of Bizet's score, but mostly creates new rap music to update the story to modern-day inner-city Philadelphia and Los Angeles. The cultural heroes are not toreadors here, but rap singers; this modern Carmen has an ambition—to be an actor.

Interestingly, unlike these versions, even some of the most benign of Hollywood's *Carmen* adaptations to film over the years retain some sense of racial or ethnic difference within the plot. Carmen was often played by stars who were or seemed exotically ethnic—Theda Bara, Pola Negri, Dolores del Rio, and Rita Hayworth. Some were sinister; others were sultry. But all were different in some way, and all were versions of the *femme fatale*. On the contrary, the other side of the stereotype, the defiant and liberated woman, has been celebrated and appropriated by performers like Madonna and Nina Hagen with rather different gender politics in mind.

Embodyings/Disembodyings Almost all adaptations of the Carmen story—no matter what the medium—inevitably focus on her singing and dancing body. So it is not surprising that the dance stage should have become a site of choice for adaptations. In 1967 the Soviet composer Rodion Shchedrin reworked and reassembled Bizet's themes into a modernist, almost abstract narrative for his wife, Maya Plisetskaya, the grand ballerina of the Bolshoi Ballet. Though this Carmen negotiates her fate in a symbolic bullring, she is curiously disembodied through her translation into the body language and gestural conventions of classical ballet. In contrast, Roland Petit's earlier (1949) version returned Carmen and *Carmen* to their French roots, but updated both in the sense that realism and eroticism now replaced exoticism. This Carmen is not racially different: she is simply beautiful and sexy. The lovers' choreographed interactions are decidedly risqué for the time. What the adaptation gains in erotic energy, however, it loses in psychological motivation: bodies cannot convey inner worlds as well as words can. We only know characters in dance by their movement and their music. Interestingly, this ballet version reassigns and thus refocuses the music, giving Don José the fate theme that is Carmen's in the opera and letting him dance a solo to her "Habañera"; Carmen dies to the strains of her earlier seduction ("Je vais danser en votre honneur"), kissing her murderer. French audiences would likely have noticed these deliberate transgressions, even if they might not have noticed the excision of most of Carmen's chromatic and orientalized music. This Carmen is differently embodied, but still very much controlled by the classical ballet movements, as she is given no distinctive dance steps of her own (see Collier 1994: 94).

Matthew Bourne's "auto-erotic thriller" *The Car Man* (2001) took the embodied and sexualized body of the Carmen of the opera and divided her into a male character (Luca) and a female (Lana), both of whom seduce the Don José character (Angelo). Seville has here been transformed into Harmony, U.S.A. in the 1950s; the tobacco factory becomes an auto repair shop and a diner. *Carmen*'s sex outside of marriage may have been shocking to the 1875 bourgeois audience at the Opéra Comique in Paris, but today (or even in the 1950s?) the drifter Luca may well have to be bisexual (as he is) to get anything like the same transgressive thrill from a ballet audience.

The best-known dance adaptation-embodiment of Carmen is likely Spanish director Carlos Saura's hispanizing and "gypsifying" flamenco dance film of 1983. The late Antonio Gades choreographed and starred as Antonio in Saura's self-reflexive film about a choreographer seeking the perfect Carmen for his flamenco version of Mérimée's story. (Gades had already produced a ballet of Act II of the opera before working on the film, and afterward, he put together a suite of the dances created for the movie and toured with that show.) The film traces the development of the dance version in workshop, but we soon realize that the plot of *Carmen* is being acted out by the dancers not only on stage but also off stage. The film's most gripping moments occur when the audience cannot tell in which narrative frame the action is taking place. French critics lamented this dispersion of the narrative over two parallel plot lines: this was not *their Carmen* (see Bertrand 1983: 106). And they were right; it isn't their *Carmen* at all.

Bizet's music is present here, reworked and reinterpreted, but it is displaced from the center by music composed and played in the film by the flamenco guitarist, Paco de Lucia. Yet the operatic music reappears whenever Antonio is obsessed with the mythic creature that is Carmen. The real woman he casts is not initially a particularly good dancer, nor is she really interested in the role. In this version, she is not so much a dangerous and conniving *femme fatale* as an indifferent, sexually liberated woman. But that change determines her final fate, as she is stabbed to the rhythm of the music of the end of the opera. The real woman is as far from Antonio's obsession/illusion as Bizet's French-exotic "Spanish" music is from Spain's actual ethnic music:

as Paco points out in the film, it is impossible to dance flamenco to Carmen's "Seguidilla" until he changes the rhythm, improvising on its themes on his guitar. Yet, the often violent, always confrontational flamenco scenes could also be said to reinscribe the opera's French clichés of Spanishness: jealousy, passion, male honor, aggressive violence, and revenge. These may be somewhat different images than those offered by the French exoticism of the Gustave Doré engravings of Spain that we see Antonio examining at the start of the film, but clichés they potentially remain nonetheless.

Yet Spanish critics saw the film as removing the French excrescences from an essentially Spanish character and making dance the perfect articulation of Carmen's passion (see Bertrand 1983: 106). It may be no accident that the year 1983 saw Spain enter the European Community, moving from its exoticized nineteenth-century role as alien to becoming an integral part of European culture. José Colmeiro has recently argued that Spain internalized the French or European orientalized image of itself, but reappropriated it (or indigenized it, in my terms) for the purposes of national identification. Like the gypsy in Spain, Spain in Europe could be seen as the internal other.

Of course, the renewal of interest in adapting Carmen's story in the 1980s was in large part the result of the fortuitous end of Bizet's copyright, but it may well also have had something to do with this context of European identity-seeking, as has been suggested (Gould 1996: 13). Yet Carmen's story has traveled widely and has therefore been indigenized ever since it was first *told* and, even more importantly, first *shown* in performance. When this narrative changes context—of time or place—it is both different and the same. Recognizably either the *femme fatale* or the liberated woman or sometimes both, Carmen is created again, but created anew each time. Her doubled stereotypical identification likely contributes to the ubiquity and power of her story—and its ability to survive major shifts in gender, ethnic, and racial politics. But it is also likely true that we cannot experience any adaptation of Carmen's story today without seeing it through the lenses of such contemporary themes as violence to women and ethnic or racial "othering." Evolutionary psychologists might be right that there is something biological about stories of male jealousy in terms of the theory of sexual competition (Barash and Barash 2005: 14–37), but responses to these stories are culture-specific.

That is why this particular story has changed over time and with new contexts. To return to a different use of a biological analogy, the one I began to develop at the end of Chapter 1, perhaps traveling stories can be thought of in terms of cultural selection. Like evolutionary natural selection, cultural selection is a way to account for the adaptive organization, in this case, of narratives. Like living beings, stories that adapt better than others (through mutation) to an environment survive: those of Carmen, Don Juan, Don Quijote, Robinson Crusoe, Dracula, Hamlet, and so on. In Richard Dawkins' terms, "some memes are more successful in the meme-pool than others" (1976/1989: 194). Though he is thinking of memes (his cultural parallel to genes) as ideas, I argue in the first chapter that stories qualify as well. If so, his list of the three qualities needed for high survival value is of interest to a theory of cultural adaptation. The first is clearly longevity, though it is the least significant; what is more important is fecundity. For adaptations, the sheer number of them or the proven appeal across cultures might qualify as evidence of this quality. The third is "copying-fidelity" (194), but even Dawkins admits that in a cultural context copying means changing with each repetition, whether deliberate or not (194–95). For an adaptation to be experienced *as an adaptation*, recognition of the story has to be possible: some copying-fidelity is needed, in fact, precisely because of the changes across media and contexts.

Natural selection is both conservative and dynamic; it involves both stabilizing and mutating. In short, it is all about propagating genes into future generations, identical in part, yet different. So too with cultural selection in the form of narrative adaptation—defined as theme and variation, repetition with modification. Also significant for the cultural adaptation of stories is the fact that "[s]election favours memes that exploit their cultural environment to their own advantage" (199). Each newly indigenized version of a story competes—as do genes—but this time for audience attention, for time on radio or television or for space on bookshelves. But each adapts to its new environment and exploits it, and the story lives on, through its "offspring"—the same and yet not.

6

FINAL QUESTIONS

[L]ovingly ripped off from the motion picture, *Monty Python and the Holy Grail.*

—Mike Nichols, about *Monty Python's Spamalot*

I begin the end of this book with two words from this epigraph: "lovingly" and "ripped off." Their mixture of affection and sense of transgression or even guilt captures well the dichotomy about adaptation with which *A Theory of Adaptation* opened: familiarity and contempt, ubiquity and denigration. Yet, as we have seen, multiple versions of a story in fact exist laterally, not vertically: adaptations are derived from, ripped off from, but are not derivative or second-rate. In offering some answers to the basic questions of the *what, who, why, how, where,* and *when* of both adaptation and this ambivalent evaluation of it as product and as process, this book invariably has provoked many new questions in turn. By way of conclusion, this chapter explores two questions that it raises for me.

What Is *Not* an Adaptation?

In answer to this question, defining an adaptation as an extended, deliberate, announced revisitation of a particular work of art does manage to provide some limits: short intertextual allusions to other works or bits of sampled music would not be included. But parodies would, and indeed parody is an ironic subset of adaptation, whether a change in medium is involved or not. After all, not every adaptation is necessarily a remediation, as we have seen. Robert Lepage's *Elsinore* (1995), an adaptation of part of Shakespeare's *Hamlet*, is still a stage play, even though a one-man, technologically driven performance. In *Foe* (1986) J.M. Coetzee adapts Daniel Defoe's 1719 novel about Robinson Crusoe, but again it is in novel form. Rex Ingram's 1921 film about the First World War, *Four Horsemen of the Apocalypse*, was remade by Vincente Minelli in 1961, substituting the Second World War, but both were films. Remakes are invariably adaptations because of changes in context. So not all adaptations necessarily involve a shift of medium or mode of engagement, though many do.

In his book, *The Fluid Text: A Theory of Revision and Editing for Book and Screen* (2002), John Bryant argues that no text is a fixed thing: there are always a variety of manuscript versions, revisions, and different print editions (1–2). In a parallel sense, live performance works are likewise fluid in that no two productions of one printed play text or musical score, or even two performances of the same production, will be alike. But there is a break between the kinds of fluidity determined by (a) the production process (writing, editing, publishing, and performing) and (b) those created by reception, by people who "materially alter texts" (7), who censor, translate, bowdlerize (3), and adapt them further. Although Bryant is interested in these latter changes primarily as "part of the energy" of the initial text (62), I am more intrigued both by the process of "cultural revision" (93) itself and by where these reception-generated changes fit along a continuum of fluid relationships between prior works and later—and lateral—revisitations of them.

The production-oriented elements of fluidity are clear in all three modes of engagement: Bryant's manuscripts, revisions, and editions are examples in the mode of telling; in a showing mode, we find those different productions of a play or musical; in the participatory mode, there are the various hypertextual possibilities created by interactive fiction creators. As we move along the reception continuum itself, however, we move from this production focus to a re-production one, as receivers begin to refashion the initial works.

At one end, we find those forms in which fidelity to the prior work is a theoretical ideal, even if a practical impossibility: (1) literary translations, which are, in fact, inevitably refractions of the aesthetic and even ideological expectations of their new audience (Lefevre 1982: 17), or (2) transcriptions of orchestral music for piano, which cannot help altering the relationship between the public and the private (T. Christensen 1999: 256). Next come forms like condensations and bowdlerizations or censorings in which the changes are obvious, deliberate, and in some way restrictive. Next along the continuum we find what Peter Rabinowitz calls "retellings" of familiar tales and "revisions" of popular ones (1980: 247–48). This is the realm of adaptation proper in all three modes of engagement, but parodies too find a place here as ironic adaptations. Here stories are both reinterpreted and rerelated.

At the other end of the continuum, but still part of this system of relations among works and thus part of a system of diffusion, are a whole series of spin-offs—and not only in the commercial sense of the term. A film like *Play It Again, Sam* (1972) that offers an overt and critical commentary on another prior film (in this case, *Casablanca* [1942]) finds a place here, but so too do academic criticism and reviews of a work. This is also the space of sequels and prequels, what Rabinowitz calls "expansions" (1980: 248–49), and of fan zines and slash fiction. There are some hybrid cases, of course. The television series of *Buffy the Vampire Slayer* (first aired in 1997) is ostensibly a sequel to the 1992 film written by Joss Whedon and directed by Fran Rubel Kuzui. But its first season, in fact, adapts parts of the film, adding new characters but keeping the same story elements. This "expansions" end of the continuum is not where videogames based on films appear—for they are adaptations in their own right. But it is where we find the Titania, Queen of Fairies, Barbie doll, inspired by the ballet of *A Midsummer Night's Dream*, or the Galadriel Barbie and Legolas Ken, inspired by *The Lord of the Rings* movies.

A continuum model has the advantage of offering a way to think about various responses to a prior story; it positions adaptations specifically as (re-) interpretations and (re-) creations. Because I have included historical accounts as possible prior stories, however, I am left with still other questions: for instance, would a museum exhibit be an adaptation? Museum professionals variously see themselves as collectors, scholar-researchers, educators, conservators, money-making entertainers, or consultants with stakeholders in a community. But are they also adapters? A museum exhibit takes material objects from the past and recontextualizes them within a historical narrative. Arguably, it is an extended interpretive and creative engagement with a past history. But does the audience experience it as such; that is, in a palimpsestic way? Or to use another metaphor developed for adaptation by Katie Kodat, does a museum exhibit provide the doubled experience of the "eidetic image," that after-image that is a kind of mental reviewing of an image that has passed (2005: 487): "The retained image is often experienced as something of a complementary 'negative' of the original image, in that there are common properties shared by both the original and its ghost (usually shape), but also clear differences (usually color)" (486). By analogy, adaptations do allow this kind of retention, but do museum exhibits? I am not convinced that the pleasure of the audience in this case relies on the "palimpsestuousness" of the experience, on the oscillation between a past image and a present one. And, in the end, it is the audience who must experience the adaptation *as an adaptation*.

What Is the Appeal of Adaptations?

I come back to this question after raising it in a number of contexts in this book, for it continues to fascinate me, especially in light of all the negative rhetoric expended on adaptation as both a product and a process. Obviously the audience for adaptations is enormous: it is not made up only of preschoolers who adore going to see mega-adaptations of children's books (*Noddy Live!* [2004]) in vast arenas. Adults are just as addicted to what have been called "sagas"—narratives like *Star Wars* or *Star Trek* that span several media (film, TV, comics, novels) and both retell and extend popular stories. George Steiner may be correct when he says that "economy of invention" is a human trait, and thus that it is "distinctly possible that the mechanics of theme and variation, essential to music, are incised also in language and representation" (1995: 14). We find a story we like and then do variations on it through adaptation. But because each adaptation must also stand on its own, separate from the palimpsestic pleasures of doubled experience, it does not lose its Benjaminian aura. It is not a copy in any mode of reproduction, mechanical or otherwise. It is repetition but without replication, bringing together the comfort of ritual and recognition with the delight of surprise and novelty. *As adaptation*, it involves both memory and change, persistence and variation.

In *The Shape of Time: Remarks on the History of Things*, George Kubler remarks that the "antipodes of the human experience of time are exact repetition, which is onerous, and unfettered variation, which is chaotic" (1962: 63). It strikes me that the combination of the two extremes in adaptations may explain part of their appeal. Kubler claims that "[h]uman desires in every present instance are torn between the replica and the invention, between the desire to return to the known pattern, and the desire to escape it by a new variation" (1962: 72). Adaptations fulfill both desires at once. Although Kubler does not address adaptations directly, he does talk about something he calls a relay: "The relay transmits a composite signal, composed only in part of the message as it was received, and in part of impulses contributed by the relay itself" (22). This is why replications—like adaptations—are never without variations.

On an experiential level as well, the conservative comfort of familiarity is countered by the unpredictable pleasure in difference—for both creator and audience. Building upon Walter Benjamin's 1933 essay, "On the Mimetic Faculty," Michael Taussig has argued that the human compulsion to behave *like* something or someone else marks a paradoxical capacity to be Other (1993: 19). His anthropological study of the power of replication is focused on how a society can maintain sameness through alterity (129). He defines the mimetic faculty as "the faculty to copy, imitate, make models, explore difference, yield into and become Other" (xiii).

What we might, by analogy, call the adaptive faculty is the ability to repeat without copying, to embed difference in similarity, to be at once both self and Other. Adapters choose to use this ability for any number of complicated reasons, as we have seen. Sometimes their cultural contexts make exercising this adaptive faculty easy: Ousmane Sembène is respected as a filmmaker in Africa because he is considered a modern-day *griot* or oral storyteller, using film to retell traditional stories (Cham 2005: 297–98). Sometimes, on the contrary, context can create real challenges: how does one adapt a written text into film images in a culture where "the very act of visual representation has been enmeshed in taboos and prohibition" (Shohat 2004: 23)? It is not that adaptations are not made within the Judeo-Islamic traditions, but in dealing especially with religious texts or figures, complications obviously do arise. Witness the aftermath of the publication of Salman Rushdie's *The Satanic Verses* (1988) or Danish cartoons (2005–2006).

We have seen that adaptations disrupt elements like priority and authority (e.g., if we experience the adapted text *after* the adaptation). But they can also destabilize both formal and cultural identity and thereby shift power relations. Could that subversive potential also be part of the appeal of adapting for adapters and audiences alike? In 1818, Percy Bysshe Shelley was attracted to a historical story told in a manuscript he found about a Roman woman, Beatrice Cenci, who was raped by her wicked father, conspired to have him killed, and, when she succeeded, was arrested and then beheaded in 1599 by papal decree. The next year, on a visit to Rome, Shelley saw a portrait of Beatrice at the Palazzo Colonna. Haunted by both the gloomy architecture of the building and the image of the young woman, he wrote his verse play *The Cenci*—a kind of historical protest play against both a private tragedy (incest and murder) and a public scandal (gender inequities, despotic authority). Several hundred years later, while studying for his doctoral examinations in English literature, a young African Canadian poet read this adaptation, responded to its themes of gendered injustice, and decided to adapt it anew, as it turned out, into both a verse play and an opera libretto. But he filtered it through another text: an abolitionist slave narrative called *Celia, a Slave*. Like the story of Beatrice Cenci, this slave narrative was a true story of an oppressed woman brutalized, in this case, by a slave master, whom she kills. With this added layer of adaptation, race was added to the gender politics of Shelley's play.

Beatrice Chancy, the adaptation by George Elliott Clarke (published in 1999), willfully grafts together history and literature, on the one hand, and an American slave narrative and a British play, on the other. It performs this graft in order to show on stage a story about the often ignored history of slavery in Canada. It breaks the conventions of both its adapted genres: there is none of their shared linguistic decorum or off-stage violence. The language of Clarke's adaptation ranges from the brutal and frank to the biblical and soaring; its dramatic action includes powerfully enacted on-stage scenes of rape and torture. The text is set to music (by James Rolfe) that adapts the spirituals sung by slaves in eastern Canada at the time (1802), eighteenth-century Scottish reels, and also blues and gospel songs. The music in fact fuses black and white traditions in a way the text refuses: in the adaptation, as in real life, Beatrice is hanged for killing her abusive father and we are not allowed to forget that fact. Power too can be adapted—that is, destabilized, disrupted—and again both memory and mutation, theme and variation are at work. Return need not be regression.

Adapters are obviously attracted to their task for all kinds of reasons, as we have seen. In other words, the appeal of adaptation cannot simply be explained or explained away by economic gain, however real that may be as a motive for some adapters. For audiences, that is the *result* of the appeal, not the cause. Because adaptations usually revisit stories, however, perhaps we should look to theories of narrative to explain the popularity of adaptations. There are basically two different ways of thinking here: either stories are considered forms of representation and thus vary with period and culture, or they are what theorists like Marie-Laure Ryan identify as timeless cognitive models by which we make sense of our world and of human action in it (2001: 242–43). If we ask what kind of "work" adaptations do as they circulate stories among media and around the world, indigenizing them anew each time, we may find ourselves agreeing that narrative is indeed some kind of human universal: "Building shape and meaning is what we do in our stories and songs" (Chamberlin 2003: 8). But that explains the *creating* of stories, not necessarily their *repeating*—especially when we already know the ordering resolution they each offer.

J. Hillis Miller offers us one possible explanation for the repetition of stories. They affirm and reinforce basic cultural assumptions, he claims: "We need the 'same' stories over and over, then, as one of the most powerful, perhaps the most powerful, of ways to assert the basic ideology of our culture" (1995: 72). But adaptations are not simply repetition; there is always change. Of course, the desire for change, as Kubler suggests, may itself be a human universal. As Prior Walter, Tony Kushner's protagonist in *Angels in America, Part Two: Perestroika*, puts it, change is life: "We're not rocks—progress, migration, motion is ... modernity. It's animate, it's what living things do. We desire. Even if all we desire is stillness, it's still desire *for*. Even if we go faster than we should. We can't wait. And wait for what?" (1992, 1994: 132). Perhaps, then, adaptations as repetitions without replication point us simultaneously to *both* possible ways of defining narrative: as a specific cultural representation of a "basic ideology" *and* as a general human universal. In this doubling may lie yet another clue to their popularity, for popular they remain.

An adaptation is not vampiric: it does not draw the life-blood from its source and leave it dying or dead, nor is it paler than the adapted work. It may, on the contrary, keep that prior work alive, giving it an afterlife it would never have had otherwise. Yet Richard Dawkins argues that because ideas propagate themselves by imitation, they are like either malign or benign parasites. When we plant a fertile idea in someone's mind, he says, we turn it into a vehicle for the idea's propagation "in just the way that a virus may parasitize the genetic mechanism of a host cell" (1976/1989: 192). Is this how some stories propagate? Adaptations reveal that stories do seem to have what he calls either high or low "infective power" (193).

Suggestive as this parasitic analogy can be (see Stam 2005b: 3), I prefer to return instead to the other biological parallel I have been suggesting throughout this book: adaptation is how stories evolve and mutate to fit new times and different places. Dawkins' postulating of the existence of those units of imitation or cultural transmission he calls "memes" seems to me to be potentially very productive. Memes are not high-fidelity replicators: they change with time, for meme transmission is subject to constant mutation. Stories too propagate themselves when they catch on; adaptations—as both repetition and variation—are their form of replication. Evolving by cultural selection, traveling stories adapt to local cultures, just as populations of organisms adapt to local environments.

We retell—and show again and interact anew with—stories over and over; in the process, they change with each repetition, and yet they are recognizably the same. What they are not is necessarily inferior or second-rate—or they would not have survived. Temporal precedence does not mean anything more than temporal priority. Sometimes we are willing to accept this fact, such as when it is Shakespeare who adapts Arthur Brooke's versification of Matteo Bandello's adaptation of Luigi da Porto's version of Masuccio Salernitano's story of two very young, star-crossed Italian lovers (who changed names and place of birth along the way). That awkwardly long lineage points not only to the instability of narrative identity but also to the simple but significant fact that there are precious few stories around that have not been "lovingly ripped off" from others. In the workings of the human imagination, adaptation is the norm, not the exception.

EPILOGUE

In order to understand how adaptation is perceived and practiced today—that is, since the 2006 publication of this book—we need to examine the forces that have changed culture—and more importantly, entertainment—in the intervening years. Since 2006, the global entertainment and media industries have seen seismic shifts with the emergence of new platforms, modes of interaction, and the changing production design of entertainment properties.

Prominent amongst these changes has been the rise of the social web with the increasing popularity of participatory media, blogs, and wikis, the increase in smart mobile devices that support these interactions, the viral dissemination of DIY content online through platforms such as YouTube, Facebook and Twitter, and the revolution of touch-screen interfaces. Because of these online and mobile platforms, audiences no longer function as regional markets; instead, audiences are potentially global, connected, and responsive, as demonstrated in the speed of transmission of viral or, as media scholar Henry Jenkins recast it, spreadable content (2009). Consider that an adaptation like the Volkswagen *Darth Vader Super Bowl* (2011) advertisement, *The Force*, has at the time of writing been viewed over 51 million times, not on television, but on YouTube, a free online platform. Or that Patrick Boivin's (2010) short video adaptation of *Iron Man*, *Iron Baby*, has been viewed over 11 million times on YouTube. While the first is the product of a global brand, the latter is not and the phenomenal reach and rapid spread of online content remains a wild card for studios and marketers. As adaptations are often undertaken to capitalize on an existing fan base (the readers of the *Harry Potter* books are a guaranteed audience for the films; the boys who play with *Transformers* will likely see the movies), tapping into the marketing potential of existing fan communities on free online platforms is a pivotal goal of industry today. The connectivity of the web has fostered a paradigm shift in the mobilization of global communities of interest, able to act and react instantly and en masse to shared delights and perceived injustices. The availability and low cost of high quality video and editing tools, combined with participatory media has fostered a shift from DIY to DIO (Do It with Others), and has had an impact on how adaptations are produced, controlled, and distributed.

Just to give a sense of the scale of what a networked fan community means in 2012, consider the following:

- Facebook's 2012 "population" of 800+ million makes it the third largest "nation" behind China and India at 1,314 billion and 1,224 billion respectively;
- People on Facebook install 20 million "apps" every day;
- Launched 2006, Twitter has over 300 million users in 2012;
- Google+ was the fastest social network to reach 10 million users at 16 days; Twitter took 780 days and Facebook 852 days.

(Bullas 2011).

Because of the rapid rate of adoption of social networking platforms, media conglomerates are scrambling to utilize these new modes of communication and to monetize content wherever possible. Instead of controlling the channels of production and distribution, industry giants operate in a space where the platforms of communication change in rapid cycles of adoption and obsolescence, where audiences remix and extend given properties creating new forms of intermedial adaptation, and where disruptive innovations launched by unknowns can alter existing business models without warning (see the scramble to use Pinterest.com). According to *Business Insider Magazine* (Davis 2011), Facebook is the most important tool in movie marketing, and major studios' forays onto this social platform lack templates for success. In today's hybrid media landscape, where fans expect films and TV series to have online components, Hutcheon's closing question of "What Is Not an Adaptation?" is even more relevant now. As her work demonstrates, if we understand adaptation as a transcoding process that encompasses recreations, remakes, remediations, revisions, parodies, reinventions, reinterpretations, expansions, and extensions (Hutcheon 2006: 171), adaptation considered on a continuum has been further complicated by the emergence of transmedia as a media conglomerate production strategy.

To clarify at the outset, although there are relatively clear definitions of adaptation and transmedia and their difference, in practice untangling where the distinction lies is often difficult. In March 2010, the Producers Guild of America created the Transmedia Producers Credit and provided this statement:

> A Transmedia Narrative project or franchise must consist of three (or more) narrative storylines existing within the same fictional universe on any of the following platforms: Film, Television, Short Film, Broadband, Publishing, Comics, Animation, Mobile, Special Venues, DVD/Blu-ray/CD-ROM, Narrative Commercial and Marketing rollouts, and other technologies that may or may not currently exist. These narrative extensions are NOT the same as repurposing material from one platform to be cut or repurposed to different platforms.

(http://www.producersguild.org/?page=coc_nm#transmedia.)

A transmedia production exists across multiple platforms and discrete components understood together comprise an integrated, interconnected narrative whole, though they are encountered separately. As a design strategy, transmedia productions have to date been primarily designed as extensions of films, TV series and console games that function as the central "tent-pole" production. Oft-cited examples are *The Blair Witch Project* (1999) and the Wachowskis' *Matrix* film trilogy (1991–2003), with video games and anime shorts, and Tim Kring and NBC's series *Heroes* (2006–2010), with supplemental storylines told via graphic novels, online games, and websites.

Alternatively, transmedia projects can be designed to extend tent-pole film or TV adaptations of prior existing content where the content is recognizable from one property to the next. The new BBC version of *Sherlock Holmes* is a recent example where each episode reworked elements drawn from various Conan Doyle stories, and other online content, including blogs for Watson, Sherlock, and other characters, was created to extend the story into the digital sphere. Watson's blogging was mentioned repeatedly throughout the two seasons, as was the content posted there; shots of Watson writing his blog and of the blog website with the number of visitors were included. In addition, official Twitter accounts posted messages, though much more interesting and equally convincing are the multiple unverified as BBC accounts seemingly tweeting as characters, who have been highly active on Twitter since January 2012, exchanging witty ripostes with each other and the interested public (see Figure 1).

A purported fan video made by the BBC about Holmes (BBC 2012a; BBC 2012b) was posted on YouTube and reposted on Watson's blog. Two other videos posted by Watson, one of Moriarty's break-in to Holmes' apartment and a BBC report on the Moriarty trial and Holmes' death, were cross-posted by fans to YouTube. In breaking the fourth wall, the strategy of many alternate reality games, the BBC *Sherlock* transmedia adaptation offers an example of how Web 2.0 platforms are being used to transcode existing projects, as characters interact in real-time with users of Twitter from potentially around the globe (see Figure 2).

Arguably, if fans are behind the current active Twitter accounts (see on Twitter: @The_Whip_Hand, @_JMoriarty, @Genius_Holmes and Irene Adler's blog 2012) and not the show's writer, Steven Moffat, fans

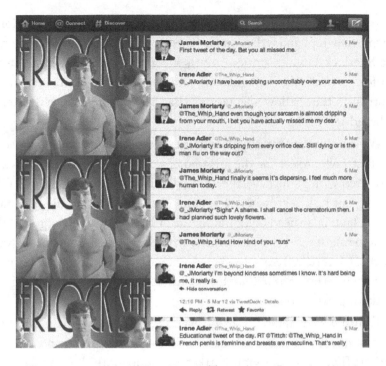

Figure 1 Exchange via @The_Whip_Hand's Twitter page. Reproduced with permission from the account holder

Figure 2 Exchange via @_JMoriarty Twitter page. Reproduced with permission from the account holder

have claimed and extended the current adaptation onto other platforms (http://thewhiphand.webs.com/). The BBC transmedia adaptation of the Sherlock Holmes stories models a compelling and effective use of platforms, audience engagement, and layered integrated content, in contrast to the shallow adaptations that drive the franchise marketing of brands.

Within this context, a mobile game or app can adapt some aspect of the tent-pole project for the affordances of a new medium. Showtime partnered with game developer Ecko Code to create *Weeds Social Club*, where your task is growing marijuana (Jackson 2011). While producer Curt Mavis (also head of digital media at Lionsgate) has suggested that the app might serve as a platform to introduce new characters or stories for the TV series, *Weeds*, the site is currently closed after a beta run. To date then, *Weeds Social Club* has been an adaptation functioning as a marketing extension.

Transmedia adaptations also exist as reworkings of the mythos and content of a given story and storyworld (see *Transformers* and *The Dark Knight: Why So Serious* viral marketing campaign). A film adaptation such as Lionsgate's *The Hunger Games* (2012) exists as the tent-pole property supporting a wider transmedia campaign currently running live on Facebook (with now over two million global fans) and other websites (http://www.thehungergamesmovie.com/index2.html). Both transmedia adaptation strategies are being used by major American production studios to connect with audiences in new ways and to monetize new content where possible. The same is true in the UK and Australia.

What further complicates the overlapping between adaptation and transmedia storytelling as distinct processes is that where unauthorized adaptation, recreation, and remixing were once viewed as infringements of copyright, a number of key players in the field of convergent media and transmedia production, Jeff Gomez and Tim Kring most prominently, have championed fan participation and fan-generated content as a welcome demonstration of fan loyalty to a given storyworld and brand. Jeff Gomez, CEO of Starlight Runner and a pivotal contributor to the establishment of the PGA Transmedia Producer credit, was promoting transmedia in 2010 as a form that would allow for the development of "robust 'story worlds' that play out across multiple media platforms" (Humphrey 2011) and that would someday soon allow fans to "touch the canon" (Gomez 2011). Less than two years later, Lionsgate announced, in February 2012, that the Cafepress online store for *The Hunger Games* merchandise would include official and fan-created designs (Sibayan 2012). Arguably, Lionsgate's inclusion of fan designs is, however, a reactive measure to the enthusiastic sharing of fan-generated content online (see Figure 3).

While the official Facebook page was launched January 2011, hardcore fans launched their own alternate reality game, PanemOctober.com, in October 2011 and registered over 55,000

Figure 3 Hunger Games fan creations – Shylah Addante on Facebook. Reproduced with permission from the account holder

players. When Lionsgate issued a cease and desist letter, the game creators changed the site name, prominently disavowed any connection to Lionsgate (Nemiroff 2011), and carried on for a number of months until the ARG shut down before completion for a variety of reasons outlined by the Gamemaster, Rowan, on Facebook (Rowan 2011). On the official site, tensions are now emerging because although the fan community is global, competitions for key roles within the fictional adapted world running on Facebook are only open to US residents (see Figure 4). Fan outrage at restricted participation is an indicator of how Lionsgate's legal protocols exist in conflict with the ethos of a Web 2.0 fan community.

What this tension reveals is that media conglomerates are now unwillingly positioned as *reactive* to the rapid ebb and flow of changing social phenomena, enabled by new technologies and platforms. Fans expect to be able to play with and adapt content and arguably, in the digital era, being a fan is demonstrated by the extent to which one

Kit Reuben Baron
I have a question for President Snow, or, if this does not concern him, whoever runs Capitol Couture and it's stylist wanted feature! I can understand why the contests to win the District Uniform and stuff were only limited to people in the US; and I was fine with that– but Capitol Couture's Stylist Wanted feature was something a WHOLE lot of people all over the world were looking forward to; and me, being the good citizen I am, just read the terms of submission for the contest. And what a surprise! You have to be a legal resident of the US to even submit an entry! I'm in Australia and have been looking forward to the stylist wanted feature ever since I missed out on becoming a) the mayor, b)the recruiter, c) winning the uniform, and d)missing out on winning tickets to the premier– and so I have put sooo much time and effort into this stylist wanted feature that I know have over 20 outfits for the females of numerous districts (not just my own which is 7) and over 15 for the males! These don't include shoes, hats, wigs, etc (which I do have as well!). So I was just wondering; for this Stylist Wanted feature(not just the first competition, but all of them), could you PLEASE make it so that people outside of the US can enter; you don't have to send over the prizes, you can keep them, because for some of us we just want to enter and possibly win!
I'd really appreciate it.
–Reuben, D7

Like · Comment · 13 hours ago · ⊛

👍 Ave Basilio likes this.

💬 View all 3 comments

Write a comment...

Figure 4 Hunger Games Outraged Fan posted February 18 2012 by Kit Reuben Baron. Reproduced with permission from the account holder

adapts and generates adapted/adaptive content. Although this partici-patory adaptation has a long history in fan culture, the reach and con-nectivity of the Internet have given fans today leverage as collaborators against those whom Jenkins terms the "prohibitionists" (2006: 134). What was once a one-way conversation controlled by authorized pro-ducers of content is now a multi-channel networked exchange between communities of fans and content producers where the expectation is that producers will respond to and accommodate fans.

An examination of the characteristics of adaptation and transmedia projects of the past six years demonstrates more overlaps and blurrings than distinctions, and while there are clear instances of different prac-tice and design at either end of the spectrum, there are many proj-ects that resist easy categorization. Fan-generated adaptations further complicate the spectrum, as some transmedia producers push for par-ticipatory content and others claim a model of authorial control. That the distinction matters is clear within the American context because the recognition of the Transmedia Producer credit vs. Film Producer is vital for many industry professionals and stakeholders. Because of the economic and professional consequences, the distinction is being debated intensely by industry professionals who are pioneering and developing transmedia practice, by academics, and in some instances, by academics who are also top tier industry professionals, such as Christy Dena, Ivan Askwith, and Geoffrey Long.

A survey of the variant interdynamics of adaptation and transme-dia as design strategies extending narrative projects/brands across media strongly supports Hutcheon's argument that adaptation can be thought of as a "system of relations among works" and "a system of diffusion" (2006: 171). Hutcheon's final questions provide a prescient framework for considering how adaptation as product and process con-tinues to evolve due to the pressure to innovate that is now demanded of global entertainment industries. This pressure is amplified because in the world of convergent media, the proven templates of traditional media are no longer adequate (screenplay, production, marketing, dis-tribution). The bind for traditional media producers is that even if there were a reliable template for multi-platform production, the repetition of any established or well-known model would be perceived as a failure to innovate. Within this context, innovation and change are givens in that industries are forced to respond to new platforms, technologies and new social networking phenomena and to an audience that is consistently described as suffering from attention deficit disorder.

This Epilogue challenges that assertion, as the number of examples of audiences devoted to ongoing multi-platform adaptive projects such as *Star Wars*, *Harry Potter*, and now *The Hunger Games* suggests that the flaw is not in technology-induced ADHD but rather in the quality of the content and the experience designed around that content. What a survey of the last six years reveals is a pattern of intermedial and intra-medial adaptation of beloved projects through authorized or intellectual property-protected iterations and the parallel claiming, co-optation, and adaptation of content by fans, regardless of copyright. Jenkins' 2006 work, *Convergence Culture: Where Old and New Media Collide*, examined fan activities in the context of convergent culture and mapped in great detail fan engagement with the *Star Wars* brand through fan fiction and fan films. In order to understand how radical recent industry shifts actually are, the story of *Raiders: The Adaptation* illustrates what was once the status quo.

In 1982, three twelve-year-old boys set out to make a shot-by-shot remake/adaptation of Steven Spielberg's *Raiders of the Lost Ark* (produced by Lucasfilm). It took them seven years to complete and $5,000 to make. *Raiders: The Adaptation* was screened once to 200 friends and family in "an auditorium at a local Coca-Cola plant in 1989" (Silverman 2007; Windolf 2004; *TheRaider.net*). The film was shelved for almost fifteen years, until *Ain't It Cool News* guru, Harry Knowles, screened it as his *Butt-numb-a-thon* festival where it was an instant hit (http://en.wikipedia.org/wiki/Butt-numb-a-thon; Silverman 2007; Windolf 2004). The filmmakers were suddenly on Spielberg's radar and invited to his ranch. Because of the film's "peculiar legal situation involving copyright" (Verschuere 2005) and despite Spielberg's favorable response, the film has had only a handful of screenings since, and finding a DVD or viewing it legally is still a challenge. Although remarkable in terms of the seven-year effort on the part of the filmmakers, the disappearance of the fan film because of possible legal prosecution is entirely typical of fan-film and -video adaptations in the last century. From then to now, however, fans have claimed the web and YouTube as distribution platforms to connect with a global community of like-minded passionate devotees.

Star Wars' rollercoaster relationship with fans provides one of the longest examples of the tension between what Lawrence Lessig (2008) has termed commercial and sharing economies, a tension that repeatedly crystallizes as a fight between fans and George Lucas (and Lucasfilm) for ownership of the content and as a struggle over the issue of fidelity to the original content (that is, as it was released). Adaptation as a process and product factors in at different moments and in different ways. What fans of *Star Wars* have claimed is a right to play with the content, adapt it via fan-fiction and fan-film remakes; they also expect that Lucas will respect fan loyalty to the brand. In this tale of contested rereleases, adaptations, and extensions, questions of intellectual property (IP) have been complicated by the perceived and demonstrated investment of fans in an immersive story world that has been at issue for over 30 years (Ryan 2011).

Lucas's early decision to trade a sizable director's fee for all sequel rights and merchandizing rights was a stroke of genius in terms of retaining commercial IP for a franchise brand. What Lucas hadn't envisioned (and why should he have?) was how proprietorial fans would become (and remain) over the storyworld, its characters, and the films as artifacts. As a mother of two boys and wife of a long-time *Star Wars* fan said to me recently, "You outgrow *Sponge Bob*. You don't outgrow *Star Wars*." In 1981, tensions peaked over fan fiction that depicted *Star Wars* characters in "X-Rated pornographic situations," an understandable hot spot for a PG brand (the original letter is archived on *Fanlore*: n.d.). As digital cameras made film production more accessible, fans created numerous homage and parody films, the history of which Henry Jenkins details in *Convergence Culture*. The merchandising generated by the *Star Wars* franchise maintained a constant brand presence and acted as a bridge between film releases and as Jenkins notes, often provided the materials used in fan films (146). In 2000, with fan remakes and extensions now in the digital sphere, Lucasfilm set up a web space offering to host fan pages. Contained within the Terms of Service was this notification:

The creation of derivative works based on or derived from the Star Wars Properties, including, but not limited to, products, services, fonts, icons, link buttons, wallpaper, desktop themes, online postcards and greeting cards and unlicensed merchandise (whether sold, bartered or given away) is expressly prohibited. If despite these Terms of Service you do create any derivative works based on or derived from the Star Wars Properties, such derivative works shall be deemed and shall remain the property of Lucasfilm Ltd. in perpetuity.

(quoted in Lessig 2008: 245)

As one blogger pointed out at the time (Durack 2000), Lucasfilm refrained from including fan fiction explicitly as a mode of transcoding, likely avoiding a greater firestorm. In 2007, Lucasfilm launched a mash-up site to host the ongoing stream of fan-generated content and again claimed IP over all content uploaded to the site (Parrish 2011; Murphy 2009). Lessig (2008) has repeatedly called for a revamping of copyright laws to reflect the hybrid sharing and commercial economy that propels much of consumer culture today. His harshest criticism in his detailing of the *Star Wars* saga is for Lucasfilm's IP claim over all original content, music, and images that fans might include with their video remakes. Ironically, tension again erupted over changes made by Lucas to the original films when rereleased, first on DVD and then in 2011 on Blu-Ray. In *Return of the Jedi*, at the moment in which the Emperor electrocutes Luke, Darth Vader's original ambiguous silence was replaced by his cry "Nooooo," transferred from *Revenge of the Sith*. Online fans debated at length the impact of this addition, with one fan stating that this change *"genuinely lessened the movies"* (Bricken 2011, italics in original; see also Faraci 2011; Miller 2011; Anders 2011). While Lucas's alterations of the original do not constitute adaptation, what is most striking about the extreme negative responses by fans to his changes (which are extensively catalogued online: Starwars.wikia. com; M. Mitchell n.d.) is that they reveal the depth of fan loyalty to the original releases and the perceived value of a fidelity to that original content and experience that Lucas, though the creator, is seen as having betrayed. Yet, as Lucas points out (Block 2012), there are numerous versions of Ridley Scott's *Bladerunner* that exist unproblematically:

"most movies when they release them they make changes. But somehow, when I make the slightest change, everybody thinks it's the end of the world." (Block 2012; see Lucas' statement to Congress archived on the website, *Saving* Star Wars 2010.)

Where this story of fan devotion/fidelity intersects again with questions of adaptation is in the phenomenon of fan remakes of *Star Wars*, where paradoxically, fidelity is desired and simultaneously unimportant. While there are now decades of fan-film remakes, parodies, and extensions, one recent remake is noteworthy for the global crowdsourcing of the content and for the recognition the production achieved in the mainstream. This collaborative adaptation marks a key break between the past, as illustrated by the fate of *Raiders: The Adaptation*, and the contemporary empowerment of fans via the social web and Web 2.0 technologies.

In July 2009, Casey Pugh invited a global audience to help remake the original *Star Wars Episode IV: A New Hope* in the form of 473 15-second clips to be posted to the film adaptation's website (http://www.starwarsuncut.com/). Pugh's project was not the first shot-by-shot remake of *Star Wars: A New Hope*, for *Toy Wars* (2002) remade the film with movie action figures (Jenkins 2006: 147). Fans from roughly 20 countries remade clips in a wide range of styles, including live action, multiple styles of animation and anime, puppets, LEGO, grindhouse, Yellow Submarine-style, stop motion—the list goes on. There was no attempt at continuity in style, location, or actors and as multiple versions were uploaded for individual clips, fans voted on what version would make the final cut. The result is a glorious, hilarious testimony to fan devotion and enthusiasm for playing with the "original" content, and to adaptation as an act of communal ownership of a story deeply embedded in the consciousnesses of multiple generations across the globe. Pugh's crowdsourced adaptation, "an official, perfectly imperfect shadow version of the original film" (Lloyd 2010), was posted live online as *Star Wars Uncut* in August 2010, and then went on to receive an Emmy for "outstanding creative achievement in interactive media" (Stelter 2010). Although restricted by an NDA, Pugh has stated that Lucasfilm supports the project and there appears to be the potential for future cinema release. The film can be viewed in full on YouTube and on the website (http://www.youtube.com/watch?v=7ezeYJUz-84; http://www.starwarsuncut.com/watch).

What the easy accessibility of Pugh and his collaborators' adaptation demonstrates is that media conglomerates no longer own the channels of production and distribution in the way that they did in the last century. Further, control of IP and thus adaptation is no longer a straightforward legal cease and desist affair, leading to prosecution. Instead, fans can and do mobilize in response to what they perceive as betrayals of their loyalty. Unlike *Raiders: The Adaptation*, *Star Wars Uncut* was made in the very public space of the Internet; production and editing were crowdsourced, meaning that the community was interconnected throughout the process. Pugh intentionally took advantage of the connectivity of the web to create an aggregate work that is the logical extension of fan-generated content posted on YouTube since its 2005 launch. The connectivity of the net has circumvented what fifteen years ago would have been a cease and desist action against copyright infringement. What *Star Wars Uncut* has achieved is a middle ground between what Grant McCracken (2010) defines as the economies of scarcity and plenitude. In the first, the corporation retains complete control (he cites Disney), believing value and revenue depend on the scarcity of content, and in the second, corporations realize they "have a right to retain copyright but they have an interest in releasing it" (McCracken 2010; quoted in Jenkins 2006: 158).

The award of the Emmy to *Star Wars Uncut* acknowledges two important shifts: the significance of participatory media in the production of what has been called the "greatest viral video ever" (Seitz 2012) and thus the profound shift to an increasingly connected and participatory global audience of "prosumers" (Suciu 2007; Gunelius 2010) and, second, the value of a phenomenon called "sweding" as a promotional strategy for mainstream brands. While *Star Wars Uncut* has been called the most extensive collaborative example of "sweding" to date (Drumb 2008), as *Raiders: An Adaptation* shows, examples exist well before the era of digital cameras and the social web. "Sweding" offers another kind of fan adaptation defined by filmmaker Michel Gondry as remaking a feature film on zero budget. In these instances, the replication of and adherence to the model of a pre-existing work in the same medium is an obvious goal. In this space, fan adaptations are no longer use-fully viewed as copyright infraction, as they are more rightfully under-stood as engagement with and promotion of a prior project. To whit, if your production has not generated fan adaptations, what are you doing wrong?

One other example demonstrates how digital technologies are empowering fans and how disruptive of industry fans now are. David Brisbin (2009), production designer on *The Twilight Saga: New Moon*, described how fans were posting images and mash-up trailers of real footage being shot on location in Rome and Montepulciano on YouTube, often within 24 hours of scenes being shot (xXAliceinthe darkXx: 2009; NASIONAL002: 2009; TWILIGHTxx00xx: 2009). As he notes, "before our negative was processed in Rome, the Art Department in Vancouver watched a version of the scene on YouTube. Someone had edited a montage of still photos, shot through hidden windows, between extras and from nooks and crannies of the piazza, into a rather effective little movie scene" (57). Recognizing the deep emotional investment fans had with the *Twilight* brand, and that leaked images and videos were a promotional boost to greater fan excitement about the upcoming film adaptation, the studios chose not to try to restrict the release of content.

Transmedia designer and scholar Christy Dena (2009) offers one of the few sustained critical inquiries into the relationship of adapta-tion and transmedia practices to date. She traces the impact of Jenkins' statement that "a simple adaptation may be 'transmedia' but it is not 'transmedia storytelling' because it is simply re-presenting an existing story rather than expanding and annotating the fictional world" (Jen-kins 2009b; quoted in Dena 95). In her reading via Hutcheon, a more complex understanding of adaptations as both products and process complicate this simplistic binary, as any adaptation that adds backstory, character- or world-development has added something new to a prior version(s) (Hutcheon 2006: 18–21; 118–19; cited in Dena 2009: 151). Drawing on Hutcheon's thinking on "the desire for repetition," Dena views this impulse as comparable to the motivations of transmedia cre-ators with the distinction that transmedia producers may transmedi-ate content from one platform or medium to others with very different audiences in mind (155). For Dena, the paradigm shift of designing transmedia works is that new projects are conceived as having multiple points of entry via unique elements of interconnected content, rather than one channel of access, as in a movie, graphic novel, or TV series. In illuminating transmedia practices, Dena's emphasis is on the fact that adaptation is not to be usefully "understood by an end-product trait such as expansion" (160). Rather, adaptation is one of a number of skills to be employed in the development of transmedia content across platforms.

Dena's perceptive understanding of the complex relationship of adaptation and transmedia is not as fully realized in contemporary debates by industry leaders. An April 2011 blog post by transmedia and experience designer, Brooke Thomson, generated a discussion thread that reveals the dissensus amongst key transmedia producers on the distinctions between adaptive practices and transmedia production. Her initiating post responded to a rant against Hollywood's upcoming franchised adaptations, and the promotion of rehashing known "rubberized action figure[s]" (Harris 2011) as transmedia storytelling in the summer's latest blockbusters. At issue was how to separate existing brand-building practices from transmedia campaigns? Steve Peters, of No Mimes Media and 4th Wall Entertainment (the agency behind the *Why So Serious?* viral campaign), made a distinction between "franchising, stunt marketing, brand building or adaptations," in contrast to transmedia as "the *new* types of *real* storytelling that we're seeing now." Responding next was Mike Monello, co-producer of *The Blair Witch Trials* (which Forbes named the Best Ever Social Media campaign in 2010) and co-founder of the marketing agency, Campfire NYC, which has received international recognition and won numerous awards for designing transmedia extensions of content for the TV series adaptations of *Trueblood* and *Game of Thrones*. For *Trueblood*, Campfire NYC set up vending machines around Manhattan, selling bottles purporting to be of Trueblood, the vampire substitute beverage. Monello challenged Peters' distinction: "Above you claim that Transmedia is being used to describe franchising, brand-building, and stunt marketing. If 'transmedia' is the movement of story across all kinds of media, then can you specifically explain the differences? Was *The Dark Knight* 'transmdia' [sic] or was it brand building, or perhaps more accurately an extensive 'advergame?' ... How thin is the line?" Campfire NYC's adaptations for HBO'S *Game of Thrones* foregrounded the distinctive characteristics of the physical world of Westeros in creating promotional wooden cases filled with vials of Westeros scents (see Figure 5) and during SXSW, food carts with a uniquely created menu of dishes purporting to be from the world's different regions (Anderson 2011). Brian Clark, founder and CEO of GMD Studios, added a further spin arguing that "[i]f it [transmedia] was developed AFTER the original IP, it's something else. It might be adaptation. It might be an extension. And it might use transmedia methods. But it isn't transmedia storytelling." Clarke's distinction recategorized many "canonical" transmedia projects and alternate reality games as "marketing utilizing transmedia tactics."

At issue throughout this long discussion thread are a series of perceived oppositions: adaptation vs. transmedia storytelling; franchise transmedia vs. transmedia storytelling (also parsed by Carrie Cutfort-Young as merchandising/objects vs. experience, which becomes problematic with game adaptations); original authorial/intentional transmedia productions vs. later add-on extensions; and in one response, franchising transmedia vs. participatory transmedia, where users/consumers are invited to participate in the story. Adaptation is

Figure 5 Campfire NYC photos of Westeros scent boxes. Reproduced under Creative Commons license

(still) positioned consistently as a lesser, more simplistic mode of reworking content, and Hollywood's ongoing catalogue of big budget adaptations of prior works with slim or juvenile content would certainly support this view.

More recently, Claire Parody's "Franchising/Adaptation" (2011) offers insights on the "particularities of adaptation in the context of the modern fictional franchise" (212). Building on what she terms Hutcheon's notion of "adaptive intertextuality," Parody teases out the logic whereby an adaptation of a franchise brand can function as a "specific franchise installment," yet exist in an intertextual relationship with other content generated within "the entire franchise multitext." Franchise adaptation across platforms can produce "chains of remediation" linked by tenuous though recognizable adaptations of "its most immediate predecessor," re-visioning the source content (212). Parody's articulation of the problems encountered in franchise adaptations accords with the criticism noted above: "Where franchise production is diasporic and development un-coordinated, canonicity, continuity, and authority become problematic concepts, constantly re-negotiated; many franchise multitexts come together as an 'array' (Collins 1991: 164; quoted in Parody 2011: 212) of versions, origin points, co-existing, overlapping, and contradictory narrative realities, rather than a master narrative and stable textual corpus". The strong expert consensus on transmedia design is that all components are narratively connected in an intentional way, and many, as noted above, would likely take issue with Parody's statement that "[f]ranchise storytelling is first and foremost transmedia practice" (213).

Parody positions world building and brand building as separate components of franchise adaptations, yet the trend in conferences, festivals, and symposia, from 2010–2012, is that these components are now viewed as inseparable, largely because of the promotion of world building as an essential component of developing a brand identity that can be extended across platforms (Gomez 2010). World (or what Hutcheon calls "heterocosm") adaptation is arguably one of the most powerful immersive adaptation strategies in use today, as the ongoing enthusiasm over J.K. Rowling's *Pottermore*, the online multi-player game and world extension, demonstrates. As *Pottermore* is still in invitation-only beta mode, the details of how the world of Harry Potter has been adapted have not been widely disseminated, though it's known that new text will be made available through the site and that those playing work their way both through the books, as interactive experiences, and through a virtual Hogwarts education in wizardry. Considered in the context of adaptation studies, *Pottermore* is an adaptation as remediation and extension, a transmedia world-building experience, and a franchise that will sell more books and merchandise, as the Pottermore Shop is slated to open soon for eBook sales (*Pottermore Insider* 2011).

While *Pottermore* exists within the canon of Rowling's imagined world, The Harry Potter Alliance is a unique example of fan adaptation for social change in the real world. Founded in 2005 by Andrew Slack, the HPA is a global activist organization committed to fighting "the Dark Arts in the real world" through interventions based on the values expressed by Rowling's characters (DeCanio 2012). The HPA has worked to raise awareness of the crisis in Darfur and partnered with Oxfam to fundraise for Haiti after the 2010 earthquake. An ongoing campaign calls on Warner Bros to use Fair Trade cocoa beans for the Potter branded chocolates it sells. As a counter move, the HPA has now created its own line of fair trade chocolate frogs (see Figure 6).

Figure 6 HPA Chocolate Frogs. Reproduced with permission from The Harry Potter Alliance

The HPA response to Warner Bros' cease and desist letters (posted online) is a testimony to the perceived changed relationship fans have with proprietorial content:

> **Now the tables have turned.** Warner Brothers may legally own the copyright to Harry Potter but we have something better – we own the love and bravery of Harry's name. Because we have loved and been changed by these stories, because we used their inspiration to change the world, Harry's name belongs to us.
>
> **SEND WARNER BROTHERS A CEASE AND DESIST LETTER.**
> Use our letter or fill in text on your own to remind them that without our love of Harry and our dedication to the stories, they would not have movies or theme parks. Their empire is built on our love of Harry Potter and it's time that we take a stand in the name of our hero.
>
>

**(http://thehpalliance.org/action/campaigns/nihn/
cease-and-desist-letter/, bold in the original)**

The HPA's identification and transcoding of essential values as a basis for adaptation aligns with the practice of one of the leading transmedia producers today. Jeff Gomez has described the process his company, Starlight Runner, takes to creating a transmedia story-bible and adapting a known brand. Speaking of his company's contributions to the adaptation and redevelopment of *Transformers* for transmedia development, Gomez's team started with a thorough survey of all media components produced as part of the *Transformers* franchise for the duration of its nearly 30-year history. Through this process, they identified key recurrent patterns and storylines and considered these in terms of their derivation from archetypal myths across cultures. In the end, Starlight Runner worked with brand owner Hasbro to recognize the essence of the *Transformers* narrative as being aligned with the kind of duality found in such transformational belief systems as Taoism. The narrative journey found in the best of this wealth of content, and perhaps most importantly in the toy-play itself (small-to-big, ignorance-to-enlightenment, novice-to-mastery), then became the foundation upon which the transmedia bible was written, mapping potential transmedia story arcs into the future (Gomez email exchange with author, 24 February 2012).

The affordances of the web and social networking platforms for viewing, remixing, sharing, and interacting with content include, in the examples of official and fan adaptations discussed so far, numerous successful examples, if one bases success on popularity, longevity, and reach of dissemination. The adaptation of almost anything else into a game is, as previously discussed by Hutcheon, much more challenging. A scan of the top 10 console games, from year to year or of all time, consistently shows original titles rather than adaptations (http://www. filibustercartoons.com/games.htm). The handful of best-selling game adaptations for console and portable systems includes Atari's *ET the Extraterrestrial*, various *Star Wars* games for different platforms, *Mighty Morphin Power Rangers*, *Jurassic Park* and *Marvel Comics X-Men*. That said, there have been hundreds of film-to-game adaptations, and Alexis Blanchet's (2011) research into film-to-video game adaptations from 1975–2010 in Western and Japanese markets reveals that this adaptive practice is overwhelmingly an American one. In this 25-year span, 547 films have generated over 2,000 games and "out of 547 films, 373 are American." The six *Star Wars* films alone have generated over 120 games. The proportional failure of game adaptations to reach the top ten in sales foregrounds the very different goals of stories in non-game media and the difficulty of transcoding non-games advantageously within the affordances of gaming platforms. Perhaps not surprisingly in terms of rights and revenue, the majority of games adapted from films are based on original screenplays—46%—with literary adaptations second, at 30%. Blanchet also notes that 90% of film adaptations to video games occur as simultaneous releases, or movie tie-in games, and the statistics indicate that most games are viewed as merchandising.

Arguably though, Hollywood's assumption that games are ancillary satellite merchandise for films that serve as promotion for game properties does a marked disservice to the fan interest in immersive console games, as the opening weekend sales of new stand-alone video games repeatedly demonstrate. For example, In 2011, Activism's 2011 console game, *Call of Duty, Modern Warfare 3* hit $1 billion in sales in

16 days (Ivan 2011), breaking the 2010 record of James Cameron's 3D feature *Avatar*, which hit $1 billion in ticket sales in 17 days (Arrington 2010). As Blanchet notes though, his study did not track adaptations to mobile and app games or, I would add, games for the iPad. Yet, media conglomerates are also acutely aware of the volume of sales in casual games, which again will drive apps as adaptation extensions for mobile platforms. Rovio's casual game *Angry Birds* had surpassed 500 million downloads on iTunes by November 2011, reaching that figure in just under two years. Currently, Rovio has just launched the Facebook app and has plans to adapt the massive global brand into a feature film adaptation (Gaudioso 2011).

The last area of innovation in adaptations to be discussed here is the impact of Apple's iPad (launched in April 2010) on adaptation as a practice and a design process with the emergence of the iBook. In the best examples, iPad book adaptations play with the material form of the book, integrating elements of film animation and touch-screen gaming with the conventions of the material book. A survey of the best reviewed and best selling iBooks since the iPad's launch maps an evolution in form and interactive design and indicates a likely trend in the future intermedial adaptations of books to interactive tablets. App designers at Atomic Antelope developed an interactive version of Lewis Carroll's *Alice's Adventures in Wonderland* in March 2010, before the release of the platform, making it the first notable and innovative iBook created specifically for the iPad; it quickly became the number one app in the iTunes store. This adaptation supplemented the text with dynamic elements in the color illustrations that respond via the touch-screen interface to the tapping and swiping of objects such as the Drink Me bottle, and the comfits awarded after the Caucus Race. These objects and others can be further manipulated by tilting the iPad from side to side as if sliding the object across a surface and bouncing it off the edges of the iPad screen, an effect made possible by the gyroscope embedded as part of the iPad's programming. The critical reception and immersive satisfaction of the iPad adaptation immediately created a rich media benchmark that later iBook adaptations have been measured against.

The affordances of the iPad's touch screen, gyroscope, video and audio support make it an extremely rich platform for adapting children's books, which can be easily oriented towards exploratory play and educational learning or edutainment. The best adaptations often combine much-beloved illustrations with dynamic interaction and audio elements, including voice-over Read to Me modes, clickable words triggering the reading of that word or sentence, and Easter Egg sounds to be discovered. App adaptations of Beatrix Potter's *The Tale of Peter Rabbit*, redesigned as *Pop Out! The Tale of Peter Rabbit* (November 2010), and Charles M. Schulz's *A Charlie Brown Christmas* (November 2011), both by Loud Crow Interactive Inc., create immersive experiences with innovative, layered audio elements and distinctively responsive cut-out figures "mounted" on the illustrated backgrounds. *Pop Out! The Tale of Peter Rabbit* uses a recording of Debussy's *Suite Bergamasque/Clair de Lune* as a constant audio element layered with bird songs. Interactive elements are linked with distinct sounds so that swiping the illustration of Peter eating Farmer McGregor's carrots triggers both the movement of Peter and the carrots he's holding, as well as satisfying crunching sounds. On the following page, a now distressed Peter, when touched, wobbles with gurgling upset tummy sounds. *A Charlie Brown Christmas* integrates original recorded dialogue, targeting potential nostalgia in parents, and a short interactive piano tutorial on an interactive keyboard that triggers the piano piece, *Linus and Lucy (Peanuts Theme)*.

The Three Little Pigs and the Secret of a Pop-Up Book (December 2010) adapts British artist L. Leslie Brookes' 1904 children's book and provides an x-ray function that purportedly reveals the mechanisms behind the screen: pulleys, gears, ropes, and springs that control the movements of the interactive objects. Of course, what we don't see here is the code that enables the dynamic interaction and the x-ray mode then reinforces the illusion of this iBook as a material object.

Numerous other titles have been successful adapted, including many of Sandra Boynton's works and those by Dr. Seuss. One last notable use of a touch-screen interface is found in Auryn Ink's iBook adaptation of Hans Christian Anderson's *The Little Mermaid* (March 2011), in which many of the full-page illustrations appear as if under water.

Swiping across the screen produces complicated ripple effects that change the physics of how the underwater world appears, according with our understanding of how our perception of focus, depth and form changes with the intervening distortion and movement of water. The convention in all of these works is to play with objects drawn from the illustrations as if they were physical cut-outs or objects in a fairly limited spatial plane that is usually structured as a single dynamic panel or page, rather than the multiple panels used in comics and graphic novels. The pre-existing stories, either in text alone or as illustrated texts, remain close to the originating work and the innovation in adaptation occurs in the innovations in form and interactivity.

Atomic Antelope's iOS adaptation *Alice in New York* (March 2011) does something different in adapting and adding to Carroll's *Through the Looking Glass* by recontextualizing the tale in the illustrations as if Alice were transposed to a 1940s or 1950s New York, though the text remains the same. Tweedle Dum and Tweedle Dee appear on the Brooklyn Bridge and Humpty Dumpty bounces off the construction girders of skyscrapers. Individual illustrations are designed as mini-games and shaking the Red Queen at the end causes a metamorphosing from Queen to kitten and back again.

The iBook adaptation of Crockett Johnson's *Harold and the Purple Crayon* (August 2011) remains very close to the 1955 original yet engages the reader/player in a different way. The illustrations are designed to invite interactivity by having elements appear in half-opacity and sometimes as unfinished, signaling the opportunity to complete the image. Swiping and tapping trigger distinct elements: swiping reveals stars and a tinkling sound, and tapping sends the stars shooting off the edge of the screen with a swooshing sound. The app also includes a "Read To Me" mode, a "Read Alone" mode, and portions of the audio are often delayed, waiting to be triggered by touch-screen interactivity. The iBook also has a tutorial on use, though the app is designed to be an exploratory and intuitive experience for small children.

Novels for a slightly older audience have also been adapted, more often those whose copyright has expired and that now exist in the public domain. *Padworx Digital Studios* have released a number of eBook titles, including *Dracula: The Official Stoker Family Edition*, which is marketed to tweens and teens, adding 600+ illustrations to the abridged text, original music and songs, and a range of interactive elements. *Pride and Prejudice and Zombies: The Interactive eBook* delivers an interactive version of the 2009 parody novel and provides Austen's original text as a running companion work. Both works play on the popularity of zombies and gore in contemporary mainstream culture, and the interactive elements are designed to be gruesome and fun. Padworx's *Alice: Madness Returns* is a more complex layered adaptation in that the iPad app is a cross-platform adaptation of a game designed for PS3 and XBox and, arguably, the free release of the iPad app is a trailer promoting the EA console game. Further, in its narrative adaptation it borrows from both Carroll's *Alice's Adventures in Wonderland* and *Through the Looking Glass*, and it is also a sequel to the popular and very dark adaptation, *American McGee's Alice*. Originally created as a game for PC and released in 2000, *American McGee's Alice* depicted an older, much more traumatized Alice who has spent her teen years incarcerated in an asylum after losing her family in a house fire. The latent violence in Carroll's world is brought to the foreground in what is reworked as a horror adaptation of the world of Alice, renegotiating again the landscape and denizens of Wonderland. The very big difference resulting from the design of the interactivity is that in order to move the story forward, trigger new pages, and the release of content, the player repeatedly has to enact violence upon Alice, shaving her hair, force-feeding her, and setting the electro-shock input at higher and higher levels. The effect is calculated to make most players feel uncomfortable at participating in the brutalization of the protagonist to whom their sympathies are directed.

The exciting potential of the iPad as an educational tool for adapting existing works as rich media or intermedial iBooks is demonstrated in a very different mode of adaptation provided by the iBook version of T.S. Eliot's *The Waste Land*. This multi-media app adds layers of supplemental content with multiple audio readings of the poem, including Eliot in two recordings, Ted Hughes, Sir Alec Guinness, and Fiona Shaw. The interface design allows one to shift on each line through varied recordings, juxtaposing the nuances of different readings. Video clips offer interpretations and responses to Eliot by Seamus Heaney, Jeanette Winterson, and others. A facsimile of Eliot's manuscript, with editing notations by Ezra Pound, gives readers insight into the process behind Eliot's published work. The adaptation of Richard Dawkins' *The Magic of Reality* further demonstrates the flexibility of the iPad as a platform for learning, as this too contains all of the text of the original book, enriched by illustrations with small animated elements (though not a high degree of interactivity), embedded audio and video clips, games that involve touch screen physics and that in one instance, use the microphone as a input device to "blow" turtles to shore. The iBook also plays with the physical layout of the page, allowing readers to pull down the main screen revealing a horizontal slider panel with each chapter's first page as an access point, and a second slider panel showing the individual pages of the book.

Here, the app designers begin to break away from the convention of the book as a material object of bound pages and utilize the affordances of the iPad as a screen that can display multiple content zones simultaneously. These rich media components can make what exist in the material book as footnotes, for example, dynamic elements that can deepen the experience of a work through audio, visual, and video stimuli and source material. These additional layers could provide a means to design book adaptations to engage more kinaesthetic, visual, and audio learners in new ways in the classroom and at home.

Al Gore's *Our Choice* iBook adaptation models the innovation possible in the adaptation and supplementation of a given text with rich media content. The iBook adds a wealth of interactive content to the book's text and images, adding zoom in/out features to photos, embedded videos and documentary content, infographics, and a further integration of geolocated content linking to Google maps. The iBook was released in May 2011, and following the immediate and widespread critical acclaim for the sophistication of the interface and content design, the design company PushPop Press was acquired by Facebook in August 2011. Although *Our Choice* received the 2011 Apple Design Award in September, as a company now integrated into Facebook's global "book" platform, PushPop Press have stated they will have no future books in development. The integration of rich media content, connectivity with the web, varied interactivity, and an innovative use of the screen space similar to that of *The Magic of Reality* established *Our Choice* as the most advanced iBook experience to date and again, established a benchmark of innovation that will impact the production design of future eBook adaptations.

The other most exciting iBook design studio to appear since the launch of the iPad is Moonbot Studios, co-founded by ex-Pixar animator and successful children's author/illustrator, William Joyce (creator of the nostalgically retro book and animated series, *Rolie Polie Olie* and *George Shrinks*), whose animated short, *The Flying Books of Mr. Morris Lessmore*, won the 2012 Academy Award for animated short. With a visual aesthetic reminiscent of the 1930s and a Wizard of Oz style tornado as an inciting incident, *The Flying Books* combines exquisite animation with casual game mechanics, responsive text, and a narrative voiceover to tell a story about the love of books through the immersive experience of an eBook. A printed book adaptation is rumored to be in production (J. Mitchell 2012). Because of the cinematic quality of Moonbot's animation, visual aesthetics, and interface design, *The Flying Books* models a new achievement in intermedial practice or media fusion in that film, text and game elements exist as equally integrated and expressive within the narrative experience. The success of Moonbot's approach to integrated design is also evident in its latest iBook, *The Numberlys*. And, although this work has not yet been adapted (a print book is projected; see J. Mitchell 2012), it too redefines what an eBook can be. Its visual aesthetic echoes the cinematic world of Fritz Lang's *Metropolis* in the scale and breadth of the cityscape depicted and its text interstitials of dialogue and narration recall those of silent films. The interaction design of *The Numberlys* supports visually seamless shifts from the black and white animated sequences to the interactive games which result in the creation of new letters, all contained within a beautifully realized immersive world. The fusion of different media in *The Flying Books of Morris Lessmore* and *The Numberlys* arguably creates a new model of practice for interactive adaptations that raises the question of whether the categorization via older models of siloed or distinct production industries (games vs. films vs. books) is still relevant, particularly in terms of how a work makes meaning as an adaptation. Although each of the eBooks discussed here refers knowingly back to a material book, the rapid evolution of interactive forms and practices and the variants of intermedial experiences of these adaptations foreground how accelerated innovations in future adaptations to digital platforms will likely be.

The rapidity of shifts and the rapid evolution of form in adaptations for the iPad to date have been contained and controlled because of the programming requirements of the platform and the required approval of Apple for entry in the iTunes store; this is obviously in contrast to the rambunctious and disruptive progress and evolution of adaptations in and between other industries and platforms. As the examples detailed in this Epilogue demonstrate, how adaptation is conceived and practiced continues to be debated, as does the value of adaptation as a practice, particularly in the context of what some are calling transmedia's messy practices. What is probably the most significant shift since the 2006 publication of *A Theory of Adaptation* is that where media conglomerates and IP holders once controlled the production and distribution of adaptations, with limited temporal, geographic or product releases, audiences now claim all aspects of ownership over content that they identify with, immerse themselves in, adapt, remix, reuse, and share. The digital world in which these practices take place is driven by "variation and repetition" (Hutcheon 2006: 177), by porousness, instability, collaboration, and participation on a global scale; the tools of production, distribution, and communication are easily accessible, networked and ubiquitous.

If this Epilogue is convincing in the evolution of adaptive practices and products it has traced, again to adapt Hutcheon, in the workings of human imagination evident in the remediation and intermedial production that define our Web 2.0 world, adaptations as remakes, swedings, memes, mash-ups, cosplay, and fan-run MMORPGs, will be recognized by media conglomerates as the most valuable form of fan investment with and extension of any given work.

REFERENCES

Aaraas, Hans. 1988–89. Bernanos in 1988. *Renascence* 41 (1–2): 15–28.

Abbate, Carolyn. 1991. *Unsung voices: Opera and musical narrative in the nineteenth century*. Princeton: Princeton University Press.

Abbott, H. Porter. 2002. *The Cambridge introduction to narrative*. Cambridge: Cambridge University Press.

Abeel, Erica. 2001. Warily adapting a scary book. *New York Times*. 20 Dec., Arts and Leisure: 22.

Adler, Irene. 2012. *The science of seduction*. http://thewhiphand.webs.com/. 5 February 2012.

Albouy, Serge. 1980. *Bernanos et la politique: La societe et la droite francaises de 1900 a 1950*. Toulouse: Privat.

Allen, Jeanne Thomas. 1977. *Turn of the screw* and *The innocents*: Two types of ambiguity. In Peary and Shatzkin 1977a, 132–42.

Allen, Richard, and Smith, Murray, eds. 1997. *Film theory and philosophy*. Oxford: Clarendon Press.

Allen, Robert C., ed. 1992. *Channels of discourse, reassembled: Television and contemporary criticism*. Chapel Hill, NC: University of North Carolina Press.

Altman, Rick. 1999. *Film/genre.* London: British Film Institute.

Amos, Tori, and Powers, Ann. 2005. *Tori Amos: Piece by piece.* New York: Broadway.

Anders, Charlie Jane. 30 August 2011. Darth Vader will lose a little more of his dignity in *Star Wars* original trilogy Blu-rays. Listen for yourself! *io9.com.* http://io9.com/5835951/darth-vader-will-lose-a-little-more-of-his-dignity-in-star-wars-original-trilogy-blu+rays-listen-for-yourself. 25 January 2012.

Anderson, Melissa. 2005. In search of adaptation: Proust and film. In Stam and Raengo 2005, 100–110.

Anderson, Michael. 3 May 2011. A walk through Westeros: Retracing "The Maester's Path." *argn.com.* http://www.argn.com/2011/05/a_walk_through_westeros_retracing_the_maesters_path/ . 5 May 2011.

Andrew, J. Dudley. 1976. *The major film theories: An introduction.* London: Oxford University Press.

_____. 1980. The well-worn muse: Adaptation in film and theory. In *Narrative strategies.* Macomb: Western Illinois Press, 9-17.

_____. 2004. Adapting cinema to history: A revolution in the making. In Stam and Raengo 2004, 189–204.

Armour, Robert A. 1981. The "whatness" of Joseph Strick's *Portrait.* In Klein and Parker 1981, 279–90.

Arrington, Michael. 4 January 2010. Bam! Avatar hits $1 billion in ticket sales in 17 days, already No. 4 all time movie. *techcrunch.com.* http://techcrunch.com/2010/01/04/bam-avatar-hits-1-billion-in-ticket-sales-in-17-days-already-no-4-all-time-movie/. 18 November 2011.

Axelrod, Mark. 1996. Once upon a time in Hollywood; or, the commodification of form in the adaptation of fictional texts to the Hollywood cinema. *Literature/Film Quarterly* 24 (2): 201–8.

Aycock, Wendell M., and Schoenecke, Michael, eds. 1988. *Film and literature: A comparative approach to adaptation.* Lubbock: Texas Tech University Press.

Babbitt, Irving. 1910/1929. *The new Laokoon: An essay on the confusion of the arts.* New York: Houghton Mifflin.

Baker, Noel. 1997. *Hard core road show: A screenwriter's diary.* Toronto: Anansi.

Baldwin, James. 1955/1975. *Carmen Jones*—the dark is light enough. In L. Patterson 1975, 88–94.

Balestrini, Nassim Winnie, ed. 2011. *Adaptation and American studies: Perspectives on teaching and research.* Heidelberg: Universitätsverlag Winter.

Barash, David P., and Barash, Nanelle. 2005. *Madame Bovary's ovaries: A Darwinian look at literature*. New York: Delacorte Press.

Bardenstein, Carol. 1989. The role of the target-system in theatrical adaptation: Jalal's Egyptian-Arabic adaptation of *Tartuffe*. In Scolnicov and Holland 1989, 146–62.

Barnes, Julian. 1998. *England, England*. London: Picador.

Barthes, Roland. 1968/1977. The death of the author. Trans. Stephen Heath. In Barthes 1977, 142–48.

———. 1971/1977. From work to text. Trans. Stephen Heath. In Barthes 1977, 155–64.

———. 1977. *Image—Music—Text*. Trans. Stephen Heath. New York: Hill & Wang.

Bassnett, Susan. 2002. *Translation studies,* 3rd edn. London: Routledge.

Bateson, F.W. 1972. *Essays in critical dissent*. London: Longmans.

Bauer, Leda V. 1928. The movies tackle literature. *American Mercury* 14: 288–94.

Bazin, Andre. 1967. *What is cinema?* Vol 1. Trans. Hugh Gray. Berkeley: University of California Press.

———. 1997. *Bazin at work: Major essays and reviews from the forties and fifties*. Trans. Alain Piette and Bert Cardullo. London: Routledge.

BBC. 8 January 2012a. The video from John's blog 16 Mar. by Moriarty. *Sherlock Series 2*. http://www.youtube.com/watch?v=enIwRGc8XlM&feature=youtu.be. 5 February 2012.

———. 15 January 2012b. Latest video from John's blog. *Sherlock Series 2*. http://www.youtube.com/watch?v=BnMmAkc1LmM&feature=related. 5 February 2012.

Beebee, Thomas O. 1994. *The ideology of genre: A comparative study of generic instability*. University Park, PA: Pennsylvania State University Press.

Begley, Louis. 2003. "About Schmidt" was changed, but not its core. *New York Times*. 19 Jan., Arts and Leisure: 1, 22.

Beguin, Albert. 1958. *Bernanos par lui-meme*. Paris: Seuil.

Benjamin, Walter. 1968. *Illuminations*. Trans. Harry Zohn, intro. Hannah Arendt. New York: Harcourt, Brace and World.

———. 1992. The task of the translator. In Schulte and Biguenet 1992, 71–92.

Bernanos, Georges. 1949. *Dialogues des Carmelites*. Paris: Seuil.

Bertrand, Denis. 1983. Les migrations de Carmen. *Le français dans le monde* 181 (Nov.–Dec): 103–10.

Bessell, David. 2002. What's that funny noise? An examination of the role of music in *Cool Boarders 2, Alien Trilogy* and *Medieval 2*. In King and Krzywinska 2002a, 136–44.

Black, Gregory D. 1994. *Hollywood censored: Morality codes, Catholics, and the movies*. New York: Cambridge University Press.

Blanchet, Alexis. 15 December 2011. A statistical analysis of the adaptation of films into video games. Trans. Christopher Edwards. *inaglobal.fr*. http://www.inaglobal.fr/en/video-games/article/statistical-analysis-adaptation-films-video-games#intertitre-7. 14 February 2012.

Blau, Herbert. 1982. Theatre and cinema: The scopic drive, the detestable screen, and more of the same. In *Blooded thought: Occasions of theatre*. New York: Performing Arts Journal Publications, 113–37.

Bluestone, George. 1957/1971. *Novels into film*. Berkeley: University of California Press.

Block, Alex Ben. 9 February 2012. 5 questions with George Lucas: Controversial 'Star Wars' changes, SOPA and 'Indiana Jones 5'. *The Hollywood Reporter*. http://www.hollywoodreporter.com/heat-vision/george-lucas-star-wars-interview-288523. 25 January 2012.

Blunck, Annika. 2002. Towards meaningful spaces. In Rieser and Zapp 2002a, 54–63.

Boivin, Patrick. 27 May 2010. *Iron Baby*. http://www.youtube.com/watch?v=SyoA4LXQco4. 30 May 2010.

Bolter, Jay David, and Grusin, Richard. 1999. *Remediation: Understanding new media*. Cambridge, MA: MIT Press.

Bolton, H.P. 1987. *Dickens dramatized*. London: Mansell Publications.

Boly, Joseph, O.S.C. 1960. *Georges Bernanos, Dialogues des Carmelites*: Etude et analyse. Paris: Editions de l'ecole.

Boose, Lynda E., and Burt, Richard, eds. 1997a. *Shakespeare, the movie: Popularizing the plays on film, TV, and video*. London and New York: Routledge.

———. 1997b. Totally clueless?: Shakespeare goes Hollywood in the 1990s. In Boose and Burt 1997a, 8–22.

Bortolotti, Gary R. and Linda Hutcheon. 2007. On the origin of adaptations: Rethinking fidelity discourse and "success"—Biologically. *New Literary History* 38: 443-458.

Boyum, Joy Gould. 1985. *Double exposure: Fiction into film*. New York: Universe Books.

Bradbury, Malcolm. 1994. The novelist and television drama. In Elsaesser, Simons, and Bronk 1994, 98–106.

Brady, Ben. 1994. *Principles of adaptation for film and television*. Austin: University of Texas Press.

Braudy, Leo. 1998. Afterword: Rethinking remakes. In Horton and McDougal 1998a, 327–34.

_____, and Cohen, Marshall, eds. 1999. *Film theory and criticism: Introductory readings*. New York and Oxford: Oxford University Press.

Brecht, Bertolt. 1964. The film, the novel and epic theatre. *Brecht on theatre*. Trans. and ed. John Willett. New York: Methuen, 47–51.

Bremond, Claude. 1964. Le message narratif. *Communications* 4: 4-32

Brett, Philip. 1984. Salvation at sea: *Billy Budd*. In Palmer 1984, 133–43.

Bricken, Rob. 31 August 2011. Confirmed: George Lucas @#$%ed with the original trilogy for the Star Wars blu-rays. *ToplessRobot.com*. http://www.toplessrobot.com/2011/08/confirmed_george_lucas_ed_with_the_original_trilog.php. 25 January 2012.

Brisbin, David. December 2009/January 2010. Instant fan-made media. *Perspective*. 55-59.

Brook, Peter. 1987. Filming a play. In *The shifting point: Theatre, film, opera, 1946–1987*. New York: Harper and Row, 189–92.

Bruckberger, Raymond. 1980. *Tu finiras sur l'echafaud*, suivi de *Le Bachaga, memoires*. Paris: Flammarion.

Bryant, John. 2002. *The fluid text: A theory of revision and editing for book and screen*. Ann Arbor: University of Michigan Press.

Bryce, Jo, and Rutter, Jason. 2002. Spectacle of the deathmatch: Character and narrative in first-person shooters. In King and Krzywinska 2002a, 66–80.

Buck-Morss, Susan. 1989. *The dialects of seeing: Walter Benjamin and the Arcades project*. Cambridge, MA: MIT Press.

Buckland, Sidney, and Chimenes, Myriam, eds. 1999. *Francis Poulenc: Music, art, and literature*. Aldershot: Ashgate.

Buhler, Stephen M. 2001. *Shakespeare in the cinema: Ocular proof*. Albany: State University of New York Press.

Bullas, Jeff. 9 September 2011. 20 stunning social media statistics plus infographic. *JeffBullas.com*. http://www.jeffbullas.com/2011/09/02/20-stunning-social-media-statistics/#.TzVbtmVT0g8.twitter. 14 February 2012.

Burroughs, William S. 1991. Screenwriting and the potentials of cinema. In Cohen 1991a, 53–86.

Bush, William. 1985. *Bernanos' Dialogues des Carmelites: Fact and fiction*. Compiegne: Carmel de Compiegne.

_____. 1988. *Bernanos, Gertrud von le Fort et la destinee mysterieuse de Marie de l'Incarnation.* Compiegne: Carmel de Compiegne.

_____. 1999. *To quell the terror: The mystery of the vocation of the sixteen Carmelites of Compiegne guillotined July 17, 1794.* Washington, DC: ICS Publications.

Butler, Robert. 2003. *The art of darkness: Staging the Philip Pullman trilogy.* London: Oberon Books.

_____. 2004. *The art of darkness: The story continues.* London: Oberon Books.

Cahir, Linda Costanzo. 2006. *Literature into film: theory and practical approaches.* Jefferson, NC: McFarland.

CampfireNYC.com. Press. http://campfirenyc.com/press.html. 10 October 2011.

Carcaud-Macaire, Monique, and Clerc, Jeanne-Marie. 1998. Pour une approche sociocritique de l'adaptation cinematographique: L'exemple de *Mort a Venise.* In Groensteen 1998a, 151–76.

Cardwell, Sarah. 2002. *Adaptation revisited: Television and the classic novel.* Manchester: Manchester University Press.

Carlisle, Janice, and Schwarz, Daniel R., eds. 1994. *Narrative and culture.* Athens: University of Georgia Press.

Carriere, Jean-Claude. 1985. Chercher le coeur profond. *Alternatives theâtrales* 24: 5–14.

Carroll, Rachel, ed. 2009. *Adaptation in contemporary culture: Textual infidelities.* London and New York: Continuum.

Carruthers, John. 1927. *Scheherazade, or the future of the English novel.* London: Kegan Paul, Trench, and Trubner.

Cartmell, Deborah, Hunter, I.Q., Kaye, Heidi, and Whelehan, Imelda, eds. 1996. *Pulping fictions: Consuming culture across the literature/media divide.* London and Chicago: Pluto Press.

_____. 1997. *Trash aesthetics: Popular culture and its audience.* London and Chicago: Pluto Press.

Cartmell, Deborah, and Imelda Whelehan. 2010. *Screen adaptation: Impure cinema.* New York: Palgrave-Macmillan.

Cartmell, Deborah, and Whelehan, Imelda, eds. 1999. *Adaptations: From text to screen, screen to text.* London: Routledge.

_____. 2007. *The Cambridge companion to literature on screen.* Cambridge: Cambridge University Press.

Cascardi, Anthony J., ed. 1987. *Literature and the question of philosophy.* Baltimore: Johns Hopkins University Press.

Casetti, Francesco. 2004. Adaptation and mis-adaptations: Film, literature, and social discourses. Trans. Alessandra Raengo. In Stam and Raengo 2004, 81–91.

Cassutt, Michael. 2004. It happens. wysiwyg://177/http://www.scifi.com/sfw/current/cassutt.html. 5 August.

Cattrysse, Patrick. 1992. Film (adaptation) as translation: Some methodological proposals. *Target* 4 (1): 53–70.

_____. 1997. *The unbearable lightness of being*: Film adaptation seen from a different perspective. *Literature/Film Quarterly* 25 (3): 222–30.

Cham, Mbye. 2005. Oral traditions, literature, and cinema in Africa. In Stam and Raengo 2005, 295–312.

Chamberlin, J. Edward. 2003. *If this is your land, where are your stories? Finding common ground*. Toronto: Knopf.

Chambers, Ross. 1998. *Facing it: AIDS diaries and the death of the author*. Ann Arbor: University of Michigan Press.

Chatman, Seymour. 1999. What novels can do that films can't (and vice versa). In Braudy and Cohen 1999, 435–51.

Christensen, Jerome. 1991. Spike Lee, corporate populist. *Critical Inquiry* 17: 582–95.

Christensen, Thomas. 1999. Four-hand piano transcription and geographies of nineteenth-century musical reception. *Journal of the American Musicological Society* 52 (2): 255–98.

Citron, Marcia J. 2000. *Opera on screen*. New Haven: Yale University Press.

Citron, Paula. 2002. A Carmen of ferocious passion. *Globe and Mail*. 29 May: R3.

Clark, Alan R. 1983. *La France dans l'histoire selon Bernanos*. Paris: Minard.

Clark, Randy. 1991. Bending the genre: The stage and screen versions of *Cabaret*. *Literature/Film Quarterly* 19 (1): 51–59.

Clement, Catherine. 1989. *Opera, or the undoing of women*. Trans. Betsy Wing. London: Virago Press.

Cohen, Keith. 1977. Eisenstein's subversive adaptation. In Peary and Shatzkin 1977, 245–56.

_____. 1979. *Film and fiction: The dynamics of exchange*. New Haven: Yale University Press.

Cohen, Keith, ed. 1991a. *Writing in a film age: Essays by contemporary novelists*. Niwot, CO: University Press of Colorado.

_____. 1991b. Introduction. In Cohen 1991a, 1–44.

Collier, Mary Blackwood. 1994. *La Carmen essentielle et sa realization au spectacle*. New York: Peter Lang.

Collins, Jim. 1991. Batman: The movie and narrative: The hyperconscious in *The many lives of the Batman: Critical approaches to a superhero and his media*. Eds. Roberta E. Pearson, and William Urrichio. New York: Routledge: 64–181.

Colmeiro, Jose F. 2002. Rehispanicizing Carmen: Cultural reappropriations in Spanish cinema. Paper read at *The Carmen Conference*. University of Newcastle upon Tyne, 25 Mar.

Conrad, Joseph. 1897/1968. The condition of art. (Preface to *The Nigger of the Narcissis*) in Morton Dauwen Zabel, ed., *The Portable Conrad*. New York: Viking Press, 705–10.

Constandinides, Costas. 2010. *From film adaptation to post-celluloid adaptation*. New York and London: Continuum.

Conte, Gian Biagio. 1986. *The rhetoric of imitation: Genre and poetic memory in Virgil and other Latin poets*. Ed. Charles Segal. Ithaca, NY: Cornell University Press.

Cooke, Mervyn. 1993. Britten and Shakespeare: Dramatic and musical cohesion in "A Midsummer Night's Dream." *Music and Letters* 74 (2): 246–68.

Coombe, Rosemary. 1994. Author/izing the celebrity. In Woodmansee and Jaszi 1994, 101–31.

Corliss, Richard. 1974. The Hollywood screenwriter. In Mast and Cohen 1974, 541–50.

Corrigan, Timothy. 1999. *Film and literature: An introduction and reader*. Upper Saddle River, NJ: Prentice Hall.

Cox, Alex. 2002. Stage fright. *Globe and Mail*. 2 Sept.: R4.

Crespin, Regine. n.d. D'une Prieure a l'autre. *L'Avant-scene Opera* 52: 106–7.

Cronenberg, David. 1996. Introduction: From novel to film (with Chris Rodley) in *Crash*. London: Faber and Faber, vii–xix.

Crozier, Eric. 1986. The writing of *Billy Budd*. *Opera Quarterly* 4 (3): 11–27. References 185

Cubitt, Sean. 2002. Why narrative is marginal to multimedia and networked communication, and why marginality is more vital than universality. In Rieser and Zapp 2002a, 3–13.

Cuddy-Keane, Melba. 1998. *Mrs. Dalloway*: Film, times, and trauma. In Laura Davis and Jeanette McVicker, *Virginia Woolf and her influences: Selected papers from the seventh annual Virginia Woolf conference*. New York: Pace University Press, 171–75.

_____. 2003. Modernism, geopolitics, globalization. *Modernism/Modernity* 10 (3): 539–58.

Culler, Jonathan. 1975. *Structural poetics: Structuralism, linguistics, and the study of literature*. Ithaca, NY: Cornell University Press.

Cunningham, Michael. 2003. "The Hours" brought elation, but also doubt. *New York Times*. 29 Jan., Arts and Leisure: 1, 22.

Darley, Andrew. 1997. Second-order realism and post-modern aesthetics in computer animation. In Pilling 1997, 16–24.

_____. 2000. *Visual digital culture: Surface play and spectacle in new media genres*. London: Routledge.

Davis, Noah. 2 November 2011. Facebook is quickly becoming the most important tool in movie marketing. *Business Insider Magazine*. http://www.businessinsider.com/facebook-is-quickly-becoming-most-important-tool-in-movie-marketing-2011-11. 4 February 2012.

Dawkins, Richard. 1976/1989. *The selfish gene*. New York and Oxford: Oxford University Press.

DeCanio, Lisa. 15 February 2012. No magic necessary: The Harry Potter Alliance inspires social change through fictional novels. *Bostinno*. http://bostinno.com/2012/02/15/no-magic-necessary-the-harry-potter-alliance-inspires-social-change-through-fictional-novels/. 15 February 2012.

Dena, Christy. 2009. *Transmedia practice: Theorising the practice of expressing a fictional world across distinct media and environments*. Ph.D. dissertation, University of Sydney. (http://www.christydena.com/phd/.)

Desmond, John M., and Peter Hawkes. 2005. *Adaptation: Studying film and literature*. New York: McGraw-Hill.

Dick, Bernard F. 1981. Adaptation as archaeology: *Fellini Satyricon* (1969). In Horton and Magretta 1981a, 145–54.

Dimock, Wai Chee. 1997. A theory of resonance. *PMLA* 112 (5): 1060–71.

Dinkla, Soke. 2002. The art of narrative—towards the *Floating Work of Art*. In Rieser and Zapp 2002a, 27–41.

Doherty, Thomas. 1998. World War II in film: What is the color of reality? *Chronicle of Higher Education*. 9 Oct.: B4-B5.

Donaldson, Peter S. 1997. Shakespeare in the age of post-mechanical reproduction: Sexual and electronic magic in *Prospero's Books*. In Boose and Burt 1997a, 169–85.

Drumb, Cole. 22 February 2008. How to Swede? Ask Michel Gondry. *Film.com*. http://www.film.com/movies/how-to-swede-ask-michel-gondry #fbid=QF_ENJwaETY. 22 January 2012.

DuQuesnay, Ian M. le M. 1979. From Polyphemus to Corydon: Virgil, *Eclogue* 2 and the *Idylls* of Theocritus. In West and Woodman 1979, 35–69.

Durack, Elizabeth. 2000. Editorial. *Echo Station*. http://lessig.org/content/columns/pdfs/118.pdf. 25 January 2012.

Dutton, Denis. 1987. Why intentionalism won't go away. In Cascardi 1987, 194–209.

_____. n.d. The smoke-free *Carmen*. *Arts and Letters Daily*. http://www.aldaily.com/smoke.htm. 7 August 2004.

Eagleton, Terry. 1996. *Literary theory: An introduction*, 2nd ed. Minneapolis: University of Minnesota Press.

Edel, Leon. 1974. Novel and camera. In Halperin 1974, 177–88.

Edelstein, David. 2001. "Remade in America": A label to avoid. *New York Times*. 4 Nov., Arts and Leisure: 3, 20.

Elliott, Kamilla. 2003. *Rethinking the novel/film debate*. Cambridge: Cambridge University Press.

Ellis, John. 1982. The literary adaptation. *Screen* 23 (May–June): 3–5.

Elsaesser, Thomas. 1994. Introduction. In Elsaesser, Simons and Bronk 1994, 91–97.

Elsaesser, Thomas, Simons, Jan, and Bronk, Lucette, eds. 1994. *Writing for the medium: Television in transition*. Amsterdam: Amsterdam University Press.

Emslie, Barry. 1992. *Billy Budd* and the fear of words. *Cambridge Opera Journal* 4 (1): 43–59.

Ermarth, Elizabeth Deeds. 2001. Agency in the discursive condition. *History and Theory* 40: 34-58.

Fanlore. n.d. Open letter to Star Wars zine publishers by Maureen Garrett. *fanlore.org*. http://fanlore.org/wiki/Open_Letter_to_Star_Wars_Zine_Publishers_by_Maureen_Garrett. 24 January 2012.

Faraci, Devin. 30 August 2011. Update: Lucas added Vader crying "Noooooo!" to Return of the Jedi. *BadassDigest.com*. http://badassdigest.com/2011/08/30/did-lucas-add-vader-crying-noooooo-to-return-of-the-jedi?utm_source=feedburner&utm_medium=feed&utm_campaign=Feed%253A+badassdigest+%2528Badass+Digest+ALL%2529. 25 January 2012.

Fassbinder, Rainer Werner. 1992. Preliminary remarks on *Querelle*. In Toteberg and Lensing 168–70.

Fawcett, F. Dubrez. 1952. *Dickens the dramatist*. London: W.H. Allen.

Feingold, Ken. 2002. The interactive art gambit. In Rieser and Zapp 2002a, 120–34.

Feldberg, Robert. n.d. A dated musical made thoroughly modern. http://www.northjersey.com/cgi-bin/page.pl?id=4718267. 8 December 2002.

Filibuster Cartoons. n.d. The best video games in the history of humanity. *filibustercartoons.com*. http://www.filibustercartoons.com/games.htm. 22 January 2012.

Fischlin, Daniel, and Fortier, Mark, eds. 2000. *Adaptations of Shakespeare: A critical anthology of plays from the seventeenth century to the present*. London and New York: Routledge.

Fish, Stanley. 1980. *Is there a text in this class?: The authority of interpretive communities*. Cambridge, MA: Harvard University Press.

Flitterman-Lewis, Sandy. 1992. Psychoanalysis, film, and television. In R.C. Allen 1992, 203–46.

Foer, Jonathan Safran. 2011. *Tree of Codes*. London: Visual Editions.

Forster, E.M. 1910/1941. *Howards End*. Harmondsworth: Penguin.

Fortier, Mark. 2002. Undead and unsafe: Adapting Shakespeare (in Canada). In Diana Bryden and Irena R. Makaryk, eds., *Shakespeare in Canada: A world elsewhere*. Toronto: University of Toronto Press, 339–52.

Foucault, Michel. 1972. *The archaeology of knowledge* and *The discourse on language*. Trans. A.M. Sheridan Smith. New York: Harper and Row.

Friedman, Susan Stanford. 2004. Whose modernity? The global landscape of modernism. Humanities Institute Lecture, University of Texas, Austin. 18 February.

Furman, Nelly. 1988. The languages of love in *Carmen*. In Groos and Parker 1988, 168–83.

Gagnebin, Laurent. 1987. *Du Golgotha a Guernica: Foi et creation artistique*. Paris: Les Bergers et les Mages.

Galloway, Priscilla. 2004. Interview with the author. 25 April.

Garber, Marjorie. 1987. *Shakespeare's ghost writers*. London: Methuen.

———. 2003. *Quotation marks*. London and New York: Routledge.

Gardies, André. 1998. Le narrateur sonne toujours deux fois. In Groensteen 1998a, 65–80.

Gaudioso, John. 10 February 2011. New Rovio exec David Maisel believes "Angry Birds" movie will change video game adaptations. *HollywoodReporter.com*. http://www.hollywoodreporter.com/news/rovio-david-maisel-angry-birds-242956. 14 February 2011.

Gaudreault, André. 1998. Variations sur une problematique. In Groensteen 1998a, 267–71.

———, and Marion, Philippe. 1998. Transecriture et mediatique narrative: L'enjeu de l'intermedialite, … . In Groensteen 1998a, 31–52.

———. 2004. Transecriture and narrative mediatics: The stakes of intermediality. Trans. Robert Stam. In Stam and Raengo 2004, 58–70.

Gaut, Berys. 1997. Film authorship and collaboration. In Allen and Smith 1997, 149–72.

Geduld, Harry M. 1983. *The definitive Dr. Jekyll and Mr. Hyde companion.* New York: Gardan.

Gendre, Claude. 1994. *Destinee providentielle des Carmelites de Compiegne dans la literature et les arts.* Jonquieres: Carmel de Compiegne.

———. 1999. *Dialogues des Carmelites*: The historical background, literary destiny and genesis of the opera. Trans. William Bush. In Buckland and Chimenes 1999, 274–319.

Gendron, Bernard. 2002. *Between Montmartre and the Mudd Club: Popular music and the avant-garde.* Chicago: University of Chicago Press.

Genette, Gerard. 1979. *Introduction a l'architexte.* Paris: Seuil.

———. 1982. *Palimpsestes: La litterature au second degre.* Paris: Seuil.

Geraghty, Christine. 2007. *Now a major motion picture: Film adaptations of literature and drama.* Lanham, MD: Rowman & Littlefield.

Gerrig, Richard J. 1993. *Experiencing narrative worlds: On the psychological activities of reading.* New Haven, CT: Yale University Press.

Gibbons, Luke. 2002. "The cracked looking glass" of cinema: James Joyce, John Huston, and the memory of "The Dead." *Yale Journal of Criticism* 15 (1): 127–48.

Giddings, Robert, Selby, Keith, and Wensley, Chris. 1990. *Screening the novel: The theory and practice of literary dramatization.* London: Macmillan.

———, and Sheen, Erica, eds. 2000. *The classic novel: From page to screen.* New York: St. Martin's Press.

Glancy, Mark. 2003. *The 39 Steps.* London and New York: I.B. Tauris.

Golden, Leon, ed. 1982. *Transformations in literature and film.* Tallahassee: University Presses of Florida.

Gombrich, E.H. 1961. *Art and illusion: A study in the psychology of pictorial representation.* New York: Panther.

Gomez, Jeff. 10 March 2010. Coca-Cola's happiness factory: Case study. http://www.youtube.com/watch?v=pYDFUvO4upY&list=PL322B492 1359703F7&index=13&feature=plpp_video. 20 March 2010.

———. Email exchange with author, 24 February 2012.

Gordon, Rebecca M. 2003. Portraits perversely framed: Jane Campion and Henry James. *Film Quarterly* 56 (2): 14–24.

Gould, Evlyn. 1996. *The fate of Carmen.* Baltimore: Johns Hopkins University Press.

Grau, Oliver. 2003. *Virtual art: From illusion to immersion.* Trans. Gloria Custance. Cambridge: MIT Press.

Greenberg, Clement. 1940/1986. Towards a newer Laocöon. *Partisan Review* July-Aug. 1940; rpt. John O'Brian, ed., *The collected essays and criticism.* Vol. 1, *Perceptions and judgements, 1939–1944.* Chicago: University of Chicago Press, 23–38.

Greenberg, Harvey R. 1998. Raiders of the lost text: Remaking as contested homage in *Always.* In Horton and McDougal 1998a, 115–30.

Greenblatt, Stephen. 1991. Resonance and wonder. In Ivan Karp and Steven D. Lavine, eds., *Exhibiting cultures: The poetics and politics of museum display.* Washington, DC: Smithsonian Institute, 42–56.

Groen, Rick. 2004. Bad kitty! Very bad kitty! *Globe and Mail,* 23 July: R1.

Groensteen, Thierry, ed. 1998a. *La transecriture: Pour une theorie de l'adaptation.* Colloque de Cerisy, 14–21 Aug. 1993, Quebec: Editions Nota Bene.

———. 1998b. Fictions sans frontieres. In Groensteen 1998a, 9–29.

———. 1998c. Le processus adaptatif (tentative de recapitulation raisonnee). In Groensteen 1998a, 273–77.

Groos, Arthur, and Parker, Roger, eds. 1988. *Reading opera.* Princeton: Princeton University Press.

Gunelius, Susan. 7 March 2010. The shift from CONsumers to PROsumers. *Forbes.com.* http://www.forbes.com/sites/work-in-progress/2010/07/03/the-shift-from-consumers-to-prosumers/. 12 January 2012.

Habicht, Werner. 1989. Shakespeare and theatre politics in the Third Reich. In Scolnicov and Holland 1989, 110–20.

Halevy, Ludovic. 1905/1987. Breaking the rules. Trans. Clarence H. Russell. *Opera News* 51 (13): 36–37, 47.

Hall, Carol. 1991. Valmont redux: The fortunes and filmed adaptations of *Les liaisons dangereuses* by Cholderlos de Laclos. *Literature/Film Quarterly* 19 (1): 41–50.

Hall, James Andrew. 1984. In other words. *Communication and Media* 1: 1.

Halliwell, Michael. 1996. "The space between" postcolonial opera? The Meale/Malouf adaptation of *Voss. Australasian Drama Studies* 28 (April): 87–98.

Halperin, J., ed. 1974. *The theory of the novel.* London: Oxford University Press.

Hammerstein, Oscar III. 1945. *Carmen Jones.* New York: Knopf.

Hamon, Philippe. 1977. Texte litteraire et metalangage. *Poetique* 31: 263–84.

Hansen, Miriam Bratu. 2001. *Schindler's List* is not *Shoah*: The second commandment, popular modernism, and public memory. In Landy 2001a, 201–17.

Hapgood, Robert. 1997. Popularizing Shakespeare: The artistry of Franco Zeffirelli. In Boose and Burt 1997a, 80–94.

Harries, Dan M. 1997. Semiotics, discourse and parodic spectatorship. *Semiotica* 113 (3–4): 293–315.

Harris, Mark. February 2011. The day the movies died. *GQ.com*. http://www.gq.com/entertainment/movies-and-tv/201102/the-day-the-movies-died-mark-harris. 24 May 2011.

Harry Potter Alliance. 2012. Cease and desist letters. *thehpalliance.org*. http://thehpalliance.org/action/campaigns/nihn/cease-and-desist-letter/. 18 February 2012.

_____. 2012. HPA Chocolate Frogs. *thehpalliance.org*. http://thehpalliance.org/action/campaigns/nihn/chocolate-frogs/. 18 February 2012.

Hawthorne, Christopher. 1996. Coming out as a socialist. Interview with Tony Kushner, *SALON* http://www.salon.com/weekly/interview 960610. html. 2 November 2004.

Hayles, Katherine N. 2001. The transformation of narrative and the materiality of hypertext. *Narrative* 9 (1): 21–39.

Hedrick, Donald K. 1997. War is mud: Branagh's dirty Henry V and the types of political ambiguity. In Boose and Burt 1997a, 45–66.

Hell, Henri. 1978. *Francis Poulenc: Musicien français*. Paris: Fayard.

Helman, Alicja, and Osadnik, Waclaw M. 1996. Film and literature: Historical models of film adaptation and a proposal for a (poly)system approach. *Canadian Review of Comparative Literature* 23 (3): 645–57.

Henderson, Diana E. 1997. A Shrew for the times. In Boose and Burt 1997a, 148–68.

Hensley, Wayne E. 2002. The contribution of F.W. Murnau's *Nosferatu* to the evolution of *Dracula*. *Literature/Film Quarterly* 30 (1): 59–64.

Hermans, Theo. 1985. Introduction: Translation studies and a new paradigm. In Theo Hermans, ed., *The manipulation of literature: Studies in literary translation*. London: Croom Helm, 7–15.

Highway, Tomson. 2003. Adaptation. Lecture to University College, 6 Oct.

Hinds, Stephen. 1998. *Allusion and intertext: Dynamics of appropriation in Roman Poetry*. Cambridge: Cambridge University Press.

Hirschhorn, Joel. 2002. Hearing a different drum song: David Henry Hwang. *The Dramatist Magazine*. Mar.-Apr. http://www.dramaguild.com/doc/mdhart1.htm. 5 August 2004.

Hix, H. L. 1990. *Morte d'author*. Philadelphia: Temple University Press.

Hodgdon, Barbara. 1997. Race-ing *Othello*. Re-engendering white-out. In Boose and Burt 1997a, 23–44.

Hoesterey, Ingeborg. 2001. *Pastiche: Cultural memory in art, film, literature*. Bloomington: Indiana University Press.

Honig, Joel. 2001. A novel idea. *Opera News* 66 (2): 20–23.

Hopton, Tricia, Adam Atkinson, Jane Stadler, and Peta Mitchell, eds. 2011. *Pockets of change: Adaptation and cultural transition*. Lanham, MD: Lexington Books.

Horkheimer, Max, and Adorno, Theodor W. 1947/1972. *Dialectic of enlightenment*. New York: Herder and Herder.

Horton, Andrew, and Magretta, Joan, eds. 1981a. *Modern European filmmakers and the art of adaptation*. New York: Frederick Ungar.

_____. 1981b. Introduction. In Horton and Magretta 1981a, 1–5.

Horton, Andrew, and McDougal, Stuart Y., eds. 1998a. *Play it again, Sam: Retakes on remakes*. Berkeley: University of California Press.

_____. 1998b. Introduction. In Horton and McDougal 1998a, 1–11.

Howard, Patricia. 1969. *The operas of Benjamin Britten: An introduction*. London: Barrie and Rockliff, the Cresset Press.

Howells, Sach A. 2002. Watching a game, playing a movie: When media collide. In King and Krzywinska 2002a, 110–21.

Humphrey, Michael. 29 July 2011. Pottermore: Expert explains how Harry Potter's website will transform storytelling. *Forbes.com*. http:// www.forbes.com/sites/michaelhumphrey/2011/07/29/pottermore- expert-explains-how-harry-potters-website-will-transform- storytelling/. 25 August 2011.

Hutcheon, Linda. 1979. "Sublime noise" for three friends: E.M. Forster, Roger Fry, and Charles Mauron. *Modernist Studies* 3 (3): 141–50.

_____, and Hutcheon, Michael. 1996. *Opera: Desire, disease, death*. Lincoln: University of Nebraska Press.

Hutchings, Anthony. 1997. Authors, art, and the debasing instinct: Law and morality in the *Carmina Burana* case. *Sydney Law Review* 19: 385–99.

Hwang, David Henry. 2002. A new musical by Rodgers and Hwang. *New York Times*. 13 Oct., Arts and Leisure: 1, 16.

Iannucci, Amilcare A., ed. 2004a. *Dante, cinema, and television*. Toronto: University of Toronto Press.

_____. 2004b. Dante and Hollywood. In Iannucci 2004a, 3–20.

Inde, Vilis R. 1998. Jeff Koons: Piracy or fair use? Is it art? Visual excess? Or a cupcake?. In *Art in the courtroom*. Westport, CT and London: Praeger, 1–47.

Innis, Christopher. 1993. Adapting Dickens to the modern eye: *Nicholas Nickleby* and *Little Dorrit*. In Reynolds 1993a, 64–79.

Iseminger, Gary, ed. 1992. *Intention and interpretation*. Philadelphia: Temple University Press.

Iser, Wolfgang. 1971. Indeterminacy and the reader's response in prose fiction. In J. Hillis Miller, ed., *Aspects of narrative*. New York: Columbia University Press, 1–45.

Ivan, Tom. 12 December 2011. Call of Duty: Modern Warfare 3 hits $1 billion in sales. *CVG.com*. http://www.computerandvideogames. com/329324/call-of-duty-modern-warfare-3-hits-1-billion-in-sales/. 24 February 2012.

Ivry, Benjamin. 1996. *Francis Poulenc*. London: Phaedon Press.

Jackson, Nicholas. 27 June 2011. Buy and sell virtual marijuana with new 'Weeds' Facebook game. *The Atlantic*. http://www.theatlantic.com/ technology/archive/2011/06/buy-and-sell-virtual-marijuana-with-new-weeds-facebook-game/241111/. 6 February 2012.

Jarman, Derek. 1991. *Queer Edward II*. London: British Film Institute.

Jenkins, Henry. 2006. *Convergence culture: Where old and new media collide*. New York: New York University Press.

―――. 11 February 2009a. If it doesn't spread, it's dead (Part One): Media viruses and memes. *Henryjenkins.org*. http://henryjenkins.org/2009/02/ if_it_doesnt_spread_its_dead_p.html. 15 February 2009.

―――. 11 September 2009b. The aesthetics of transmedia: In response to David Bordwell (Part One). *HenryJenkins.org*. http://henryjenkins. org/2009/09/the_aesthetics_of_transmedia_i.html. 19 November 2009.

―――. 2011. Transmedia 202: Further reflections. *Henryjenkins.org*. http:// henryjenkins.org/2011/08/defining_transmedia_further_re.html.   13 March 2012.

Jinks, William. 1971. *The celluloid literature: Film in the humanities*. Los Angeles: Glencoe.

Joe, Jeongwon. 1998. Hans-Jurgen Syberberg's *Parsifal*: The staging of dissonance in the fusion of opera and film. *Musical Research Forum* 13 (July): 1–20.

Jost, Francois. 2004. The look: From film to novel: An essay on comparative narratology. Trans. Robert Stam. In Stam and Raengo 2004, 71–80.

Kauffmann, Stanley. 2001. *The Abduction from the theater*: Mozart opera on film. In *Regarding film: Criticism and comment*. Baltimore: Johns Hopkins University Press, 175–87.

Kerman, Judith B., ed. 1991. *Retrofitting* Blade Runner: *Issues in Ridley Scott's* Blade Runner *and Philip K. Dick's* Do Androids Dream of Electric Sheep? Bowling Green, OH: Bowling Green University Press.

Kerr, Paul. 1982. Classical serials to-be-continued. *Screen* 23 (1): 6–19.

Kestner, Joseph. 1981. The scaffold of honor. *Opera News* 56 (9): 12, 14, 16, 26–27.

King, Geoff, and Krzywinska, Tanya, eds. 2002a. *ScreenPlay: Cinema/ videogames/interfaces*. London: Wallflower Press.

_____. 2002b. Cinema/videogames/interfaces. In King and Krzywinska 2002a, 1–32.

_____. 2002c. Die hard/try harder: Narrative spectacle and beyond, from Hollywood to videogame. In King and Krzywinska 2002a, 50–65.

Kirby, Michael. 1981. Reinterpretation issue: An introduction. *Drama Review* 25 (2): 2

Klein, Michael. 1981. Introduction. *The English novel and the movies*. New York: Frederick Ungar, 1–13.

Klein, Michael, and Parker, Gillian, eds. 1981. *The English novel and the movies*. New York: Frederick Ungar, 1–13.

Kodat, Catherine Gunther. 2005. I'm Spartacus! In Phelan and Rabinowitz 2005, 484–98.

Kracauer, Siegfried. 1955. Opera on the screen. *Film Culture* 1: 19–21.

Kramer, Lawrence. 1991. Musical narratology: A theoretical outline. *Indiana Theory Review* 12: 141–62.

Kristeva, Julia. 1969/1986. *Semiotike: Recherches pour une semanalyse*. Paris: Seuil.

Kubler, George. 1962. *The shape of time: Remarks on the history of things*. New Haven: Yale University Press.

Kucich, John, and Sadoff, Dianne F., eds. 2000. *Victorian afterlife: Postmodern culture rewrites the nineteenth century*. Minneapolis: University of Minnesota Press.

Kushner, Tony. 1992, 1994. *Angels in America, part two: Perestroika*. New York: Theatre Communications Group.

Lachiusa, Michael John. 2002. Genre confusion. *Opera News* 67 (2): 12–15, 73.

Lackner, Chris. 2004. Here's one guy who doesn't like a sexy Catwoman. *Globe and Mail*. 23 July: R5.

Landon, Brooks. 1991. "There's some of me in you": *Blade Runner* and the adaptation of science fiction literature into film. In Kerman 1991, 90-102.

Landy, Marcia, ed. 2001a. *The historical film: History and memory in media*. London: Athlone Press.

_____. 2001b. Introduction. In Landy 2001a, 1–22.

Large, Brian. 1992. Filming, videotaping. In Sadie 1992, 2: 200–205.

Larsson, Donald F. 1982. Novel into film: Some preliminary reconsiderations. In Golden 1982, 69–83.

Laurel, Brenda. 2005. New players, new games. http://www.tauzero.com/ Brenda_Laurel/Recent_Talks/New Players. 3 June 2005.

LeClair, Tom. 2000/2003. False pretenses, parasites and monsters. http:// www.altx.com/ebr. 22 May 2005.

Leclerc, Gerard. 1982. *Avec Bernanos*. Paris: Hallier, Albin Michel.

Lee, M. Owen. 1998. *A season of opera: From Orpheus to Ariadne*. Toronto: University of Toronto Press.

Lefevre, Andre. 1982. Literary theory and translated literature. *Dispositio* 7 (19–21): 3–22.

_____. 1983. Why waste our time on rewrites? The trouble with interpretation and the role of rewriting in an alternative paradigm. In T. Hermans, ed., *The manipulation of literature: Studies in literary translation*. London: Croom Helm, 215–42.

LeGrice, Malcolm. 2002. Virtual reality—tautological oxymoron. In Rieser and Zapp 2002a, 227–36.

Leicester, H. Marshall, Jr. 1994. Discourse and the film text: Four readings of *Carmen*. *Cambridge Opera Journal* 6 (3): 245–82.

Leiris, Michel. 1963. *Manhood: A journey from childhood into the fierce order of virility*. Trans. Richard Howard. New York: Grossman.

Leitch, Thomas M. 2007. *Film adaptation and its discontents: From* Gone with the Wind *to* The Passion of the Christ. Baltimore, MD: Johns Hopkins University Press.

_____. 2008. Adaptation studies at a crossroads. *Adaptation* 1 (1): 63-77.

Lejeune, Philippe. 1975. *Le pacte autobiographique*. Paris: Seuil.

Lentricchia, Frank, and McLaughlin, Thomas, eds. 1995. *Critical terms for literary study*, 2nd ed. Chicago: University of Chicago Press.

Lessig, Lawrence. 2008. *Remix: Making art and commerce thrive in the hybrid economy*. London: Bloomsbury. Also at http://www.scribd.com/ doc/47089238/Remix. 11 December 2011.

Lessing, Gotthold Ephraim. 1766/1984. *Laocöon: An essay on the limits of painting and poetry*. Trans. Edward Allen McCormick. Baltimore: Johns Hopkins University Press.

Levy, Wayne. 1995. *The book of the film and the film of the book*. Melbourne: Academic Press.

Limbacher, James L. 1991. *Haven't I seen you somewhere before? Remakes, sequels, and series in motion pictures, videos, and television, 1896–1990*. Ann Arbor, MI: Pierian Press.

Linden, George. 1971. The storied world. In F. Marcus 1971, 157–63.

Lindley, Craig. 2002. The gameplay gestalt, narrative, and interactive storytelling. In Mayra 2002, 203-15.

Lionsgate. 2011. *The Hunger Games Movie.* http://www.thehungergamesmovie. com/index2.html. 26 January 2012.

Livingston, Paisley. 1997. Cinematic authorship. In Allen and Smith 1997, 132–48.

Lloyd, Robert. 26 August 2010. 'Star Wars Uncut': The world remakes a classic. *LA Times: Hero Complex.* http://herocomplex.latimes.com/ 2010/08/26/star-wars-uncut-the-world-remakes-a-classic/. 19 January 2012.

Lodge, David. 1993. Adapting *Nice Work* for television. In Reynolds 1993a, 191–203.

Loehlin, James N. 1997. "Top of the world, Ma": *Richard III* and cinematic convention. In Boose and Burt 1997a, 67–79.

Loney, Glenn. 1983. The Carmen connection. *Opera News* 48 (3): 10–14.

Lord, M.G. 2004. Off the canvas and onto the big screen. *New York Times.* 19 Dec., Arts and Leisure: 40.

Lorsch, Susan E. 1988. Pinter fails Fowles. *Literature/Film Quarterly* 16 (3): 144–54.

McCracken, Grant. 2010. *Plenitude 2.0.* http://cultureby.com/site/ wp-content/uploads/2010/05/Plenitude2.0-for-pdf-may-2010.pdf. 10 October 2011.

McEachern, Martin. 2007. Game films. *Computer Graphics World* 30 (2): 12–14, 16–18, 20–22, 24, 26–28.

Mackrell, Judith. 1 November 2004. Born in the wrong body. *The Guardian.* http://www.guardian.co.uk. 2 November 2004.

Mactavish, Andrew. 2002. Technological pleasure: The performance and narrative of technology in *Half-Life* and other high-tech computer games. In King and Krzywinska 2002a, 33–49.

Maingueneau, Dominique. 1984. *Carmen: Les racines d'un mythe.* Paris: Editions du Sorbier.

Manovich, Lev. 2001. *The language of new media.* Cambridge, MA: MIT Press.

———. 2002a. The archeology of windows and spatial montage. http://www. manovich.net/texts_00.htm. 22 May 2005.

———. 2002b. Spatial computerization and film language. In Rieser and Zapp 2002a, 64–76.

———. n.d. Cinema as a cultural interface. http://www.manovich.net/ TEXT/cinema-cultural.html. 21 May 2005.

———. n.d. From the externalization of the psyche to the implantation of technology. http://www.manovich.net/TEXT/externalization.html. 21 May 2005.

_____. n.d. Who is the author? Sampling/remixing/open source. http://www.manovich.net/texts_00.htm. 21 May 2005.

Marcus, Fred H., ed. 1971. *Film and literature: Contrasts in media*. New York: Chandler.

Marcus, Millicent. 1993. *Filmmaking by the book: Italian cinema and literary adaptation*. Baltimore: Johns Hopkins University Press.

Martin, Robert. 1986. Saving Captain Vere: *Billy Budd* from Melville's novella to Britten's opera. *Studies in Short Fiction* 23 (1): 49–56.

Mast, Gerald, and Cohen, Marshall, eds. 1974. *Film theory and criticism: Introductory readings*. New York: Oxford University Press.

Mayer, Sophie. 2005. Script girls and automatic women: A feminist film poetics. Ph.D. diss., University of Toronto.

Mayra, Frans, ed. 2002. *Computer games and digital cultures*. Tampere, Finland: University of Tampere Press.

McClary, Susan. 1992. *Georges Bizet: Carmen*. Cambridge: Cambridge University Press.

McCracken-Flesher, Caroline. 1994. Cultural projections: The "strange case" of Dr. Jekyll, Mr. Hyde, and cinematic response. In Carlisle and Schwarz 1994, 179–99.

McDonald, Jan. 1993. "The devil is beautiful": *Dracula*: Freudian novel and feminist drama. In Reynolds 1993a, 80–104.

McFarlane, Brian. 1996. *Novel to film: An introduction to the theory of adaptation*. Oxford: Clarendon Press.

McGowan, John. 2000. Modernity and culture: The Victorians and cultural studies. In Kucich and Sadoff 2000, 3–28.

McGrath, Patrick. 2002. Inside the spider's web. *Globe and Mail*. 30 Oct: R1, R9.

McKee, Robert. 1997. *Story: Substance, structure, style, and the principles of screenwriting*. New York: ReganBooks.

McLuhan, Marshall. 1996. *Essential McLuhan*. Ed. Eric McLuhan and Frank Zingrone. New York: Basic Books.

McNally, Terrence. 2002. An operatic mission: Freshen the familiar. *New York Times*. 1 Sept., Arts and Leisure: 19, 24.

Meadows, Mark Stephen. 2003. *Pause and effect: The art of interactive narrative*. Indianapolis: New Riders.

Meisel, Martin. 1983. *Realizations: Narrative, pictorial, and theatrical arts in nineteenth-century England*. Princeton: Princeton University Press.

Mele, Alfred R. 1992. *Springs of action: Understanding intentional behavior*. New York: Oxford University Press.

_____, and Livingston, Paisley. 1992. Intentions and interpretations. *Modern Language Notes* 107: 931–49.

Mellers, Wilfrid. 1993. *Francis Poulenc*. Oxford and New York: Oxford University Press.

Melville, Herman. 1891/1924/1958. *Typee* and *Billy Budd*. Ed. Milton R. Stern. New York: E.P. Dutton.

Metz, Christian. 1974. *Film language: A semiotics of the cinema*. Trans. Michael Taylor. New York: Oxford University Press.

Miller, Arthur R., and Davis, Michael H. 1990. *Intellectual property: Patents, trademarks and copyright in a nutshell*. 2nd ed. St. Paul, MN: West Publishing Co.

Miller, J. Hillis. 1995. Narrative. In Lentricchia and McLaughlin 1995, 66–79.

Miller, Jonathan. 1986. *Subsequent performances*. London: Faber and Faber.

Miller, Julie. 31 August 2011. Talkback: Is Darth Vader screaming "Noooo" really such an insult to Star Wars? *movieline.com*. http://www.movieline.com/2011/08/31/is-darth-vader-screaming-noooo-really-such-an-insult-to-star-wars/. 25 January 2012.

Minghella, Anthony. 1997. *The English patient: A screenplay*. London: Methuen Drama.

Mitchell, Jon. 11 January 2012. The Numberlys invent the alphabet in a world run by numbers. *ReadWriteWeb.com*. http://www.readwriteweb.com/archives/the_numberlys.php. 3 March 2012.

Mitchell, Maurice. n.d. Updated: Want to see the full list of changes to the Star Wars films? *Thegeektwins.com*. http://www.thegeektwins.com/2011/09/want-to-see-full-list-of-changes-to.html. 24 January 2012.

Mitchell, W. J. T. 1994. *Picture theory*. Chicago: University of Chicago Press.

_____. 2005. *What do pictures want? The lives and loves of images*. Chicago: University of Chicago Press.

Moore, Michael Ryan. 2010. Adaptation and new media. *Adaptation* 3 (2): 179-192.

Morris, Sue. 2002. First-person shooters—a game apparatus. In King and Krzywinska 2002a, 81–97.

Morrissette, Bruce. 1985. *Novel and film: Essays in two genres*. Chicago: University of Chicago Press.

Most, Andrea. 2004. *Making Americans: Jews and the Broadway musical*. Cambridge, MA: Harvard University Press.

Mulvey, Laura. 1975. Visual pleasure and narrative cinema. *Screen* 16 (3): 6–18.

Münsterberg, Hugo. 1916/1970. *The film: A psychological study.* New York: Dover.

Murphy, Brian. 21 December 2009. 28 Great *Star Wars* video mash-ups. *blastr.com.* http://blastr.com/2009/12/28-gr-star-wars-video-mas.php. 12 February 2012.

Murray, Janet H. 1997. *Hamlet on the holodeck: The future of narrative in cyberspace.* New York: Free Press.

Murray, S. Meredith, O.P. 1963. *La genese de "Dialogues de Carmelites."* Paris: Seuil.

Nadeau, Robert L. 1977. Melville's sailor in the sixties. In Peary and Shatzkin 1977, 124–31.

Naremore, James, ed. 2000a. *Film adaptation.* New Brunswick, NJ: Rutgers University Press.

———. 2000b. Introduction: Film and the reign of adaptation. In Naremore 2000a, 1–16.

NASIONAL002. 29 May 2009. KISSING SCENE Robert Pattinson & Kristen Stewart GOING UNDER New Moon set pic's Italy. http://www.youtube.com/watch?v=swI0nytT9vc&feature=related. 10 November 2011.

Nattiez, Jean-Jacques. 1990. *Music and discourse: Toward a semiology of music.* Trans. Carolyn Abbate. Princeton: Princeton University Press.

Nemiroff, Perri. 21 September 2011. "The Hunger Games" countdown: Panem October is coming! *movies.com.* http://www.movies.com/movie-news/the-hunger-games-panem/4594. 3 February 2012.

Nepales, Ruben V. 2001. "Flower Drum Song" blooms with praises. www.inq7.net/lif/2001/nov/05/text/lif_1–1-p.htm. 14 November 2003.

Neuschaffer, W. 1954–55. The world of Gertrud von le Fort. *German Life and Letters* 8: 30–36.

Newman, Charles. 1985. *The postmodern aura.* Evanston, IL: Northwestern University Press.

Nietzsche, Friedrich. 1888/1967. *The birth of tragedy* and *the case of Wagner.* Trans. Walter Kaufmann. New York: Vintage.

O'Boyle, Ita. 1964. *Gertrud von le Fort: An introduction to the prose work.* New York: Fordham University Press.

Ollier, Jacqueline. 1986. Carmen d'hier et d'aujourd'hui. *Corps ecrit: L'opera* 20: 113–22.

Ondaatje, Michael. 1997. Foreword to Minghella 1997: vii-x.

———. 2002. *The conversations: Walter Murch and the art of editing film.* Toronto: Vintage Canada.

Orr, C. 1984. The discourse on adaptation. *Wide Angle* 6 (2): 72–76.

Osborne, Laurie E. 1997. Poetry in motion: Animating Shakespeare. In Boose and Burt 1997a, 103–20.

Pack, Harry. 1996. Liner notes to recording of Rodion Shchedrin, *The Carmen ballet*. Delos DE 3208: 4–7.

Palmer, Christopher, ed. 1984. *The Britten companion*. London: Faber and Faber.

Palmer, R. Barton, ed. 2007a. *Nineteenth-century American literature on screen*. Cambridge: Cambridge University Press.

_____. 2007b. *Twentieth-century American literature on screen*. Cambridge: Cambridge University Press.

Parody, Clare. 2011. Franchising/Adaptation. *Adaptation* 4 (2): 210-18.

Parrish, Robin. 18 July 2011. 50 more Star Wars mashups. *ForeverGeek.com. http://www.forevergeek.com/2011/07/50-more-star-wars-mashups/.* 24 January 2012.

Pasolini, Pier Paolo. 1991. Aspects of a semiology of cinema. In K. Cohen 1991a, 191–226.

Patterson, Annabel. 1990. Intention. In Frank Lentricchia and Thomas McLaughlin, eds., *Critical terms for literary study*. Chicago: University of Chicago Press, 135–46.

Patterson, Lindsay, ed. 1975. *Black films and film-makers*. New York: PMA Communications.

Pavis, Patrice. 1989. Problems of translations for the stage: Interculturalism and post-modern theatre. In Scolnicov and Holland 1989, 25–44.

Peary, Gerald, and Shatzkin, Roger, eds. 1977. *The classic American novel and the movies*. New York: Frederick Ungar.

Peckham, Morse. 1970. The intentional? Fallacy? *The triumph of romanticism: Collected essays*. Columbia, SC: University of South Carolina Press, 421–44.

Perlmutter, Tom. 2011. Will digital kill Hollywood? Keynote address. Canadian Association of American Studies annual conference, 3 November on "The Aesthetics of Renewal".

Perriam, Chris. 2002. "With a blood-red carnation 'tween his lips … ": A queer look at *Carmen, la de Ronda*, 1959. Paper read at *The Carmen Conference*. University of Newcastle upon Tyne, 27 Mar.

Phelan, James. 1996. *Narrative as rhetoric: Technique, audiences, ethics, ideology*. Columbus, OH: Ohio State University Press.

_____, and Rabinowitz, Peter, eds. 2005. *A companion to narrative theory*. Oxford: Blackwell.

Pilling, Jayne, ed. 1997. *A reader in animation studies*. London: John Libbey.

Pirie, David. 1977. *The vampire cinema*. New York: Crescent Books.

Portis, Ben. 2004. Eddo Stern. *Present tense*. Contemporary Project Series No. 29, Art Gallery of Ontario.

Potter, Sally. 1994. *Orlando*. London: Faber and Faber.

Pottermore Insider. December 2011. Like reading Harry Potter? Take part in our survey. *pottermore.com*. http://insider.pottermore.com/2011_12_01_archive.html. 4 January 2012.

Poulenc, Francis. 1954. *Entretiens avec Claude Rostand*. Paris: Rene Julliard.

_____. 1959. *Dialogues des Carmelites*. New York: Ricordi.

_____. 1991. *"Echo and source": Selected correspondence 1915–1963*. Trans. Sidney Buckland. London: Victor Gollancz.

Pramaggiore, Maria. 2001. Unmastered subject: Identity as a fabrication in Joseph Strick's *A Portrait of an Artist as a Young Man* [*sic*] and *Ulysses*." In Michael Patrick Gillespie, ed., *James Joyce and the fabrication of an Irish identity*. Amsterdam and Atlanta, GA: Rodopi, 52–70.

Praz, Mario. 1970. *The romantic agony*, 2nd ed. Trans. Angus Davidson. London and New York: Oxford University Press.

Producers Guild of America. 2010. Transmedia. *Code of Credits: New Media*. http://www.producersguild.org/?page=coc_nm#transmedia. 6 April 2010.

Pugh, Casey. 2011. Director's Cut. *StarWarsUncut.com*. http://www.starwarsuncut.com/watch. Video also posted on YouTube: http://www.youtube.com/watch?v=7ezeYJUz-84. 10 December 2011.

Pullman, Philip. 2004. Let's pretend. *The Guardian*. http://www.guardian.co.uk. 24 November 2004.

Rabinowitz, Peter J. 1980. "What's Hecuba to us?": The audience's experience of literary borrowing. In Susan R. Suleiman and Inge Crosman, eds., *The reader in the text*. Princeton: Princeton University Press, 241–63.

TheRaider.net. n.d. Raiders of the Lost Ark: The Adaptation. http://www.theraider.net/films/raiders_adaptation/. 24 January 2012.

Raval, Suresh. 1993. Intention. In Alex Preminger and T.V.F. Brogan, eds., *The New Princeton Encyclopedia of poetry and poetics*. Princeton: Princeton University Press, 611–13.

Raw, Laurence, ed. 2012. *Translation, adaptation and transformation*. London and New York: Continuum.

Redmond, James. 1989. "If the salt have lost its savour": Some "useful" plays in and out of context on the London stage. In Scolnicov and Holland 1989, 63–88.

Rentschler, Eric, ed. 1986. *German film and literature: Adaptations and transformations*. New York: Methuen.

Reynolds, Peter, ed. 1993a. *Novel images: Literature in performance*. London and New York: Routledge.

_____. 1993b. Introduction. In Reynolds 1993a, 1–16.

Rhetorica ad Herennium. (*Ad C. Herennium: de ratione dicendi.*) 1964. Trans. Harry Caplan. London: Heinemann; Cambridge: Harvard University Press.

Rieser, Martin, and Zapp, Andrea, eds. 2002a. *New screen media: Cinema/art/narrative.* London: British Film Institute.

_____. 2002b. Foreword: An age of narrative chaos? In Rieser and Zapp 2002a, xxv–xxvii.

Robbe-Grillet, Alain. 1963. *Pour un nouveau roman.* Paris: Gallimard.

Robinson, Peter. 1996. Merimee's *Carmen.* In McClary 1996, 1–14.

Ropars, Marie-Clair. 1970. *De la litterature au cinema.* Paris: Armand Colin.

Ropars-Wuilleumier, Marie-Clair. 1998. L'oeuvre au double: Sur les paradoxes de l'adaptation. In Groensteen 1998a, 131–49.

Rosmarin, Leonard. 1999. *When literature becomes opera.* Amsterdam and Atlanta, GA: Rodopi.

Roth, Lane. 1979. Dracula meets the *Zeitgeist*: *Nosferatu* (1922) as film adaptation. *Literature/Film Quarterly* 6 (4): 309-13.

Rovio. 2 November 2011. Angry Birds smashes half a billion downloads. *rovio.com.* http://www.rovio.com/en/news/blog/95/angry-birds-smashes-half-a-billion-downloads. 4 November 2011.

Rowan, Gamemaster, *PanemOctober.com.* 11 December 2011. Panem government. https://www.facebook.com/panemoctober/posts/261238 243930080. 16 February 2012.

Rowe, John Carlos. 1994. Spin-off: The rhetoric of television and postmodern memory. In Carlisle and Schwarz 1994, 97–120.

Russell, D.A. 1979. De Imitatione. In West and Woodman 1979, 1–16.

Ruthven, K.K. 1979. *Critical assumptions.* Cambridge and New York: Cambridge University Press.

Ryan, Marie-Laure. 2001. *Narrative as virtual reality: Immersion and interactivity in literature and electronic media.* Baltimore: Johns Hopkins University Press.

_____, ed. 2004a. *Narrative across media: The languages of storytelling.* Lincoln: University of Nebraska Press.

_____. 2004b. Introduction. In Ryan 2004a, 1–40.

_____. 2004c. Will new media produce new narratives? In Ryan 2004a, 337–59.

_____. 2005. Narrative and digitality: Learning to think with the medium. In Phelan and Rabinowitz 2005, 515–28.

Ryan, Mike. 24 August 2011. A sneak peek at the deleted scenes we hope are on the Star Wars blu-rays. *MovieFone.com.* http://blog.moviefone.com/2011/08/24/a-sneak-peek-at-what-deleted-scenes-we-hope-are-on-the-star-wars/. 24 January 2012.

Sadie, Stanley, ed. 1992. *New Grove dictionary of opera*. 4 vols. London: Macmillan.

Sadoff, Dianne R., and Kucich, John. 2000. Introduction: Histories of the present. In Kucich and Sadoff 2000, ix-xxx.

Said, Edward W. 1983. Traveling theory. In *The world, the text, and the critic*. Cambridge: Harvard University Press, 226–47.

_____. 1985. *Beginnings: Intention and method*. 1975; rpt. New York: Columbia University Press.

Sanders, Julie. 2006. *Adaptation and appropriation* (The New Critical Idiom). London and New York: Routledge.

_____. 2011. Preface. Dynamic repairs: The emerging landscape of adaptation studies. In Hopton, et al. 2011: ix-xiii.

Saving *Star Wars*. 2010. The greatest speech against the special edition was from George Lucas. *savestarwars.com*. http://savestarwars.com/lucasspeechagainstspecialedition.html. 12 February 2012.

Savran, David. 1985. The Wooster Group, Arthur Miller, and *The Crucible*. *Drama Review* 29 (2): 99–109.

Schechter, Joel. 1986. Translations, adaptations, variations: A conversation with Eric Bentley. *Theater* 18 (1): 4–8.

Schell, Jesse, and Shochet, Joe. 2001. Designing interactive theme park rides: Lessons learned creating Disney's *Pirates of the Caribbean—Battle for the buccaneer gold*. http://www.gdconf.com/archives/2001/schell.doc. 31 August 2004.

Schickel, Richard. 1992. *Double indemnity*. London: British Film Institute Publishing.

Schiff, Stephen. 2002. All right, *you* try: Adaptation isn't easy. *New York Times*. 1 Dec, Arts and Leisure: 28.

Schmidgall, Gary. 1977. *Literature as opera*. New York: Oxford University Press.

Scholes, Robert. 1976. Narration and narrativity in film. *Quarterly Review of Film Studies* 1 (111): 283–96.

Schor, Hilary M. 2000. Sorting, morphing, and mourning: A.S. Byatt ghostwrites Victorian fiction. In Kucich and Sadoff 2000, 234–51.

Schulte, Rainer, and Biguenet, John, eds. 1992. *Theories of translation*. Chicago: University of Chicago Press.

Scolnicov, Hanna, and Holland, Peter, eds. 1989. *The play out of context: Transferring plays from culture to culture*. Cambridge: Cambridge University Press.

Searle, John R. 1983. *Intentionality: An essay in the philosophy of mind*. Cambridge: Cambridge University Press.

Seger, Linda. 1992. *The art of adaptation: Turning fact and fiction into film*. New York: Henry Holt and Co.

Seitz, Matt Zoller. 24 January 2012. The fan-made *Star Wars Uncut* is the greatest viral video ever. *vulture.com*. http://www.vulture.com/2012/01/fan-made-star-wars-recut-is-the-greatest-viral-video-ever.html. 28 January 2012.

Shaughnessy, Nicola. 1996. Is s/he or isn't s/he?: Screening *Orlando*. In Cartmell, Hunter, Kaye, and Whelehan 1996, 43–55.

Shaw, Jeffrey. 2002. Movies after film—the digitally expanded cinema. In Reiser and Zapp 2002a, 268–75.

Shawcross, J.T. 1991. *Intentionality and the new traditionalism: Some liminal means to literary revisionism*. University Park, PA: Pennsylvania State University Press.

Shohat, Ella. 2004. Sacred word, profane image: Theologies of adaptation. In Stam and Raengo 2004, 23–45.

Sibayan, Genevieve. 15 February 2012. Lionsgate to open Hunger Games Cafepress store. *Cult Hub*. http://www.culthub.com/lionsgate-to-open-hunger-games-cafepress-store/4539/. 15 February 2012.

Sidhwa, Bapsi. 1999. Watching my novel become her film. *New York Times*. 5 Sept., Arts and Leisure: 21.

Siegel, Carol. 1994. From pact with the devil to masochist's contract: *Dangerous Liaison*'s translation of the erotics of evil. In Carlisle and Schwarz 1994, 238–49.

Silverman, Jason. 17 May 2007. Ultimate 'indy' flick: Fanboys remake *Raiders of the Lost Ark*. *Wired*. http://www.wired.com/entertainment/hollywood/news/2007/05/diy_raiders. 24 January 2012.

Simon, Sherry. 1996. *Gender in translation: Cultural identity and the politics of transmission*. New York: Routledge.

Simpson, Alexander Thomas, Jr. 1990. Opera on film: A study of the history and the aesthetic principles and conflicts of a hybrid genre. Ph.D. dissertation, University of Kentucky.

Sinyard, Neil. 1986. *Filming literature: The art of screen adaptation*. London: Croom Helm.

———. 2000. "Lids tend to come off": David Lean's film of E.M. Forster's *A Passage to India*. In Giddings and Sheen 2000, 147–62.

Smith, Murray. 1995. *Engaging characters: Fiction, emotion, and the cinema*. Oxford: Clarendon Press.

Smith, Patrick J. 1970. *The tenth muse*. New York: Knopf.

Smith, Sarah W.R. 1981. The word made celluloid: On adapting Joyce's *Wake*. In Klein and Parker 1981, 301–12.

Smith, Zadie. 2003. "White Teeth" in the flesh. *New York Times*. 11 May, Arts and Leisure, 2: 1, 10.

Somigli, Luca. 1998. The superhero with a thousand faces: Visual narratives on film and paper. In Horton and McDougal 1998a, 279–94.

Sontag, Susan. 1999. Film and theatre. In Braudy and Cohen 1999, 249–67.

Sorensen, Sue. 1997. "Damnable feminization"?: The Merchant Ivory film adaptation of Henry James's *The Bostonians*. *Literature/Film Quarterly* 25(3): 231–35.

Sorlin, Pierre. 2001. How to look at an historical film. In Landy 2001a, 25–49.

Speaight, Robert. 1973. *Georges Bernanos: A study of the man and the writer*. London: Collins and Harvill Press.

Spiegelman, Art. 2004. Picturing a glassy-eyed private I. In *Paul Auster, city of glass*. Adaptation by Paul Karasik and David Mazzucchelli. New York: Picador.

Stallman, R.W. 1950. *Critic's notebook*. Minneapolis: University of Minnesota Press.

Stam, Robert. 2000. The dialogics of adaptation. In Naremore 2000a, 54–76.

_____. 2005a. *Literature through film: Realism, magic, and the art of adaptation*. Oxford: Blackwell.

_____. 2005b. Introduction: The theory and practice of adaptation. In Stam and Raengo 2005, 1–52.

_____, and Raengo, Alessandra, eds. 2004. *A companion to literature and film*. Oxford: Blackwell.

_____. 2005. *Literature and film: A guide to the theory and practice of film adaptation*. Oxford: Blackwell.

Starwars.wikia.com. n.d.. List of changes. http://starwars.wikia.com/wiki/List_of_changes_in_Star_Wars_re-releases. 25 January 2012.

Steiner, George. 1995. *What is comparative literature?* Oxford: Clarendon Press.

Steiner, Wendy. 2004. Pictorial narrativity. In Ryan 2004a, 145–77.

Stelter, Brian. 27 August 2010. An Emmy for rebuilding a galaxy. *NY Times. com*.   http://www.nytimes.com/2010/08/28/arts/television/28uncut.html?_r=1. 26 January 2012.

Suciu, Peter. 15 June 2007. The rise of the prosumer. *TechCrunch.com*. http://techcrunch.com/2007/06/15/the-rise-of-the-prosumer/. 15 January 2012.

Syberberg, Hans-Jurgen. 1982. *Parsifal: Notes sur un film*. Trans. Claude Porcell. Paris: Gallimard, Cahiers du cinema.

Tambling, Jeremy. 1987. *Opera, ideology and film*. Manchester: Manchester University Press.

_____, ed. 1994a. *A night in at the opera: Media representations of opera*. London: J. Libbey.

_____. 1994b. Introduction: Opera in the distraction culture. In Tambling 1994a, 1–23.

Taruskin, Richard. 2005. *The Oxford history of western music*. 6 vols. Oxford: Oxford University Press.

Taussig, Michael. 1993. *Mimesis and alterity: A particular history of the senses*. New York and London: Routledge.

Taylor, Andrew. 2004. Reflections on Phillips' and Greenaway's *A TV Dante*. In Iannucci 2004a, 145–52.

The Greatest Speech Against the Special Edition was from George Lucas. n.d. *Saving Star Wars*. http://savestarwars.com/lucasspeechagainst specialedition.html. 25 January 2012.

Thomas, Bronwen. 2000. "Piecing together a mirage": Adapting *The English patient* for the screen. In Giddings and Sheen 2000, 197–232.

Thomas, Ronald R. 2000. Specters of the novel: *Dracula* and the cinematic afterlife of the Victorian novel. In Kucich and Sadoff 2000, 288–310.

Thompson, Ann. 1997. Asta Nielsen and the mystery of *Hamlet*. In Boose and Burt 1997a, 215–24.

Thompson, John O. 1996. "Vanishing" worlds: Film adaptation and the mystery of the original. In Cartmell, Hunter, Kaye, and Whelehan 1996, 11–28.

Thompson, Kristin. 2003. *Storytelling in film and television*. Cambridge, MA: Harvard University Press.

Thomson, Brooke. 25 April 2011. Transmedia is killing Hollywood will kill Transmedia. *giantmice.com*. http://www.giantmice.com/archives/2011/04/transmedia-is-killing-hollywood-will-kill-transmedia/. 24 May 2011.

Thomson, Virgil. 1982. On writing operas and staging them. *Parnassus: Poetry in Review* (fall): 4–19.

Tong, Wee Liang, and Tan, Marcus Cheng Chye. 2002. Vision and virtuality: The construction of narrative space in film and computer games. In King and Krzywinska 2002a, 98–109.

Toteberg, Michael, and Lensing, Leo A., eds. 1992. *The anarchy of the imagination: Interviews, essays, notes*. Trans. Krishna Winston. Baltimore: Johns Hopkins University Press.

Toye, Frances. 1934. *Rossini: The man and his music*. New York: Dover.

Trowell, Brian. 1992. Libretto. In Sadie 1992, 1185–1252.

TWILIGHTxx00xx. 28 May 2009. NEW MOON – BIG KISSING SCENE!! – 5-27-09. http://www.youtube.com/watch?v=aKhmIBmmf uI&feature=related. 10 November 2011.

Verone, William. 2011. *Adaptation and the avant garde*. London and New York: Continuum.

Verschuere, Gilles. 8 August 2005. Interview with the Raiders Guys. *TheRaider.net*. http://www.theraider.net/films/raiders_adaptation/interview_02.php. 24 January 2012.

Vinaver, Michel. 1998. De l'adaptation. In *Ecrits sur le theatre*. Vol. 1, ed. Michelle Henry. Paris: L'Arche, 80–85.

Vincendeau, Ginette. 2001. Introduction. In Ginette Vincendeau, ed., *Film/literature/heritage: A sight and sound reader*. London: British Film Institute, xi-xxxi.

Vineberg, Steve. 2002. On screen, on stage: The double virtuosity of Andrew Borell. *Chronicle of Higher Education*. 1 Feb: B16.

Volkswagen. 2 February 2011. Darth Vader Super Bowl: The force. http://www.youtube.com/watch?v=x0EnhXn5boM. 5 February 2011.

von le Fort, Gertrud. 1956. *Aufzeignungen und Erinnerungen*. Koln: Benzingen.

Wagner, Geoffrey. 1975. *The novel and the cinema*. Rutherford, NJ: Fairleigh Dickinson University Press.

Wagner, Heather. 10 November 2010. Jonathan Safran Foer talks *Tree of Codes* and conceptual art. *Vanity Fair*. http://www.vanityfair.com/online/daily/2010/11/jonathan-safran-foer-talks-tree-of-codes-and-paper-art. March 10, 2012.

Wand, Eku. 2002. Interactive storytelling: The renaissance of narration. In Rieser and Zapp 2002a, 163–78.

Ward, Paul. 2002. Videogames as remediated animation. In King and Krzywinska 2002a, 122–35.

Weibel, Peter. 2002. Narrated theory: Multiple projection and multiple narration (past and future). In Rieser and Zapp 2002a, 42–53.

Weinbren, Grahame. 2002. Mastery (sonic c'est moi). In Rieser and Zapp 2002a, 179–91.

Weisstein, Ulrich. 1961. The libretto as literature. *Books Abroad* 35: 16–22.

West, David, and Woodman, Tony. 1979. *Creative imitation and Latin literature*. Cambridge and New York: Cambridge University Press.

Whipp, Glenn. 2002. Director remains faithful to Harry. *Toronto Star* 21 Sept.: H4.

Whittall, Arnold. 1990. "Twisted relations": Method and meaning in Britten's *Billy Budd*. *Cambridge Opera Journal* 2 (2): 145–71.

_____. 1992. *The turn of the screw*. In Sadie 1992, 4: 846–49.

Willeman, Paul. 2002. Reflections on digital imagery: Of mice and men. In Rieser and Zapp 2002a, 14–26.

Williams, Raymond. 1977. *Marxism and literature*. New York: Oxford University Press.

Wills, David. 1986. Carmen: Sound/effect. *Cinema Journal* 25 (4): 33–43.

Wimsatt, William K., Jr. 1976. Genesis: An argument resumed. In *Day of the leopards*. New Haven, CT: Yale University Press, 11–39.

_____, and Beardsley, Monroe C. 1946. The intentional fallacy. *Sewanee Review* 54: 468–88.

Windolf, Jim. March 2004. Raiders of the lost backyard. *Vanity Fair*. http://www.vanityfair.com/culture/features/2004/03/raiders200403. 5 February 2011.

Witchell, Alex. 2000. An "Aida" born of ecstasies and explosions. *New York Times*. 19 Mar., Arts and Leisure: 7.

Wittkower, Rudolf. 1965. Imitation, eclecticism, and genius. In Earl R. Wasserman, ed., *Aspects of the eighteenth century*. Baltimore: Johns Hopkins University Press, 143–61.

Wober, J.M. 1980. Fiction and depiction: Attitudes to fifteen television series and the novels from which they were made. *Special Report*. Audience Research Department, Independent Broadcast Authority.

Wollen, Peter. 1969. *Signs and meaning in the cinema*. London: British Film Institute.

Woodmansee, Martha, and Jaszi, Peter, eds. 1994. *The construction of authorship: Textual appropriation in law and literature*. Durham, NC: Duke University Press.

Woolf, Virginia. 1926. The movies and reality. *New Republic* 47 (4 Aug.): 308–10.

Wright, Nicholas. 2003. Introduction. In *His Dark Materials*. London: Nick Hern Books, vii–ix.

Wunderlich, Eva C. 1952. Gertrud von le Fort's fight for the living spirit. *The Germanic Review* 27 (4): 298–313.

xXAliceinthedarkXx. 29 May 2009. Shirtless Robert Pattinson films sexy scene for New Moon! http://www.youtube.com/watch?v=09kt7 CnpzTU. 10 November 2011.

Y'Barbo, Douglas. 1998. Aesthetic ambition versus commercial appeal: Adapting novels and film to the copyright law. *St. Thomas Law Review* 10: 299–386.

Zalewski, Daniel. 2002. Can bookish be sexy? Yeah, says Neil LaBute. *New York Times*. 18 Aug., Arts and Leisure: 10, 22.

Zapp, Andrea. 2002. net.drama://myth/mimesis/mind_mapping/. In Rieser and Zapp 2002a, 77–89.

Zhang, Hsia Yang. 1996. *Shakespeare in China: A comparative study of two traditions and cultures.* Newark: University of Delaware Press.

INDEX

www.routledge.com/literature